Say you'll Wait for Me,

A Memoir

Say you'll Wait for Me,

A Memoir

SAMANTHA ROSALIA

Archway Publishing books may be ordered through booksellers or by contacting:

Archway Publishing
1663 Liberty Drive
Bloomington, IN 47403
www.archwaypublishing.com
844-669-3957

Because of the dynamic nature of the Internet, any web addresses or links contained in
this book may have changed since publication and may no longer be valid. The views
expressed in this work are solely those of the author and do not necessarily reflect the views
of the publisher, and the publisher hereby disclaims any responsibility for them.

This book is a work of non-fiction. Unless otherwise noted, the author and the publisher
make no explicit guarantees as to the accuracy of the information contained in this book
and in some cases, names of people and places have been altered to protect their privacy.

Any people depicted in stock imagery provided by Getty Images are models,
and such images are being used for illustrative purposes only.
Certain stock imagery © Getty Images.

ISBN: 978-1-6657-5269-5 (sc)
ISBN: 978-1-6657-5270-1 (e)

Library of Congress Control Number: 2023921515

Print information available on the last page.

Archway Publishing rev. date: 11/06/2023

Contents

Part 04: Bad Parts

Part 05: Travel Diaries

PART 1

Life In Louisiana, Growing Up Samantha

CHAPTER 1

Returning to the Past

"*You* will find me in every member of my family. My extended family is no different than me, like each one of my heart beats." Daniyal used to say.

Relocating to Louisiana allowed me to daydream about having an ordinary childhood, making friends and succeeding in school. I left a life of instability with my mom in Florida behind and moved in with relatives who lived in Louisiana. A good portion of my upbringing, I was raised by a single mother, Casandra who worked as a waitress. Casandra made rent with tip money from regular customers. On Saturdays Casandra worked double shifts at a busy Barbeque restaurant and was seldom home. Years later, my biological mother achieved her goals of entrepreneurship and opened her own small business grooming and boarding pets.

At a local thrift shop in Louisiana, I accidentally ran into my dad, Joseph. Joseph remarried by the time I entered middle school. "Be realistic, it's not that you can't indulge in fantasy. Don't let unattainable dreams blind you to how hard the rest of us work for a living," Joseph said, referencing my impractical aspirations of entrepreneurship and future goals of publishing novels. Spending free time at a village area of Pakistan envisioning myself publishing books someday, I found contentment in a quiet village area of Ganish. Joseph's motto growing up was work hard and live below your means but don't expect your creative aspirations to necessarily materialize.

Daniyal told his family from his native land of Pakistan, a diluted version of his life in the United States, lying about securing a well-paying job working for cultured people from Faisalabad. I lied to my own family about hardships I faced during my marriage to Daniyal because I didn't want to tell my relatives and network of friends from Louisiana that my once outwardly successful marriage and family was falling apart. Cultured people, I thought to myself. Daniyal's motivation for achieving legal status in the United States was the commitment and sense of loyalty he had for his sisters and mother from Faisalabad, Pakistan.

Toward the end of my stay in Faisalabad, I no longer missed Nadia's brother or cared to remember the life we shared in Louisiana. My curiosity got the best of me when I wanted to learn more about Daniyal, a Pakistani immigrant from a rural village few heard of before called Ganish. When first receiving a visa to the States, Daniyal had no plans and no place of refuge to call home. The oldest brother was looking to escape a shared living arrangement with an abusive relative.

Daniyal talked about struggling to find acceptance and familiarity while living away from his country of origin. A Pakistani migrant in his 20's searched to uncover what the American dream meant to him. For immigrants and minorities, the jobless and working class, according to Nadia's brother, the United States was nothing more than an open jail.

While pushing a shopping cart full of old photographs, wall art and house décor, I ran into my dad. Joseph rarely showed emotion. I didn't know the reasons behind why I met him again after leaving home when I moved away from my childhood residency to build a life with Daniyal. Joseph spotted me in the store first, trying not to make eye contact. Joseph rarely socialized and kept to himself except when there were things to be repaired around the house. I knew Joseph as an avid reader, an intellectual and creative.

Yard work and fixing things was his area of expertise. When I returned home, Joseph avoided conversations with me like that day in the store. Joseph preferred cutting grass, and repairing things around the house, setting aside days for time consuming projects, like remodeling our basement, adding rooms or installing a bathroom downstairs. Joseph was standing in the check–out line, purchasing tools he probably found bargain priced. He was most likely going home to work on a new project, fixing a leaky faucet or putting in new flooring. It was a weekend.

New projects involving home improvement were escapes from Joseph's mundane nine-to-five desk job. While I was browsing for used furniture and synthetic flowers to decorate a room, I assumed Joseph was most likely visiting a hardware store, or secondhand shop where he could find supplies for new home projects.

Joseph sold valuable antiques online for passive income. When I began dating Daniyal, I was a first-year college student. After joining the Air National guard and graduating High School with honors, I knew military life wasn't for me. Joseph was a veteran and boasted about how the armed services gave him much back in the form of education, training and job skills. During the earlier years of my life, I liked the prospect of settling down, building a family of my own and being a housewife. I was content helping Daniyal run the gas station. I came from a long line of proud military service members.

I planned to buy a tranquil home in the rural countryside with a lake in the backyard like the home where I grew up, keep wishing, Joseph's voice repeated in my head. It will most likely never happen. A framed poem I wrote in childhood sat above the fireplace mantel in our living room beside a high school graduation photo of me. Joseph used to say, "Your poem deserved, something, for someone to see it."

Daniyal informed me out of the blue that he could not yet go back to his birth country of Pakistan. I wondered what he meant by that.

On the way out of the Hardware store, I hesitated to approach Joseph. Before I could say anything, he started tearing up, reluctant to acknowledge who I was or make it clear that he ran into me at the store one afternoon, by chance. After an unexpected encounter with Joseph years ago, after leaving the house of my youth behind for good, I thought about what I should have said to Joseph. It was a good thing Joseph left the store before me because I would have said something like, I'm sorry I left home with little warning in the harsh manner that I did. I will come for a visit soon. Since leaving home, I am doing better. You should be excited for me too. Joseph walking out of the store that afternoon before me was the better option because I would have gotten emotional. There was no point in seeing a distant family member again after the day I left my childhood home in Louisiana for good this time.

Parental love should never be conditional, in this case I knew it was. Psychological abuse for a child was like walking around with invisible scars no one could see, not knowing who to trust, never being good enough. That afternoon in the store, I chose not to let Joseph see me fall apart. I parked the shopping cart full of house decorations I would never use for the new apartment I was moving to with Daniyal in a week's time, leaving the store abruptly. I chose not to let Joseph know I was sorry about the way I left home. Since leaving my hometown, I cried all the time.

Daniyal was operating the cash register, with a long line out the door when I walked in, visibly shaken. On weekdays we experienced our slowest afternoons with gas prices skyrocketing. "Where were you when I could have used your help around here?" Daniyal complained. Daniyal reminded me that meeting me at his place of business was lucky. We were like every other youthful couple, spontaneous and carefree when we first started dating. When I met Daniyal, he ran a gas station down the road from my childhood home in Louisiana. Daniyal invested most of his savings into the gas station. Unlike some foreigners who came to the United States with little savings or family support, Daniyal traveled to the United States from his village of Ganish, Pakistan with a large amount of money he used to invest in a business.

When we began dating, I was a first-year college student. All Daniyal seemed to talk about was how much he missed his homeland of Pakistan. Inaya and her three children, practicing Islamic women, prayed namaz five times a day since Daniyal left his village of Ganish. I never thought to ask the oldest brother about reasons he couldn't return to his homeland of Pakistan. No one did.

When work was slow, we ate spicy, ethnic cuisines with homemade naan or roti bread. Daniyal cooked on a stove himself, making dinner for the two of us on most nights after work. We sat on the floor in the evenings sharing naan bread and indigenous food together while watching foreign films, like I assumed Daniyal did back home in Faisalabad with family and relatives.

Years before when Daniyal ran the gas station, working long hours, it took me back to a time when we were young and couldn't seem to get enough of one another. At the same hour every afternoon, my immigrant husband brewed a pot of coffee for us on his slowest afternoons. The business next door was packed, with long lines at each register and customers waiting outside the door. We didn't have financial setbacks then. In early years, when we first met, I knew little about Pakistan or problems over inheritance and property. Depending on the market, property owners in some parts of Faisalabad earned the equivalent to what a doctor, or lawyer earned annually in areas throughout provinces of Punjab. Children of rich property owners typically attended private schools and were considered the lucky few among a margin of what constituted upper middle-class Pakistani society.

Busy afternoons were spent helping to run the gas station, looking forward to evening walks together. During breaks, Daniyal and I shared lunches at eating places within walking distance. Daniyal seemed to know every businessperson in the area. Nadia's brother was charismatic, hardworking and kind. Customers seemed to like him.

During our walks, Daniyal talked about how it didn't matter all he lost financially because he met and fell in love with me at his workplace. Despite his affection for me back then, I knew the truth. The gas station meant everything to him. Daniyal invested a good portion of family money into the service station.

Daniyal partnered with a family member, a Pakistani immigrant, his nephew Idris. Daniyal's nephew, Idris from Faisalabad left the franchise business to his relative to manage. A couple days after money from a safe was stolen, an auto mechanic employed by Daniyal walked off the job without notice. The franchise owner of the company asked Daniyal to take a lie detector test to clear his name. Daniyal took a tremendous loss financially and couldn't sustain the gas station. Nadia's brother called the franchise owner he'd purchased the company from to explain that he would have to walk away from the gas station for good this time, empty handed.

I tried my best to make Daniyal happy so that he wouldn't think about losing family money and a business that meant a great deal to him. We were moving out of the confinement of the small living space we shared. Although our living situation was temporary, I would be missing the place.

Going back to the beginning of my relationship with Nadia's oldest brother, I thought about falling in love with a migrant from Pakistan. Daniyal reminded me of the earlier part of my upbringing, and my feelings of sentiment and longing for a country like Pakistan.

A cashier took over my shift and was busy cleaning out pots and brewing a fresh batch of coffee for new customers. My choices were clear after that day. I would start a new life for myself and build a future with the hardworking, Pakistani man I grew to adore. I looked forward to Daniyal's cultural food and having someone to rely on who cared about my wellbeing. Abuse started to become normalized in more ways than I accepted in my twenties.

It took me until I reached adulthood to realize my parents cared about me in their own way, and fully trusted Daniyal. Joseph wanted me to have a successful married life and never stopped worrying about my safety when I started traveling to Faisalabad, Pakistan. I would re- assure Joseph that on Christmas and holidays I didn't miss home in Louisiana and was settling into married life in a rural village area of Pakistan. I feel bad about that part.

After my divorce, I thought about why I was in such a hurry to leave home where I lived a quiet existence in a farmhouse where horses grazed in the backyard, out in the middle of nowhere. Secretly, I wished to return home again. Where I grew up, few strive for greatness, most are content to work hard and learn to be satisfied with what they have. While I was away from Sameer and Asad in Louisiana, I returned alone to places only the three of us went to together. In the United States, I spent afternoons at the local eatery or mall with my oldest son Sameer where I watched Sameer ride the carousel.

I walked by the carousel and saw a different version of myself and my children. Sameer was on his second round sitting on the mechanical ride grinning up at me. Sameer and Asad's presence was everywhere, in every child's laughter. Joseph purchased Sameer's favorite tractor bicycle toy at a garage sale and fixed it up like new. After I journeyed back from Pakistan, I thought about how much Sameer adored the junky tractor bike, still sitting in our yard. The thought of leaving Sameer and Asad behind in Pakistan tormented me. The same boulevard I passed dozens of times where Sameer rode his bicycle in a circle, was now a vacant lot. Buried in familiar places we visited together in Louisiana, my children's voices and laughter stayed with me. I wanted Sameer and Asad to know, I tried to get back to them.

I planned to buy a house out in the countryside where no one would think to look for me until I couldn't remember the people who betrayed me. I danced but only for myself. I wrote fiction stories but only for myself, thinking about publishing novels and escaping what turned into a severely abusive marriage to Nadia's brother, Daniyal.

Years later, I learned of the village girl back home the oldest of three brothers, Daniyal, was given to in marriage. Romance outside of arranged marriages was a foreign concept to my then immigrant husband that I mistook for kindness, friendship and support I needed in my early twenties.

I thought remorsefully about what it must have been like as a child from a village of Ganish who came to America for the first time, with no preconceptions about the western world.

A long line of customers started to die down. It was only the two of us in the gas station. I let myself sob, with only the two of us in the store. I never told Daniyal about meeting Joseph earlier, or reasons surrounding why I left my childhood home in Louisiana and couldn't return. Daniyal was a different person. Nadia's big brother didn't think to ask what was wrong a second time.

CHAPTER 2

Labor Abuse and Side Effects

On religious holidays and family functions in Louisiana I spent with a close-kinit group of friends, Daniyal walked toward a forest of trees and tall grass in my backyard, past projects Joseph left incomplete. A couple of miles past a local convenience store, hidden behind a winding gravel road, was my childhood home, a farmhouse surrounded by vast stretches of land. Being back in my home state served as a reminder of the family I grew up with in Louisiana and lifelong childhood friends I reunited with. After years of living in an isolated village area of Faisalabad with my children, I was eager to settle back into life in the United States.

On holidays and birthdays, Daniyal insisted on doing yard work for Joseph. With an array of manual labor jobs under his belt, Daniyal's interpretation of the contemporary woman may have been skewed. Daniyal's favorite chore was tree cutting. Through my discomfort, I reminded Daniyal, he didn't work for my dad. He could relax, my parents were family.

Daniyal described a woman who helped groups of undocumented workers get legal status. Some illegal workers were unaware of labor laws. Undocumented migrants from poor countries employed by Maryam, narrowly escaped death and poverty. Illegals came from third world countries seeking political asylum and could no longer safely return to their countries. In the United States, undocumented laborers were stuck somewhere in the middle, considered illegal aliens but fearful enough to do whatever it took not to be deported back to their countries of origin.

When we met, Daniyal arrived in Louisiana on a work visa from a rural village area of Pakistan. I wondered after his experience with labor abuse, how an immigrant from Pakistan viewed western women. I remembered our meeting.

"You may have heard stories about me from Daniyal."

"I run a business and each person seeking my help understands they must work extremely hard to stay in this country. I remember Daniyal well. He worked for my husband several years ago. We took him in, helped him get his papers. Daniyal, he's like family."

"Your husband, Daniyal has always been a hard worker." Maryam said.

A Pakistani man with a dark mustache dressed in plain color salwar kameez appeared in the driveway of Maryam's home. Maryam's husband walked toward me. Daniyal put the car in park and got out before I could protest. As Maryam's husband reached out his hand as a form of greeting, I wanted to convince Daniyal to turn around and drive home. That's when I remembered our meeting.

"Don't worry there's a woman I want you to meet, Maryam. She helped me get my green card when I arrived here on a work visa." Daniyal reassured

Hidden from plain sight, in the couple's plush backyard, near one area of neglected land, I spotted Daniyal. Daniyal was mowing grass. He already started on yard work, practicing how to gear up the push lawnmower, pulling the string back, sighing in frustration when the lawn mower wouldn't start up again.

Appearing out of reach, I couldn't yell loud enough for Daniyal to hear.

Maryam was a migrant from Daniyal's city of Faisalabad. I knew her husband worked for the US government at the embassy in Washington DC. Maryam didn't appear to be a wealthy foreigner. She looked to be finishing up yard work and household chores. Maryam's dark, cropped hair and salwar kameez was lined with dirt. The slender Punjabi woman didn't' bother fixing herself up before our visit. Maybe she wasn't expecting guests.

"Assalamu alaikum," Maryam greeted

Daniyal's friends from Faisalabad were known for being hospitable to guests. How Pakistani people treated their guests reflected on their upbringing and sometimes was an indication of education, social class and their place in society. I sat on a bar stool in the kitchen. Maryam stared blankly at me. I thought Maryam may have been offended by my perceived lack of culture. The Punjabi woman's large home was neatly decorated.

Maryam was a few feet away in the kitchen, making tea. I could sense something was wrong. What I knew about Pakistani culture was that house guest were considered close to God, like cleanliness was next to Godliness.

Daniyal returned a few hours later, sweaty and tired, complaining about not being able to restart the lawn mower. The motor was shot. He almost gave up after the third or fourth try, until Daniyal finally got the motor running and began cutting another portion of yard out of my sight. Daniyal wouldn't see my feelings of anxiety in being alone with Maryam, a Punjabi woman who he considered a gracious neighbor from Faisalabad.

Maryam strained loose leaf tea leaves from a pot of boiling water into the sink and sighed, flinching as she spilled some hot liquid on her hand. Maryam poured hot tea strait from the pan into a mug. She handed me a plate of desserts. Out of courtesy, I drank the cup of tea and left the decadent sweets on the table.

"I assume you and Daniyal showed up here this afternoon to talk to my husband about the process of applying for US citizenship. My husband works for the government, he can better guide you and Daniyal."

"I told Daniyal already; he only must apply for US citizenship in a few more years and pass a test. There is no need to marry a US citizen to stay in this country permanently. Believe me, I went through the immigration process myself. I wouldn't be the one to turn to for advising green card holders." Maryam explained.

Daniyal is not using me for a green card, I wanted to yell at Maryam, but kept my composure, choosing not to say anything. Maryam sat down next to me, apologetic that she had nothing else for me. When I got up to go find Daniyal, Maryam asked me to talk about myself. "Why don't you want to work?" Maryam asked rudely.

I explained calmly to Maryam that I was a housewife and cared for Sameer while Daniyal worked a full-time job. I told Maryam that Daniyal didn't tell me why we came to her home for a surprise visit on short notice.

Maryam went to the kitchen, towel drying dishes.

As I began piecing together Daniyal's experience with labor abuse, I assumed Maryam was not a well- meaning woman who helped undocumented workers pave out a way to citizenship as Daniyal described. Maryam prayed on fears and vulnerabilities of the less fortunate, exploiting unsuspecting foreigners seeking a place of safety and fair work opportunities for an honest salary. I knew Daniyal worked more than forty-hour weeks with no benefits, doing hard labor jobs. When Daniyal arrived in the United States on a work visa, he made scarcely enough to get by, sending what he could afford home to Aaliyaa and three sisters back home to his village of Ganish, for the promise of U S citizenship.

Maryam was someone who pretended to accommodate guests while subtly tearing them down. Maryam and her husband used and discarded undocumented workers who entered the United States illegally, employing them under the table to work for their businesses. Illegals put in long hours, accepted unfair pay and mistreatment, for the right to stay in America and a chance at citizenship. Undocumented workers, like Daniyal had no knowledge of labor laws when he first came to the country.

After Daniyal achieved his goal of US citizenship, there was really no need to take me along on a visit to the home of Maryam, a Punjabi woman from Faisalabad.

Like some Pakistani families I befriended, Maryam assumed Daniyal married me for a green card. Many of Daniyal's friends from Faisalabad held deep seated prejudices about foreigners marrying out of their race. Other friends of Daniyal's thought he used me to establish or secure US residency. When I got up to use Maryam's bathroom, I noticed two books sitting on a bookshelf. One book was about spirituality, filled with encouraging passages for getting through tough times. I took notice of Mariam's meticulously clean bathroom. I wanted to find Daniyal and make an excuse to leave. I would tell Daniyal that I felt out of place at his friend's home. Maryam didn't know anything about me or my marriage to Daniyal and had no right to make assumptions.

Maryam followed me out of the bathroom, shuffling things around, like she was searching for something I stole or misplaced. Daniyal's friends from Faisalabad intended to purposely shame me. I understood enough about customs and elite societies of Pakistan by now after traveling around to progressive cities of Faisalabad with Ayaan, to know how my marriage to Daniyal was viewed by wealthy foreigners. I understood enough about Pakistani culture to know that Maryam intended to shame me about my marriage to Daniyal who entered the country illegally.

My experience with labor abuse reminded me of a close friend who lived in Faisalabad and the few weeks I spent at her home in Pakistan during long power losses. Asma told sarcastic stories about life in Luton, England when she was newly married to an upper-class entrepreneur who lived and worked In England. Before tying the knot, Asma shuffled back and forth between Pakistan and England on short visits to a strange new country where her husband went to earn money.

Asma described her first trips to England as uncomfortable, considering cultural

and social differences between Pakistan and England. Asma talked about a group of upper-class British Pakistani's who watched in judgement as my friend Asma micromanaged housekeepers when she stayed in England. Asma double checked behind housekeepers to ensure rooms and bathrooms were cleaned thoroughly, reprimanding maids for rooms or spots in her home that weren't cleaned to her standards. In England how one treated respected house guests and maids differed significan' especially in the provinces of Punjab. Some Pakistani families abused houseke' they hired and refused to share bathrooms or living quarters with them.

Some middle – upper class society families in Faisalabad considered lage workers to be dirty. Other middle upper-class families I knew from treated maids like their own children, helping poor villagers with st' educating and caring for village children alongside their kids. Fi ters and women in charge of running middle -class households Ganish, managed employees and juvenile housekeepers who ' ditions. Most poor village children and agriculture worker' like social etiquette, good hygiene practices and manners

Daniyal's friend Maryam insulted me indirectly. Th of Maryam's misconceptions about my family status t' Faisalabad, intended to embarrass me. My marriag' of his foreign friends as a relationship of conver' of Daniyal's assumed an immigrant from Pak' illegally, wasn't looking to settle down with a' Pakistani culture. Daniyal swore Maryar' from his home city of Faisalabad, profe' I understood what it was like to mar' of desperate circumstances seeking' or putdown Maryam directed at ' I knew about caste systems, w'

Daniyal was a foreigner ' States. Maryam's behavic' interactions with a fam'' papers. Daniyal spen' abused and ridiculed h.

Every enjoyable holiday . ing somewhere to do yard work .

Faisalabad the pleasure of seeing me fall apart in front of them, knowing a stranger's judgements deeply impacted me. After five years of working for wealthy Pakistani foreigners, reaching his goal of US citizenship didn't seem to be worth it in the end. American Pakistani's who treated their own people poorly made me think of wealth disparities I encountered while traveling around to places in Pakistan with Ayaan. I thought back to dinners I shared with Joseph in Louisiana and yard work.

My Pakistani spouse preferred wandering off by himself, doing yard work for wealthy foreigners rather than socialize with Americans who judged Daniyal for his status in society. For more than five years Daniyal worked for rich Pakistanis for a green card, foreigners from his city of Faisalabad who placed judgments on who they thought he was. Daniyal was proud of his Pakistani heritage and the fact that he was part of a large extended family with a solid reputation in the community.

CHAPTER 3

Failure and a Cab Ride Home

Strangers hidden behind the guise of friendly restaurant service workers offered Daniyal acceptance to Louisiana in the form of a welcoming smile, a hot meal, and a thoughtful gesture. If you didn't know what it was like to marry a Pakistani, loving an immigrant from Ganish was facing down a community who laughed, drew assumptions and made snide remarks in Urdu about a white woman who wasn't successful or smart, only pretty. When we were dating, Daniyal told me never to close my eyes for too long. "Open your eyes," Daniyal whispered, when I fell asleep in the passenger's seat on a long drive out- of state to pick up one of his best paying clients. He must've been afraid I would miss out on something.

I didn't know the truth surrounding why Daniyal traveled to Louisiana, or what he was fighting for in dollars. I became like a war-torn country seeking safety and new beginnings. I became like a piece of stolen property that my migrant husband fought for.

Daniyal worked a series of blue-collar jobs until he got his license to drive a taxi-cab in Washington D.C. I rode along with him on out of state pickups to Virginia. If I knew the types of customers he called regulars, the only people who called cabs at late hours, or early hours of the morning, I wouldn't have agreed to ride along. Like the gas station Daniyal ran, he appreciated and cared for his new taxicab, driving the Toyota into the ground, accumulating over 300,000 miles on the vehicle. I noticed Pakistani people from Faisalabad valued and took good care of material possessions, living modestly, careful not to waste. I saw driving a commercial vehicle you owned as independent work, a side- hustle that wasn't permanent employment but something for the time being.

Daniyal carried with him in the strangers he came across, a longing for home, knowing he may never return to his country of origin. Nadia sobbed over the phone when I informed her that her oldest brother, Daniyal, was still driving a taxicab in Washington DC. I knew Daniyal drove in unsafe districts of Washington DC. The day Nadia's brother got his taxicab license, he added a fresh coat of red primer to his brand-new Toyota Hybrid. A silver stripe ran along the middle of the car's body along with Daniyal's name and license number.

To most status conscious middle class Pakistani families, the concept of success in the United States didn't equate to driving uber or a taxicab for an extended period. There was a great deal of shame experienced by foreigners from prideful, middle-class families attached to getting up in the morning and driving a taxicab every day for a living. Because Daniyal was home infrequently, long drives through the countryside of Louisiana when I rode as a passenger in Daniyal's taxicab, were sometimes the only quality time we spent together.

The kids and I were what kept Daniyal going another day. Tomorrow, next week, our family would be in a better place financially, I told myself. When I was newly married, Daniyal took me along for day long car rides, acting like a tour guide, showing me around wealthy neighborhoods of Louisiana where he chauffeured around his best tipping customers. During busy weekdays and holidays, typically on Thursdays and Fridays, Daniyal drove around lawyers and doctors. While Daniyal escorted rich businessmen to different areas of Washington DC during breaks, I sat on park benches at a pedestrian trail in crowded suburban neighborhoods of Louisiana, waiting for my cab driver husband to complete his last pick-up for the day. I thought about what it would be like to purchase a home in a quiet subdivision of Louisiana one day. I imagined what it would be like for my family to live in a house in a wealthy neighborhood.

In the dating phase of our relationship, Daniyal chauffeured me around almost every part of Louisiana and Washington DC like I was one of his cab customers or a tourist visiting America for the first time. Daniyal commuted to Washington DC from Louisiana showing me the white house. If you were lucky, you might catch a glimpse of the US President and first lady taking a stroll out in the yard, waving to admirers' or foreign tourists snapping photos.

Daniyal pointed out his favorite monuments, landmarks and memorials reading a short biography inscribed below the statue or picture of a slayed war hero, veteran or figure related to American history. Sometimes Daniyal and I walked around out-door shops and cafes in Washington DC window shopping, wasting away afternoons while waiting for another pick- up. On the drive home, when I drifted off to sleep in the car and started to shut my eyes, Daniyal whispered under his breath, "Don't fall asleep. Look around, Washington DC is stunning."

At our next destination, we stopped at a farm area and sat by the pond, watching people pass by. I knew Daniyal missed his native land when he was quiet for too long, deep in thought, looking out at empty fields where construction workers built new homes. I thought about what it must have felt like to experience life as a foreigner in the US for Daniyal as a newcomer from Pakistan, during his first few weeks when he arrived in Louisiana.

Daniyal must have driven around parts of Washington DC aimless, in his down time thinking about places throughout the United States that reminded him of home.

"You will like where I'm taking you next, don't shut your eyes very long. Don't fall asleep, Samantha," Daniyal said.

Daniyal never liked saying goodbye, he left short handwritten notes behind, like the day he went away to the United States. My first time driving around our village property with Ayaan was like cab rides with Daniyal, stopping for kulfi ice cream and junk food along the way. After my divorce to Daniyal, I replayed the beginning of our relationship, holding onto a memory of a humble foreigner from Pakistan and his first days arriving to the United States of America. Daniyal must've driven around every place in Louisiana that felt like home, thinking about heritage, family and ancestral land.

I didn't fully understand Daniyal's connection to his birth country until I traveled to Faisalabad, Pakistan and called my in-laws family. No matter how much my relatives from Faisalabad hurt me, I would go back to Pakistan again. According to Daniyal, the United States was a country he traveled for the purposes of earning money in the form of US currency. After years of working dead end jobs, Daniyal must have concluded that living as a foreigner in a country like America wouldn't be worth the risk of crossing the border illegally a second time.

Daniyal talked about farmers who labored on his property of Ganish, plowing fields and selling rice and milk to market, employed by his middle-class family in

Faisalabad. Daniyal claimed to never look down on people because of their place in society, like some of his wealthy friends from Faisalabad living in Louisiana who were US citizens and held dual citizenship. My migrant spouse swore he never mistreated agriculture workers or maids employed by relatives in Ganish. Daniyal's cab customers and rich friends placed prejudices on Daniyal based on his standing in society as a taxi driver. Building a new life together in the United States meant I understood Daniyal was willing to die for what belonged to him. The rest didn't matter.

We drove around a while, as Daniyal pointed out elegant homes in safe neighborhoods of Louisiana where children played outside on newly paved cement sidewalks, different than my memory of littered village backroads. Children of wealthy businessmen who Daniyal considered his best paying cab customers, seemed to play without a care in the world.

"When I get my land back, we will move to this neighborhood." Daniyal promised.

When Daniyal called me from prison in Texas, I thought of the cash he saved to buy a house for our family. I let myself fantasize, like Nadia did, about walking into a house and seeing Daniyal in every room, recalling with anguish the better times we shared as a family.

I used to advise Daniyal constantly saying things like, "You can't drive a taxicab forever. Driving late nights in certain areas of Washington DC is unsafe. I worry about you."

Circumstances rarely changed for the better. I shared in feelings of degradation for what my cab driver husband faced within the Pakistani community as a man from a respectable caste, a tribe called Sheikh. Marrying a Pakistani was like facing down the embarrassment of hearing conversations spoken in Urdu loud enough to understand jokes made at my expense aimed at my husband and children.

On a commute from Faisalabad to Karachi, I sat in silence in the backseat troubled by put downs made by Malak about Pakistani cab drivers who came from good families and went to America, still driving a taxicab for a living. During the car ride, Rani's husband, Malak gushed about finishing his law degree. Malak was currently looking for work at a prestigious law firm in Faisalabad.

Rani's husband, Malak mentioned having no desire to visit a place like America because if he couldn't succeed in the United States, it wouldn't be worth the risk to leave one's good standing in society as a proud Pakistani from an upper middle-class family. On our ride home to Faisalabad, foreigners spoke jokingly about Daniyal as a cab driver who went away to America, still driving a taxicab for work married to a contemporary woman. Malak's fears of becoming a cab driver or low wage earner himself as someone who came from a good caste wasn't the life he wanted.

Malak Pulled into the embassy in Karachi, talking in Urdu about his friends from Faisalabad who were US citizens but embarrassed themselves and the Pakistani community by staying in jobs below their skillsets while holding college degrees. I was humiliated by Malik's friends and relatives who spoke a foreign language in front of me and labeled me a gora, who married a lowly Pakistani cab driver. Some of Malak's friends and relatives from Faisalabad referred to me as white trash, a person who lacked culture.

Daniyal did side jobs for extra cash, picking up groceries for his regular cab customers. A few of his best tipping customers made traditional food or treated me like a guest in their house. Some of Daniyal's best paying customers made tea and engaged in friendly banter about my interests and married life with Daniyal and my two children.

One of Daniyal's most unusual customers was a Punjabi woman pursuing a pharmaceutical degree suffering from face paralysis. Until recently I had never heard of paid work as a taxicab driver, running errands and picking up caged pigeons, Daniyal bought for a cheap price at a local farm. Fatima was Daniyal's most unusual client. A well- meaning Pakistani living in Louisiana, a friend and regular customer of Daniyal trivialized stories of greedy relatives from village areas of Faisalabad who hoarded wealth and property for themselves saying things like; "Small-minded people kill each other over land in parts of Faisalabad. "This is not uncommon."

Daniyal's most unusual customer, Fatima referenced problems she encountered with in-laws from Faisalabad. Fatima talked about her battle with postpartum depression and genetics resulting in facial paralysis that wasn't' getting better. "I tried everything, face massages, prayers to Allah, talking to my physician. Nothing works." Fatima complained.

Caged pigeons sitting on the balcony of Fatima's apartment exaggerated my feelings of hopelessness. I didn't worry about having a perfectly symmetrical face, or meeting beauty standards. I wanted to put our financial troubles and problems over stolen land behind me. I couldn't stop thinking about the caged pigeons Daniyal brought over to Fatima's apartment in Louisiana. Soon wild pigeons will be used in a sacrificial blood ritual.

Daniyal left a modest way of life in the village of Ganish behind for a life of struggle in the states. Before the car ride to Karachi, Daniyal told foreigners who came to America struggling to find work, some with college degrees, "Keep going, you're doing this for your family back home."

I reminded myself that driving a taxicab for work was temporary, our situation would change. A better opportunity would come along. I thought about many times Daniyal's cab was broken into and our rent money was stolen. The nights I knew Daniyal slept overnight in his cab was the worst feeling, especially after our children came along. As the oldest of three brothers, from a large extended family, Daniyal carried the weight of having to provide financially for his mother and three siblings. It was the oldest brother's financial obligation to fund both his sisters' arranged marriages.

Years later, I sat in the passenger seat, taking in what cab customers said in Punjabi trying to tune out jokes, not wanting to let on that their comments affected me. I would tune out whispers spoken about a modern woman married to a cab driver. I didn't want to look at what was happening in my marriage. Daniyal talked about his native land like a fairy tale saying things like;

"Pakistan like a kind of heaven; you will go there and never remember why you would want to come to a place like America."

I started to open my eyes during the best moments of my marriage to Daniyal. I learned to close my eyes when things got too painful.

CHAPTER 4

Religious Doctrine, When Things Fall Apart

*E*id holidays fall on random Fridays. Bright red blood from a sacrificial animal covered quiet sidewalks of Faisalabad where a succession of children played on a Muslim holiday meant for devotion to Allah, Eid. Hours later, the last traces of animal blood drained from sewers. Specks of animal blood lined sidewalks and entryways of bazaars. A heavy fog lifted. The air was clear.

On his down time, Daniyal watched spiritual leaders on television in Louisiana, shouting in Urdu while reading religious doctrine from the holy Koran, preaching about damnation and hell for sinners and non-followers. Out of nowhere, Daniyal called from a prison in Texas consoling me when I tried not to let him hear me cry on the other end of the line. Not to worry, he would return home the following morning when he could afford bail money, Daniyal told me.

Like natural disasters and earthquakes in Pakistan, the worst moments of my journey to a rural area of Faisalabad were the possibilities I didn't want to believe about Nadia's brother. I suspected Daniyal may have been earning money illegally under the false pretense of a taxicab driver. Daniyal called from a prison in Texas again. This time around, I didn't bother answering the phone. A lingering odor of animal blood followed me through a day meant for celebration. Kids returned to play outside in anticipation of a major Muslim holiday, marked on a calendar. The

sight of animal blood was everywhere. When the commotion of laughter and festivities died down, Muslim families feasted together.

During my marriage to Daniyal at a mosque down the block from our apartment, I pictured myself wearing a head scarf, given the Muslim name Kasra by my
husband. The old version of me named Samantha was down to earth and optimistic
about the future. This new version of me, was an Islamic woman my in laws called
Kasra. Kasra was meek, subservient and unusually sad most of the time. Hearing the
innocence come through my voice as a newly married woman when I read passages
from the Koran, I understood that I was no different than Aaliyaa. When I married
Daniyal, I was easy to manipulate and take advantage of. I was too innocent in my
adolescence to see Daniyal for all the terrible things he did to me and other family
members. Blood spilled over onto the highways of Faisalabad

I wore a pair of new salwar kameez and sat feeling out of place in a room of
Islamic women who prayed and cried out to Allah. The group of women who made
up the prayer circle cried almost in unison, in an eerie chant that sounded like the
cries of small children. Muslim women who made up the prayer group brought
homecooked food like in laws from Faisalabad. Like my time living in Ganish, I
chose not to show up to religious celebrations where hard-core followers of Islam
offered prayers for Daniyal and our family. Strangers extended Muslim prayers for
Daniyal and our family over problems involving the ownership of land in Ganish.

I told Daniyal that I loved him and grew to care about his three sisters and their
children in Faisalabad despite our differences in religious beliefs.

On initial trips to Faisalabad, Pakistan, joy surrounded me in the form of
Muslim prayers and blessings for a fulfilling married life put forward to me by
elders. Early Friday mornings one Eid holiday, Farah went through the motions of
namaz prayer, muttering a Muslim prayer in Urdu under her breath. Farah bent
down, extending her open hands out to Allah; a gesture that meant Farah received
blessings and forgiveness from Allah for sins of family members. Religion wasn't
something you could teach by modeling a motion or following a systematic way of
reciting prayers to Allah in Urdu.

Farah's relationship with her oldest brother, Daniyal came with feelings of confusion and betrayal. There was hesitancy and grief in Farah's tone of voice when
she talked about her oldest brother from America. Daniyal was unlike Nadia who
showed a childlike adoration for her brother. The smallest of three children, still

told satirical stories about growing up with her big brother at their village home of Ganish.

In neighboring villages of Ganish, oldest brothers and Fathers of large middle-class families bore the financial obligation of funding lavish weddings of sisters and daughters. Women of Ganish who couldn't keep their marriages or families intact because of abusive in laws or husbands, were sometimes sent back to their childhood villages. That's where Rani ended up, sent to live with senior male relatives at Ganish. The stigma of being a female Muslim divorcee meant that as a disadvantage Muslim woman, you were viewed as a problematic partner who couldn't keep your marriage together in the eyes of the community.

Eid celebrations fell on a Friday when Aaliyaa's husband returned from a hospital in Pakistan, a diabetic seizure left him paralyzed on the left side of his body. Every few hours on Eid, a day meant for celebration, Aaliyaa took a break from prayers to Allah to turn, feed and bathe her husband. Aaliyaa never could face her brother Daniyal and tell him the truth. Nadia hated what he did.

Aaliyaa assumed Allah's will for her life was spending afternoons cooking meals for guests, male relatives and friends, reciting Muslim prayers five times per day, never asking for what she wanted or deserved in life. Aaliyaa rarely let on that she had hobbies of her own. Aaliyaa thought Prophet Muhammad handed her the duties of turning her husband over every few hours, changing bed sheets and preparing meals for him and male guests. Handfuls of guests showed up randomly throughout the day of Eid, offering Islamic prayers for Aaliyaa's husband's swift recovery. Aaliyaa went about her routine of reciting namaz prayer. She checked in on her husband every couple of hours like nothing was the matter.

I married a wealthy landowner, that's what Nadia told me about Daniyal who lost a good portion of his wealth and property but loved me dearly. When I questioned Daniyal about cash lying around our apartment, Daniyal lashed out in a rage episode shouting, "stay out of my business from now on!"

Instructing me to open the door of our apartment at select hours of the day for friends and regular cab customers who needed to retrieve something from our apartment urgently, like a faithful Muslim wife I did what I was told. I wasn't ready to face the realities of what was happening in my marriage. Compared to a once sensible man who managed a gas station and cooked flavorful dinners on quiet nights after work, there was a darker side to a version of a faithful practicing Muslim. I no longer saw Daniyal as a loving Father and trusted companion.

I questioned why strangers showed up to our apartment at random daytime hours frequently. I asked Daniyal about the piles of cash stashed in areas throughout our apartment. Daniyal offered a good enough explanation. He said the only people who called cabs at all hours of the night lived in rough neighborhoods, out of state. Daniyal explained that his best cab customers paid large sums of cash as a form of down payment. Building a steady customer base comprised of out- of state pickups. According to Daniyal, his clients who lived out of state were his customer base, and the only way he made good money.

When my oldest son, Sameer started Elementary school, I began finding empty liquor bottles concealed inside kitchen cupboards throughout our apartment. I learned about Daniyal's alcoholism and opioid addiction from friends and relatives years later. Concerned family members of Daniyal's were afraid he was hiding an addiction that seemed to drastically change his behavior, causing erratic mood changes that shifted in the blink of an eye, from jovial to terrifyingly provoked.

Nadia told a story during my stay in Faisalabad about a serene village where she spent her childhood with Daniyal, a protective big brother who I grew to respect.

Reemerging after weeklong absences, Daniyal came home carrying heavy boxes of religious books inside. For Sameer and Asad, I looked the part of an obedient Muslim woman, dried my eyes and faced in-laws from Faisalabad, forcing a smile. I never could accept a religion like Islam in my heart. On my next trip to Pakistan, I told each of my in-laws that my marriage to Daniyal was a success. I fabricated instances of a stable family life to relatives from Faisalabad, highlighting all the ways I was content and settled into life with Daniyal in Louisiana. I lied to family and friends in Pakistan not because I was a devoted Muslim woman or that I bothered reading the Koran, I was determined to make my marriage work at any cost. I held onto my marriage to Daniyal long after it was over, to the detriment of my health and safety.

Listening to myself as an immature woman, hearing the vulnerability come through in my voice when I read verses from the Koran in Urdu, I thought about Daniyal's secretive life. When I recalled my first times traveling to rural areas of Pakistan with my children, I was flooded with emotions. As a busy housewife and Mother during the better part of my marriage, I was practically a single Mom who lived for the happiness of my two children, Sameer and Asad. Shortly after our Islamic wedding called nikah, Daniyal took me to a mosque he attended every

Friday for prayer. He bought a new pair of salwar kameez for me, insisting I cover my hair with a veil.

A man dressed in white prayed namaz over us for a successful married life. I listened closely. Daniyal used to say things like, "It will mean a lot to me if you study the Koran, so you have a better grasp of Islam when you travel to Faisalabad and meet my three siblings. As much as you enjoy reading, I thought you would like to study the written word of the holy Koran and learn how to pray namaz." I pushed boxes of Islamic books under the bed.

On Friday mornings, Daniyal went about his morning routine of showering, ironing his white salwar kameez and leaving for the afternoon to a mosque not far from our apartment in Washington DC. We traveled out of state on Fridays, his day designated for worship. Daniyal introduced me to a women's prayer group every Friday at a stranger's home in Virginia. A Muslim man welcomed me as a guest in his home and reminded me of religious gurus on television who preached about Islamic faith being the only way to heaven. As a survivor of narcissistic abuse early in my life, looking back at my marriage to Daniyal, I was too prideful to reach out to friends or family members when the belittling started. Acclaimed Spiritual leaders Daniyal watched on Fridays preached in Urdu about catastrophic outcomes for sinners and nonbelievers.

After returning one Friday from a prayer group at a different region of Louisiana, I decided to tell Daniyal that I would never come around to converting to his Muslim faith. Daniyal smiled, proclaiming that he accepted me despite our differences in beliefs, even if I never chose to convert to Islam. After traveling to Pakistan, I realized my Pakistani in-laws never accepted that I rarely prayed namaz in public. Kasra, the Muslim version of me, was a defiant woman who purposely chose not to participate in religious functions when I was extended an invitation.

An Islamic woman named Zainab from the prayer group in Virginia switched on the international news channel. Zainab told me to pay close attention to news about our City of Faisalabad. Relatives from Faisalabad who had relatives still living in Pakistan, offered to pray for my in laws safety. While throwing a shawl over her hair, Zainab returned shortly with a plate of rice, fried pakoras and sweets for guests who showed up to the couple's home to join in the prayer group.

Daniyal's friend and regular cab customer, Eli, came to our apartment in Louisiana regularly to pick something up. Eli kept large amounts of cash, random appliances and furniture stockpiled at our apartment like he was renting out a storage unit. Daniyal's cab customer told me about the wife and children he left behind in Africa, sharing stories about a distant childhood he spent in Africa. He wore his hair in cornrows and flipped houses for a living.

According to Eli, he made a solid income, restoring and selling foreclosed homes, sending a portion of his salary back to Africa to his wife and children. Daniyal's friend parked outside of our apartment complex in designated spots; his body was hidden inside the tinted windows of his SUV. My husband's friend and customer blasted music, sitting for hours at a time in the parking lot of our apartment complex. Eli looked to be waiting for someone to show up outside of our apartment building, counting his cash in US currency from inside the parked SUV.

Daniyal was shrewd about hiding things from me, like piles of cash stuffed in coat pockets, hidden in different spots of the apartment we shared in Louisiana. Looking back at the life I lived with Daniyal in the United States, he was unusually vigilant most of the time about strangers leaving our apartment unlocked, with loads of cash lying around. Daniyal disappeared for days, sometimes weeks at a time, telling me he had to pick up an important customer in another city or state for a large amount of money.

Family and friends from Louisiana didn't know that I was living a mysterious life with a man who was only good at pretending. For years, I was married to a con man who lied about nearly every aspect of his upbringing and what he did for work. In my adolescence, when I first met Daniyal at a gas station, I could only see a sincere man from a village who I adored. Daniyal was kind-hearted with traditional family values who cooked ethnic food like his sisters made back home. Things were good at the beginning.

Daniyal taught me how to cook Pakistani food like his relatives from a village in Ganish. Daniyal taught me how to cherish a country that was once filled with tradition, family and a simpler existence. A child from Ganish left his native land of Pakistan, without warning leaving a note behind. The man who wore his hair in cornrows, Eli, played music from inside the tinted windows of his SUV. Daniyal's friend waited in the same spot outside our apartment building, always appearing the same, paranoid that he may have left something behind. Eli came across as jumpy, not thinking about going back for whoever seemed to be missing from his life.

My parents, who represented old-fashioned values, once considered Daniyal a part of our family. Daniyal lied to his joint family for years while Inaya and three sisters took the blame, asking and praying for Daniyal's return to Faisalabad.

I think about the years Nadia spent estranged from her husband when guards took him away to prison and what it must've felt like as a new bride, waiting to go on a honeymoon to Murree. Nadia stored away cash in rupees for the day when her husband would return from prison. I was like Inaya during my marriage to the oldest of three brothers, watching Nadia in agony waiting for her husband.

When I traveled back to Louisiana, nothing changed. I hoped my two sons didn't suffer and miss me in the same way I did. In the end, I imagine Daniyal went away, never to be heard from or spoken about again.

I wanted to tell my two kids in Faisalabad, let's start over, with a clean slate. I'm here for you. I wanted a new beginning with Sameer and Asad. One day, I would have to tell my children something about their father, Daniyal. The answers couldn't be found in a religious book of Islam. I used to stay up nights thinking about the cruelty of people.

CHAPTER 5

Returning to the Past, Abuse and Indirection; Abdullah

The oldest of three brothers was living a moderately comfortable lifestyle in an upper middle-class suburban neighborhood of Minnesota, a house he shared with Abdullah, his wife Rashida and their children. Daniyal described his arrival to America, summarizing what it was like living in Minnesota as an immigrant from a rural area of Faisalabad, Pakistan. Abdullah took Daniyal into his home and agreed to look after him. Wife beatings must have been the norm in some provinces of Punjab. Disciplining your spouse wasn't viewed as a big deal.

Family members from Minnesota didn't bother calling the police over trivial marital disputes and disagreements. Before I traveled abroad and witnessed what life was like for some women and daughters born of Pakistani descent, I didn't realize Nadia's oldest brother went through what he described as a traumatic experience living in a violent household. Daniyal lived in a state of constant fear, under the control of a once respected family member, his cousin Abdullah.

The oldest brother had no knowledge of his legal status in the United States while living in Minnesota with Abdullah and Rashida, claiming Abdullah was hiding and throwing away mail to sabotage his ability to gain legal residency. After getting denied for his green card, Daniyal told me he had had enough of watching Abdullah's wife, Rashida, withstand her husband Abdullah's beatings. Nadia's brother stood protectively in front of Rashida, looking Abdullah dead in the eye, warning him this was the last time he would raise a hand to Rashida.

I was sorting through what was useful enough to pack in a small carry on. Family members from Minnesota who stood in front of me turned into inanimate images of Pakistani relatives I recollected hearing stories about. Daniyal must have temporarily forgotten his circumstances. He had no other place to live and no legal status in the United States. Ther oldest brother couldn't return to his homeland of Pakistan, a failure. Daniyal never loved me.

The following morning, Daniyal was made to collect his things and leave the family's shared residency in Minnesota. Nadia's brother spoke about drifting away from close knit relatives he grew up with, Abdullah and Rashida near his village property of Ganish, blood relatives he once considered inseparable.

Returning to Minnesota to face an agonizing new beginning must have been heart-breaking

When Daniyal glanced over at me, it was as if he was seeing a version of Rashida. Daniyal couldn't take Rashida along with him wherever he ended up after leaving Minnesota. The oldest brother couldn't look after Rashida in all the ways she needed protecting. He was made to vacate the family's shared residency for good, leaving a close relative from Ganish to quite possibly withstand Abdullah's beatings. Daniyal was forced to leave the home he shared with Abdullah and his family with no plan, or destination.

The oldest of three brothers set out on a journey. Daniyal was forced to leave a woman from his neighboring village of Ganish who he promised to Abdullah in an arranged marriage behind. Rashida was an innocent village woman with a basic level of education who he could no longer shield from harm. Daniyal cared deeply for Rashida.

Gestures of sincerity and affection in Pakistani culture were made up of un-spoken emotions and horror stories about arranged marriages and the pitfalls of finding happiness after marriage. The definition of love according to Daniyal was growing up in a village and accepting the concept of arranged marriages, a type of self- sacrifice and dedication to family and religious teachings of Islam. There were questions I knew not to ask Daniyal about long held beliefs and religious teachings taken from the holy Koran. There were strict rules about being a new follower of Islam, a Muslim woman I chose not to disclose to close friends or family.

For years, I listened to accounts about a man named Abdullah who was the instigator of a more than decade long property dispute. I decided to give Daniyal's cousin, Abdullah, a chance.

Piles of unwashed clothes were spread around our living room, mixed in with mismatched dress pants and collared shirts with price tags attached. I watched secretively, as Daniyal sorted through a heap of unwashed clothes. He still couldn't seem to decide what to discard or take along for a last-minute road trip to Minnesota. We had to be packed and out the door in a few hours.

Sometimes I thought it was better to see Daniyal express a range of emotions rather than to refuse to talk about the reasons we were traveling to Minnesota. At times, I wanted to reassure Daniyal that I would be there for him. Even when he was a nervous wreck, Nadia's brother never showed that he wasn't coping well, struggling to pick out the right outfit. I was undecided about whether I should offer to help Daniyal get ready or concentrate on my packing. Last-minute planning of important events infuriated me.

I held my tongue and focused on getting ready for our trip. Insisting I go along with Daniyal and Idris on a road trip out of state was like asking me to travel back to a better memory of marital life. I was regretful that weeks prior I agreed to go on a road- trip to Minnesota. Daniyal's nephew was a soft-spoken, Pakistani immigrant cab driver who arrived ahead of schedule.

Idris owned an inexpensive piece of property in an adjacent area of Ganish. Idris was more like a brother than a nephew to Daniyal. Given the unwelcoming attitude toward Muslims and Islamophobia on the rise, the chances of Idris being granted a visa to the United States was like winning the lottery.

We finally arrived in Minnesota in the early hours of morning, before sunrise. I stood in front of a closed garage door. I remembered Rashida from a family photograph Nadia's brother showed me when we first started dating. Rashida was a heavy-set Punjabi woman from Daniyal's village home of Ganish. When I met Rashida in Minnesota, she resembled her picture and was wearing a light pair of salwar kameez most women from Ganish dressed in when at home. Rashida had a smooth complexion and high cheek bones like her picture. Auntie threw a shawl over her hair quickly, "Assalamu alaikum," Rashida greeted yawning, forcing a smile. Rashida wore her long black hair in a single braid that ran past the curve of her back. I walked through the house, careful not to wake up sleeping family members.

I imagined incidents that took place when Daniyal talked about his first cousin from Ganish, Rashida, years ago. Daniyal described Rashida as a lighthearted village woman who enjoyed cooking indigenous food for guests, known for being an accommodating and generous host to friends and relatives in Ganish and Faisalabad. Rashida served as a reminder of the abuse I experienced in my early upbringing. There was an air of sadness Rashida carried present in subtle ways she smiled and moved through the family home in Minnesota. There was a childlike vulnerability I noticed in her mannerisms when she spoke that was noticeable in women who grew up in villages.

I couldn't help but picture tragic occurrences that must have happened in Abdullah's home when Daniyal stayed here. I envisioned Rashida beaten, pleading for her husband to stop. Abdullah's demeanor shifted from terrifyingly cruel, laughing menacingly at his wife's perceived frailties. When he caught his breath and snapped out of a rage episode, Abdullah returned to his role as a calm and loving husband. The worst of what may have taken place before I arrived, made me want to leave the family's shared residency in Minnesota right away.

Rashida must have quietly pleaded for her husband to stop. The sheer strength of Abdullah's body overpowered Rashida's, each time he struck her. Abdullah would come to, suddenly remorseful, promising to do better next time. I couldn't forget the accounts Daniyal told me about Abdullah. There were moments I knew Abdullah hit his wife as a form of punishment, to keep Rashida in line. I questioned why Rashida chose to stay in an abusive marriage as a US citizen. In tribal areas of Pakistan, indigenous women carried the honor and responsibility of marriages arranged by relatives. Staying in an abusive arranged marriage must have been about survival, upholding family traditions and honoring hard working men and male providers. Rashida must have agreed to stay quiet no matter the cost. It was an arranged marriage.

Most close relatives from provinces of Punjab questioned what Rashida had to complain about. Living in a big house in a primarily white suburban neighborhood meant most within the Pakistani community assumed you were financially provided for, or at the least taken care of. Compared to how women from villages of Ganish lived, Abdullah's wife should count her blessings. I assumed Rashida made the best of her circumstances with Abdullah and their children. Abdullah's wife was like women in Faisalabad, yet different.

Rashida was hesitant to speak English, busying herself in the kitchen, no different than any of the girls I taught in Pakistan at a government school. When Auntie switched on the bright kitchen light, she stood veil-less and timid. I looked at Rashida and peered around at the house Daniyal shared with family members when he first came to Minnesota.

Daniyal never loved me.

Abdullah appeared nothing like I imagined. He was a gaunt man dressed in solid white salwar kameez with a long, graying beard. Abdullah had luminescent eyes when he looked directly at me. He had just finished reciting namaz prayer. and greeted me by touching the top of my head, a symbol of respect and blessings for a new daughter-in-law.

I thought of my late father-in law, Abbas, and remembered the only time I witnessed Daniyal open up was the day he learned of his father's passing. I couldn't be there in person to participate in the oldest son's duty and religious obligation of leading in a prayer ritual for the sake of assuring a loved one's peace in the afterlife.

Abdullah from Minnesota resembled Abbas, my late father-in-law. He had the same slender physique and brown eyes. I couldn't believe any of the earlier stories Daniyal told of Abdullah were accurate.

My first impression of Daniyal's cousin, Imran was that of a high strung, college age, man with the emotions of a child. Imran descended the steps, overtaken with excitement. Daniyal's cousin greeted me with a broad smile, snuggling me close on the leather sofa. Imran switched the channel from the international news to a cartoon, hiding his bone thin body inside a heavy throw blanket. Imran spoke fluent English, in an American accent and went on about all we would do during my stay at the family's home in Minnesota, as if no time passed. I felt like the two of us knew each other before meeting for the first time in Minnesota.

Imran was diagnosed at an early age with autism. Imran immediately noticed Daniyal reclined on the sofa in the living room and jumped into Daniyal's arms, burying his head in his lap like a kid. In a soothing motion, Daniyal stroked his hair, like a parent calming a disobedient child, who had begun winding down from a -tantrum. I couldn't comprehend half of what Daniyal went through the day he left Minnesota. I was certain that Imran missed Daniyal more than any other family member I met while visiting estranged relatives in Minnesota.

"Not enough oxygen to the brain," Abdullah remarked, caught off guard, afraid I may have suspected something being off with his little son.

The rest of our three-day long visit with relatives in Minnesota entailed eating traditional food cooked using organic ingredients that tasted like curry dishes I shared with relatives in Faisalabad. Later that afternoon, I went along with family members who drove down the block to the neighborhood tennis court to play a doubles match, a jovial game of tennis. No one kept score. We returned home to Minnesota a few hours later.

Male guests congregated together rolling out prayer mats, watching international news channels, resting and finally reciting evening Muslim prayers. Imran preferred to be on his own and excluded himself from large groups or crowded places. When possible, Imran chose to ride his bicycle around familiar cold de sacs and highways in a neighborhood of Minnesota he knew well.

I informed relatives I was going for a walk through the neighborhood. Before making it out the door to a local family park, I fell asleep. Abdullah hopped on his bicycle, riding, through the neighborhood, conducting his own missing persons search, only to discover me soundly sleeping in the guest bedroom. The long drive to Minnesota wore me out. Before I could make it to the door for my afternoon walk, without telling anyone, I slept for longer than I can remember.

On our commute back to Louisiana Daniyal confided to me that he regretted not intervening when he was informed that Imrans' school placed him in a separate class for special needs kids. "He didn't belong there, with those kids."

"Imran should have been placed in a regular school with the rest of his peers and classmates. If Abdullah would have thought to reach out to me years ago, everything would have been different." Daniyal explained.

We were within home stretch; the last road signs told me we were a few miles from Louisiana. This incident reminded me of my encounter with security at the US airport, where I thought the same thing, home was just within reach. I could almost extend my hand out to breathe in unpolluted air. Highways of Louisiana were smooth and free of liter, unlike dusty back roads of Faisalabad, Pakistan. There were no children waiting to greet me from our village of Ganish, bright eyed and curious about a stranger from America, a worldly person called gora.

My flight landed as scheduled. I made it through a grueling sixteen-hour long flight back from the village of Faisalabad to my home-state of Louisiana. before stepping on US soil, I was stopped and interrogated. My passport was confiscated by a security guard at the airport and locked in a glass case. I was led down a long corridor and made to sit with a group of foreigners for hours. I was asked a series of personal questions about in- laws from Faisalabad, Pakistan.

Officer, it's called marona, a type of sweet dessert in Pakistan, Aaliyaa must have packed it last minute, I explained as the security guard closed my suitcase, eyeing me with a look of suspicion, while stuffing my clothes and personal things back inside the suitcase. The officer hesitated to hand back my US passport. Fear overtook me when flashing sirens emitting from a nearby police car meant something was wrong.

"Expired Tags," a police officer stated, shining a bright flashlight in my face. The officer wrote something down on a notepad. "License and registration please." The police officer requested.

We drove all the way to Minnesota without renewing the tags, "No officer, that's already been taken care of," Idris said, pulling a piece of paper from the glove compartment. After almost an hour of waiting for the officer to return and tell us why we' had been pulled over, Idris was issued a hefty fine. I couldn't wait to return home to Louisiana.

"Let's not talk about this anymore," I interrupted, barely able to keep my eyes open.

"You're too tired to drive, pull over, it's my turn to drive," I insisted, letting the silence of the deserted roads and the two sleeping men, sprawled out in the back of the SUV quiet my mind. After our time visiting relatives in Minnesota ended, I decided I would never agree to go back to Minnesota again even for a visit. I would be there for Daniyal when he needed

PART 2

First Introductions

CHAPTER 6

Life in Faisalabad, Pakistan

*E*arlier days I spent in Faisalabad, Pakistan was full of excitement like visiting outdoor bazaars and the taste of mangoes at the start of summers. In the beginning, each time we visited a new region of Pakistan, my sister-in-law, Nadia greeted me with flowers, white and yellow dandelions taken from a neighbor's yard, until the sentiment of appreciation and welcoming wore off. One of the neighbors told us never to step foot in his yard again, flower thieves, is what he called us. Kasra was a Muslim name given to me by Abbas, my late father-in-law. Translated in English, Kasra meant fragrant flower.

Nadia passed a vendor selling fresh juice from a pushcart on humid summer days. I close my eyes and think of Farah's girls and stealing flowers from an irate neighbor's yard. Sana got away with stealing many times before. Daniyal wanted to gift me the most valuable pieces of his lost childhood, an upbringing he left behind in a Village area of Pakistan, Ganish where Daniyal spoke of the commitment and sacrifice of his three siblings and mother. Daniyal never told anyone, why he ultimately left his beloved homeland of Pakistan for a life of uncertainty in the United States. Pakistan was a country filled with strife, turmoil and political unrest; a country where I found community and tradition.

A recurring dream I have is of placing my hand over Sameer's chest to monitor his breathing before kissing my son on the forehead, trying my best not to let my children hear me sob quietly. I would have to leave in the middle of the night to catch a flight back to Louisiana. My mind replays an image of Asad walking in and out of empty rooms of our family home, searching for his birth Mother. In each room he finds a different version of a female parent, the wrong surrogate Mother as he cries out, searching for me. Every one of my family members from Pakistan were bound to a culture made up of feudal lords, a group of wealthy landowners who showed up one day to take everything away from me.

When I walked by newly blossomed sunflowers, I rejoiced in the thrill of my first days traveling to Faisalabad, Pakistan as a foreigner from the United States. Years living in a secluded farm village of Ganish taught me I became no different than any Pakistani who lived on farmlands hidden away in handcrafted mud houses. A large group of cheerful family members showed up at an airport in Lahore excited to show me around.

A security guard followed behind me every place I traveled alone during initial visits to Faisalabad. There were endearing moments of happiness wrought with sadness for those left behind a fond memory of white garlands of flowers intricately woven into a hair piece I was gifted on each trip to Pakistan. During my first visits to Nadia's village home of Ganish, I got dressed up in newly sown salwar kameez, excited to attend upper middle class Pakistani wedding parties when extended an invitation.

Neighboring middle class families of our city sent wedding invitations wrapped in lace, written in neat cursive lettering for the fun of seeing a worldly woman in person. Each Pakistani family member who constituted upper middle-class society wanted to know the same things, like why I came to Pakistan as an US citizen. People wanted to know how long I would last after living in tribal areas of Ganish, enduring long periods of electricity and water losses.

Arriving to Pakistan a US citizen and the newness of everything intriguing about life in a village of Ganish was beginning to wear off. I started to become like a devoted Pakistani woman, thinking only about others' well- being and happiness, having a warped idea of romance, family loyalty and marriage. Nadia worried most that I wasn't adjusting well to culture and day to day life in Faisalabad. Sitting alone for long periods at a time, lost in daydreams, writing stories during time allotted for socializing with family meant I wasn't happy. I wasn't adjusting well to cultural norms.

On walks in the village, when I stayed for long periods, I saw Daniyal every-where. Each time a child from our ancestral home said the word America, his voice broke midsentence, like the word America was synonymous with the act of leaving someone behind. This paradoxical land was like a time capsule, a picture in my mind of a country I could go to be seen or remain invisible. I made a mental note of the village kids' dirty, once white, shalwar kameez and his aversion to the word America. Traveling to a place like the United States virtually disappearing, never returning to where you originated was all that remained of my memory of Pakistan and Daniyal's ties to his birth country.

Nadia asked about how I was doing after I went to my room early before the last guest left and welcomed me to Pakistan offering prayers for my health, marriage and family. Nadia would check on me after weeks of meeting guests, strangers who offered prayers and reassured me I too would come to accept Faisalabad and Pakistani people, eventually. Nadia would find me during prayer, a large gathering or at a time meant to mingle with important people or guests sitting alone off to myself writing.

On my last day in Pakistan, Idris, Daniyal's nephew, traveled with me to Faisalabad to inform me of my flight departure time. I saw a different image of my two children, Sameer and Asad running into my arms, as we left for a promised land together, in hopes of starting a new life without the memory of ever meeting Danyal's family. Members of my joint family didn't need to remind me that I was an outsider and my Muslim name Kasra held little value. Farah was there to inform me of how I was not Islamic and still couldn't cook ethnic food. There was no use for my presence. This new sister- in law was a better version of me, a devoted Islamic woman who was highly intellectual with a respectable job as a schoolteacher.

All I could think about was going back to the beginning where I met Daniyal at a gas station in a part of Louisiana where I spent my childhood. I waited for Daniyal to tell me the truth about who he was and why he entered to the United States. Like a housekeeper employed by my Pakistani in-laws, I saw Daniyal handcuffed and taken away. When I opened my eyes, Daniyal was gone. Like the protagonist from my fiction book, I should have been angrier. I wanted to forget the day I left home in the idyllic countryside of Louisiana to start a life together. I stopped asking for a better way of life for myself and my sons, Sameer and Asad. On my last visit, Ayaan spoke of purchasing a house in a City like Karachi a few years after he made rank and became an officer.

Daniyal's idea of his country of origin, Pakistan was playing music from Hindi films and circling around his portion of land with his big brother, Ayaan piled in the back of a truck, armed with rifles. On the hottest summer days, large groups of children waited in anticipation for any signs of rain after a drought. On heavy showers, sewers poured grimy water into the open roads of Faisalabad. Teenagers employed by my in-laws splashed in deep pockets filled with rainwater. Kids of Ganish laughed and danced outdoors for hours in rain showers, coming inside when I felt the last drizzle of rain. Children of our village, Ganish would create lives of their own, progressing, no longer stuck in an endless vortex of the same, never needing to think of me- a westernized woman from Louisiana again.

When I traveled back to Louisiana this final time I waited, reluctant to tell the children of Ganish the truth, I moved on with my life before the first day I lived in a rural village. Teenage girls who worked for Pakistani relatives sat with me during their down time watching new Bollywood movies, showing off choreographed dance moves. I no longer embraced Daniyal and wouldn't be welcome back by my Pakistani family who once greeted me with flowers woven into my hair, bought for a couple hundred rupees from a street vendor. On this final trip to our ancestral village home, I wouldn't bother asking relatives why they never told any member of my joint family the truth about problems over property and inheritance. Daniyal made me a target and put my life and safety in danger.

Distant relatives from Faisalabad who owned more property than Daniyal considered me an enemy by association. Every time I stepped foot on uncharted soil or unmarked territory owned by relatives, a caste called sheikh, a tribe of wealthy landowners spanning back generations, I thought of Daniyal with regret. In the end, I pictured Nadia back at her ancestral village home of Ganish, sitting around a group of poor kids. Nadia placed the apple in her palm wearing salwar kameez from last season, carefully peeling back apple skin with sharp edges of a pocketknife. Nadia sat a bowl of fruit on a wooden table we kept outside looking to the distance dreamily, as if waiting for the arrival of a white woman she never met.

"Your American sister will be arriving any minute now." A lively crowd of village kids announced. Smallest sister- in law, Nadia dropped a pocketknife she used for cutting apples, using her kameez top to wipe off sharp edges of the knife's blade.

"Kasra is here," one girl from our village shouted, making sure to equally distribute a fair amount of fruit for each villager who would arrive to meet me for the first time that day. In my mind, I returned to Pakistan once more. I took one last trip to the market, savoring my first taste of sugarcane. I walked past a food seller purchasing another cup of freshly squeezed orange juice for a few rupees. My students from the government school showed up to tell me not to go. "Your home is here in

Faisalabad. I am afraid of what might happen to you and your children if you don't return to Pakistan," Nadia said.

No one thought to ask when Daniyal would return to Faisalabad. A security guard hired by Ayaan followed me everywhere. A child a few years older than my son, Sameer who sold snacks as a vendor and fresh produce, served as my final memory of traveling to Pakistan and returning an American.

A domestic worker employed by Nadia's brother came and went, returning to his village as a poor farmer, reemerging again at our home in Faisalabad after a few months employed temporarily as a housekeeper, cook and helper hired by Ayaan. Rohan was the same age as my teenage son hired as a new employee who showed me the right technique of shaping bread for guests who would arrive that afternoon. Rohan liked to roll out dough to make bread for guests coming to our home in the city. A man hired by Ayaan watched me a lot. He barely spoke.

I wondered what it must've been like working for a middle-class family in Faisalabad. Ayaan took the domestic worker back each time claiming he was only looking for a handout and had no home to return to. There wasn't one thing that brought a domestic worker employed by Ayaan happiness, that I could think of.

On the morning Ayaan drove me back to the airport in Faisalabad, I looked at the third story balcony to see Nadia hanging damp clothes. Nadia must have been double checking to make sure I looked well- put together, dressed in the new salwar kameez she sewed for me. Nadia waved goodbye from high above me on the third story terrace. Hours before, Aaliyaa helped condense my clothes into a small suitcase. Each piece of clothing Sameer and Asad needed to take back to Louisiana was folded and laid out neatly on the bed.

All I could think about was every criticism aimed at me during my last days as a Pakistani woman living in Ganish. "Don't think about returning to our city of Faisalabad even as a guest for a short time to live in Pakistan again," Farah threatened, before traveling back to Saudi Arabia.

On my last day in Faisalabad, an agriculture worker insisted he ride along on the day Ayaan drove me to the airport. I smiled, waved goodbye and shed a few tears. I turned to glance back at a poor farm worker employed by Ayaan tasked with carrying heavy luggage onto a baggage cart. A poor farmer employed by my extended family nodded and walked away, waving goodbye after piling my final piece of luggage onto the top of the cart.

"You could have had a good life in Pakistan. Besides, you're upper middle class.

You don't have to worry about help around the house or a tutor for your sons."
Chandra from the Vocational school where I taught in Faisalabad tried to convince
me. I wondered if my most enthusiastic student, Chandra would show up on my last
day in Pakistan. I waited for her to arrive on my last day so I could tell my student
from the vocational school in person I wouldn't be traveling back to Pakistan any
longer.

When I first began visiting Faisalabad, everything was new and exciting. Like
a guest who had worn out their welcome, my presence was no longer wanted in my
in-law's country of origin. A security guard who worked for relatives told me some
of my students from the government school where I taught English classes showed
up at random hours after I went back to Louisiana. Chandra waited outside the gate
of our home, probably thinking about whether they should knock on our front door,
wondering if our housekeeper would let her inside.

Before Ayaan drove off, Aaliyaa ran outside, covering her hair with a shawl,
claiming she forgot to recite a Muslim prayer of protection in Urdu for me, blowing
on the top of my head, whispering something in Punjabi under her breath. Aaliyaa
explained in Punjabi about needing to assure that I return to Louisiana safely and
in good health. I didn't know what to think about calling Pakistan my home and
relatives from provinces of Punjab where I lived, family. Sometimes I wondered if
relatives thought of me like an agriculture worker brother hired who returned for a
handout. Finding affection outside of arranged marriages in some parts of Punjab
where I stayed was like going with Sana to family parks and recreational places
where no one would think to find juvenile couples intimate, sitting on a park bench
with the person they desired to marry, outside of loveless arranged marriages to a
first cousin.

"You care a great deal for Daniyal. I know you miss him," Nadia teased, refer-
ring to the westernized concept of intimacy that according to Nadia didn't exist
in a country like Pakistan. I wanted to tell my Pakistani in-laws the truth, I cared
about them and wanted a more prosperous life for family members away from a
village where my three sister- in law's struggled for necessities, enduring weeklong
power and water shortages. On this last trip to Faisalabad, I meant to tell Nadia not
to waste years in prayer to Prophet Muhammed for a blessed married life to her
brother, Daniyal any longer. I moved on from my life with Daniyal a long time ago.

Students from the government school would never escape poverty and I would
likely never get out of an abusive marriage to Daniyal with two small children.

Months after arriving to Faisalabad, I stopped waiting for Daniyal to call or write and decided I wouldn't become like relatives who spent years reciting namaz prayer for a man who set out to destroy our lives over a piece of property in Karachi. Like poor students from a school where I taught English classes, I desired a better future for myself and two sons. When I returned to instruct English classes, poor students from the Vocational training school where I taught English wanted to know the reasons I arrived as a worldly person to their city of Faisalabad.

Attending social wedding parties meant I was obligated to talk about my educational background and qualifications like I was going to a job interview. What I enjoyed most were the years I spent back in Louisiana as a stay-at-home Mom to my two children, cooking and spending quality time together. Tagging along with Ayaan to meet upper- class Pakistani families made me understand that I wasn't successful or ambitious and didn't have much to offer as a westernized woman in the eyes of the middle-class community of Pakistan except for beauty. Although Inaya insulted poor students, I befriended at a Vocational school when they showed up at our home in Faisalabad at odd hours, arriving each morning to teach girls from poor communities to speak in English was something I was proud of.

"You made us believe that we would be free to marry the person of our choice, no matter what caste we're born into," Chandra complimented on the day before I left for the United States. Adolescent women from impoverished regions of Punjab were fleeing arranged marriages believing that a Pakistani from a good caste could have defied tradition and married, a woman who Daniyal met at a gas station.

Housekeepers wanted to know how my journey as an American woman living in the provinces of Punjab would end. During weeklong electricity shortages or Islamic holidays when I disappeared somewhere to work on my writing, I thought of the tragedy of my life with Daniyal and how I seldom thought of him any longer except during day long power outages when he existed as a character in my fiction books. I made a point to compose endings to my fiction books to include heartfelt goodbyes even if the characters didn't end up together any longer. I kept imagining different scenarios to add to the ending of my books. For the ending to my fiction book, I wrote about Daniyal disappearing from my life, so he couldn't hurt me any longer.

The second born daughter would still be at her village wearing outdated salwar kameez, slicing apples, carefully placing them in a bowl of fruit.

Rohan asked me what I liked most about Pakistani culture. I remembered the hundred thousand dollars cash Daniyal was carrying on him and a promise to buy the kids and I a house someday in an area of Louisiana where Daniyal drove around wealthy clients when he was pulled over and taken into custody. "We lost everything, our entire savings," Daniyal cried over the phone to me on my last day in Pakistan.

Like a taxicab driver from a part of Faisalabad I never heard of before, chauffeuring around rich customers, I told poor farm workers about how I liked to remain hopeful about what a future without Daniyal could bring. A tranquil life at Nadia's village was not possible. My marriage to Daniyal is over. I would no longer be a part of my Pakistani family. The hardest part was telling my family and friends from Louisiana about how Daniyal earned money under the table to make rent when I was a stay-at-home mom.

There was no excitement in getting dressed, cooking food and celebrating another Islamic holiday. Today was nothing out of the ordinary. A girl from Louisiana was no longer worth the hassle. My in-law's memory of me as a foreigner must've been in every way Daniyal made us suffer. Nadia never bothered inviting me back to her village. Daniyal called me from prison telling me he made bail money.

Like every lie Nadia told her sons about their father getting out of prison in Faisalabad, each good and bad memory I kept of my time living from Pakistan remained the same after the day Nadia and villagers of Ganish stopped celebrating my arrival. I thought Nadia was stunning in the way I remembered her sitting among a group of poor kids, cutting fruit into a bowl. I thought Nadia was vulnerable and child-like when I was first introduced to her.

Last, I remember seeing Nadia cheerful was the day I realized what finally broke her, it was never being able to tell her children the truth about when their father would be returning home from the prison, they moved him to. Nadia couldn't protect her children from knowing their father was in a jail cell not far from our city of Faisalabad. Nadia told Zahid that her husband, Aabid was in another country earning money for his family. Nadia's kids finally discovered their dad was in a prison not far from their home in Faisalabad. That's what was what finally broke Nadia. I wonder what happened to Nadia after I left Pakistan. I assumed sister-in-law forgot about me, a foreigner who ventured to a land called Pakistan, disappearing to a quiet village of Ganish where I could be alone to write, where no one would think to look for me.

"We don't speak about Daniyal anymore, not in Faisalabad," Nadia warned.

CHAPTER 7

Daniyal, The Guardian

*D*aniyal was the fighter of three brothers. As a kid, Daniyal used to sleep with large amounts of cash concealed in different areas of his village home of Ganish. The oldest brother spoke about family inheritance in Pakistan he had but couldn't spend, wealth that wasn't his to keep.

The oldest of three brothers talked about generational wealth buried in the soil of Ganish. From an early age, Daniyal learned what it meant to be the eldest of three brothers and to carry the honor of the family name. In hopes of crossing the US border, Daniyal spoke of paying a man from a well-known agency a large sum of cash to import him across the border illegally. Nadia's oldest brother didn't make a sound when a customs officer asked the driver to get out so he could inspect the vehicle. Nadia's brother's body was hidden inside a truck of international goods. I never thought to ask how Daniyal came to the promised land when we first met. Hidden inside a secret compartment, behind fold out seats in the back of a truck of imported goods was Daniyal eager to start a life in the United States, holding his breath like I did in childhood when I was learning to swim underwater. Daniyal must have been scared. Maybe a once humble kid from Ganesh was always fearless, never knowing when to come back up for a breath of air.

"This is where our property starts and stretches out for miles."

"My brother, Daniyal owns more land than all of us combined." Ayaan said.

Inaya was an illiterate village girl, searching for ways to escape, dreaming of one day settling abroad or in a city of Pakistan. Pakistani in-laws told me they rarely spoke to or heard from Daniyal for years as he grew into adulthood after Daniyal disappeared to live with his father at his ancestral village home Of Ganish. I knew Inaya missed her oldest son dearly. It was naïve of Inaya to expect

Daniyal to return to Faisalabad after all these years. The oldest of three brothers, must have thought there was a better life someplace, leaving his family's generational property unprotected and vulnerable to relatives, thugs and domestic terrorist groups who didn't feel they got their fair share of land. "It was my destiny to come here and meet you. Meeting you was the reason behind why I risked my life to come to the United States." Daniyal once said.

I knew what it was like to miss a place and to hate it at the same time. My relatives rom Faisalabad never accepted that Daniyal left for America and still hadn't returned to Pakistan. Nadia shared a story about Daniyal's upbringing, growing up in a quiet village area of Ganish. For a girl from a village who was uneducated and spoke little English, I would listen with intrigue as Nadia told another story about her oldest brother, Daniyal who left for a foreign country, never bothering to return to his birthplace of Pakistan. Nadia described her brother, Daniyal as a surrogate Father figure growing up, now an estranged big brother who lived in another country.

Years before, Daniyal left his ancestral village home of Ganish for the US, he composed a farewell letter to his family in Urdu. Daniyal wrote in the letter to his family about his desire to live in the United States promising to return to Pakistan shortly, unhappy with life in Ganish. Daniyal grew up in a village no different than any humble villager I met in Ganish. The oldest of three brothers wrote about how he wanted to see the rest of the world and experience what it was like to work an ordinary nine-to-five job.

In the letter, Daniyal wrote about going away to America for the betterment of Inaya and her three daughters. Like everything else I learned about Pakistani culture, sending money home in the equivalency of US currency was a good enough reason behind almost any decision an oldest son from a prideful middle-class family made. I wondered if Daniyal ultimately left Pakistan because time stood still, and he stopped living. Daniyal's life was in a village. I pictured the oldest of three brothers skimming through magazines featuring white people shown on the front covers of magazines and women dressed in racy clothing. Buried in the contents of his farewell letter to the United States, Daniyal swore his journey to The US was for the women of his family. Nadia's brother remarked once about his oldest sister, Farah who used to pray a Muslim prayer for him every place, he traveled in Pakistan that was unsafe. Each member of the family lied. Nothing was a surprise anymore. We were all lying to one another.

It was the oldest brother's obligation to be there in Pakistan in person to recite namaz prayers at his father's burial site. There was no good enough explanation for why Daniyal couldn't return to his homeland of Faisalabad, Pakistan. The oldest of three brothers was supposed to go back to his birthplace of Faisalabad, Pakistan eventually.

CHAPTER 8

Nadia, The Storyteller

*N*adia cared about me, but couldn't get close. She didn't want to reveal too many of her secrets. I was still an outsider, not Islamic or religious enough. I arrived at a place where people waited, and life came to a standstill. Out of the many entertaining stories depicting everyday struggles of life growing up in a village of Pakistan as the smallest of three children, I enjoyed a story Nadia told called burning man most. Near the end of my marriage, I began to perceive my marriage to Daniyal like an account Nadia talked about a memory of her oldest brother, who she called burning man. There was no time to carry buckets of water inside to douse out a spreading fire, without the hired help around, Daniyal may have died.

Nadia narrated a story about her arranged marriage in Faisalabad, Pakistan. During a celebratory occasion while everyone was preparing for her wedding day, Nadia's brother, Daniyal caught on fire after falling asleep at his village of Ganish. Daniyal was so exhausted after entertaining guests and helping decorate his sister Nadia's wedding venue, he caught on fire and continued sleeping. A housemaid woke Daniyal up screaming, smothering the last of the flames with his shawl.

In my dreams, I return to our ancestral village home of Ganish and find my little sister, Nadia, there. This time the land wasn't barren. Nadia planted her favorite crops, and the trees villagers chopped down grew tall, shielding Nadia's childhood home. In my dreams, I found Nadia there. This time the sun shone on everything, and time stood still. Nadia no longer waited. There would be nothing but laughter surrounding the two of us, not the same haunting Muslim prayer, that played. Nadia deserved better.

I Knew Nadia was going to meet who she called important people, the elite society of Pakistan. The first born of three daughters wore long, braided hair extensions, and brightly colored salwar kameez that she saved for wedding parties and Muslim holidays. I was told Nadia would attend outings and visit family when her husband, Aabid returned from prison in Faisalabad. Nadia stopped asking me to tag along with her to places, knowing that my answer would be a resounding no. The youngest daughter was naturally pretty, especially when made up on the occasions she bothered to apply light foundation, and lipstick. I noticed high heel shoes Nadia wore. My sister-in-law only wore flats, and an outdated shalwar kameez from last season when at Ganish. Nadia never worried about her appearance because she was still mourning the absence of her husband. Throughout the years, Nadia convinced herself Aabid wasn't in jail but living in another country with a well-paying job.

Reality was hard to face when raising two little kids all alone. Nadia was intent on learning to speak English proficiently, settling in a progressive city with her sons, Zahid and Dameer and one day having access to a higher level of education. I watched as Aabid returned from prison a different man, bitter and resentful. When I think of returning to Faisalabad one final time, I imagine gathering the strength to tell the smallest of three children that I waited for her in Louisiana thinking about how challenging it was growing up in a village, trying to raise two adolescent sons without a father. Nadia recited prayers five times per day and wept for days at a time for a man to return from prison who hated her. When I first met Nadia, she was innocent and weary of me, a foreigner from the United States. I understood that after all these years I couldn't face Nadia in person and tell her I divorced her brother, Daniyal. After she gave us her blessing in the form of reciting a namaz prayer for a successful marriage and accepted my children as her own, I couldn't bring myself to tell her the truth.

Nadia was right, this was my fault. Although I would never be part of my Pakistani family again, I wanted to tell Nadia in person, I cared about her. I was eager to visit Pakistan as a nonnative again. Hoping, like me, she would escape an abusive marriage and controlling in-laws. I kept a space for Nadia. I missed the company of Daniyal's little sister.

Inaya grew up an illiterate village girl never learning to read or write, considered fortunate to be courted and married to a wealthy landowner. Inaya talked often about how much she loved her oldest son, Daniyal and prayed for years for her sons return to Pakistan. Inaya carried prayer beads around, whispering namaz prayer to herself when I knew she missed her son. Inaya worked hard during her first pregnancy doing household chores and catering to guests. Inaya lost the pregnancy.

The only time the first-born daughter shared anything personal was about her oldest brother from Louisiana which made me think she cared a little about me. During our walks with the kids, my little sister showed me around the rich neighborhood. We stayed too long at the park until it was already late in the evening. I decided to head home. Nadia insisted we stop by one more home, a three-story bungalow style house with a newly painted white balcony. Streetlights blinked out right before it was too late to see a clear path home. All the homes in the rich neighborhood looked the same, lacking color or vibrancy. Nadia and I stood around for a while, like shadowy figures, in the dark in front of a house. Dust and debris from village roads made my white feet appear char-coal black when I wore flats.

"This is the house my husband, Aabid is going to buy me. Next month we're moving to the city," Nadia said in Urdu. Later I found out from Sana that during a visit home from prison, when traveling someplace, Aabid asked his wife to look out the window. "Do you like this house?" Aabid asked condescendingly.

Purchasing a house in the city away from a life without resources in a village was a sham like everything else. Nadia and her children never moved to a big city. Village life was challenging. The youngest of three sisters' reason for wanting to move to the city was so her kids, Zahid and Dameer could go to better quality schools and didn't have to struggle for basic needs. Nadia would be in closer proximity to her family of origin in Faisalabad. Every time my sister's in-law's relatives from Ganish abused her; she moved in with in laws from Faisalabad for long periods. Nadia arranged meetings with her in- laws at Ganish.

Family meetings were held to discuss Nadia's brother- in-law, Malak, who was blowing all the family's inheritance to fund his extravagant lifestyle, what she said rightfully belonged to her two sons. While Nadia's oldest brother was in prison, Malak was going to fine dining establishments, buying the newest model cars and wearing name brand clothes. Little sister was a saver and lived modestly, careful not to purchase things that weren't useful, and hand sewed most of her clothes including our family's shalwar kameez. Nadia copied the newest clothing designs from fashion magazines. Getting a menial job as a wealthy landowner was laughed at by the rest of the upper- middle class society in Faisalabad. "Malak is still not working. Pretty soon there will be nothing left for my kids." Nadia told Sana in Urdu. Nadia got into screaming matches with her father- in law, Abbas who always had the final say.

"A daughter and a sister give up everything for her brother and husband," little sister remarked. Nadia's portion of land was entrusted to the men of her joint family who were meant to provide financially. On different occasions, Nadia showed up unannounced at our city home in Faisalabad where she stayed for months at a time. Nadia went back to her village, without warning, when she informed me that she was needed. The cost of being a disadvantaged village woman meant you could be punished for speaking out boldly in the presence of powerful men.

Nadia was no longer her carefree, spirited self, making it her job to see that everyone in the family was provided for. Nadia's outspoken demeanor changed when her in–laws started fighting back. As a disadvantaged woman from Ganish, she had no right to speak up, not about family inheritance she claimed no right to. In Pakistan without land, you didn't have much, a mutual friend, Asma once said. I remembered it.

I stopped believing Nadia when she shared stories of a fulfilling home life with Aabid that didn't exist. When Nadia's husband, Aabid went away to jprison she re- cited namaz prayer and cried softly in the room next to mine. Nadia went out of her way to make my stay in Pakistan enjoyable by cooking what she called my favorite meals, hemming new salwar kameez together and helping care for Sameer and Asad. Zahid and Sameer were around the same age. The two cousins were inseparable. All these years the smallest of three sisters told herself and her children the same story, that Aabid was away in another country earning a substantial salary for the family. Nadia showed me her secret hiding place where she stashed away money. Little sis- ter saved money gifted to her by wealthy relatives who gave her cash in rupees on holidays and weddings. I never attended wedding parties.

"My husband's going to get out of prison this week. They are moving him to a better-quality prison, this way he'll be closer to home. I can cook his favorite meals." Nadia gushed. Every morning the little sister packed home-cooked lunches and dinners for Aabid to be sent to prison in Faisalabad.

Nadia double knotted a colorful handkerchief and handed a bundle of home cooked traditional food off to an adolescent housekeeper. I didn't know what was really going on with my favorite sister- in law's husband, Aabid. I was like everybody else in the family, waiting, told different versions of a story. Aabid was innocent, someone else committed the crime and the police wouldn't do anything but accept bribes. We all knew she was a liar. Nadia's small sons knew before Nadia could lie again that their father, Aabid was in a jail cell in Faisalabad. I despised Daniyal for what he did to his little sister, Nadia. I stopped thinking of a house or a plot of land of my own.

Nadia returned to her village home of Ganish as though searching for the trees she planted a long time ago, thinking of newly planted flowers and crops at Ganish that must have grown tall. I wanted the first born of three girls to break away from a cycle of abuse she tolerated from in-laws who lied about a better life in a city, forcing Nadia to work as a hired maid back at Ganish. Villagers she never met before chopped down most of the trees and crops she planted. I didn't blame Nadia for the way she treated me.

Sana filled me in on everyone's secrets. My three sisters wanted to forget about their own pain and make my stay in Pakistan memorable, that's what I thought at the beginning of my travels. I cared about Nadia but couldn't get too close. Applying for a visa to America would have meant years of waiting and possibly being rejected. There would be no houses in the big city. There most likely would be no visa granted to Nadia no matter how many times she reapplied for a passport to another country, listing a different reason for wanting to visit the United States. Nadia couldn't go back and plant trees or flowers. At least Nadia could go back to Ganish again.

"I'm going to dress- up for Aabid when he returns home for good this time," Nadia said, putting on glitzy clip-on earrings from a box of wedding jewelry, spinning around, asking again. "How do I look?"

Sana never took anything Nadia said or did seriously. I was good at keeping quiet and watching from a distance. Inaya announced that the entire family was moving from Faisalabad to Dubai suddenly. Inaya convinced me that Malak had a thriving printing and marketing business in Dubai. "The business flopped," Farah exclaimed in English. I thought the business was doing well.

"Stop wasting your money at this medical center for no good reason. I tell you the same thing every time, save your money and go to a government hospital free of charge. He's a healthy kid, a little on the pudgy side. Put him on the bicycle," the Canadian doctor advised Nadia, scribbling jotting something down on a notepad. I was guilty of running to the most popular international children's doctor in Faisalabad for my oldest son's, Sameer's more serious health issue. The overbooked Canadian doctor spoke in a British accent, explaining how to adequately feed and care for small children from villages of Ganish. The worst cases of indigenous women were the rare diseases or cases of malnutrition and tuberculosis. The Canadian doctor took time to educate women from Villages of Ganish.

Only people who could afford outrageous fees upfront would be seen by the best foreign doctor in Faisalabad for miles. There was a pretentious way of speaking by women in positions of authority who worked and lived in Faisalabad that came across as arrogant. Wel-respected teachers and doctors spoke bluntly to some disadvantaged women from villages regarding the care of children. Village women were looked down on despite coming from wealthy families. Nadia's indulgence and coddling of her sons came with a compulsion to find things that were wrong and blow them out of proportion. Little sister took whoever was available along with her to a private center to see the leading foreign doctor, who Nadia called an expert in the field.

Along with thinking any day now her husband, Aabid would get out of prison, Nadia took her pudgy son to the hospital intent on finding a solution. Despite seeking a resolution to her adolescent son's weight problem, Nadia fed her oldest son junk food. When Sana told Nadia to stop feeding her son unhealthy treats and snacks, little sister responded by saying her oldest son's indulgence of processed food had to do with missing his father who was still in prison. Nadia was gullible and easier to deceive than a child at times, convinced her husband, Aabid would get out of prison, and she could begin her newly married life where she left off.

The little sister was a new bride and had just returned from a honeymoon in Murree when her husband was soon after, taken to a prison in Faisalabad. There were rumors, Aabid was innocent and tried to flee before police could imprison him or try Aabid for the death penalty. "No one knows what's wrong with the third daughter," Sana said. Nadia got dressed up and planned her husband's surprise dinner when he was given a new date to be sent home for a visitation. This went on for years. He's not coming home, I wanted to tell her.

It was too late. Nadia created scenarios of celebrations and fantasies of a blissful married life. The worst part was the two children, Zahid and Dameer who waited alongside for their father to come home from prison. Nadia told her children that their father was away in a foreign country earning money for the family. She rarely told the truth.

Aabid finally came home from the more state of the art jail they moved him to in Karachi a few months later. Smallest sister's husband didn't have to go back to prison. More than five years passed. I thought back to the years Nadia spent cooking homemade food packed tightly in plastic containers every afternoon around lunch time. Nadia double knotted the end of a scarf that held plastic containers of food together. Maybe the fear of her children growing up and never seeing their father again, or the unimaginable possibility of Aabid getting the death penalty were the worst outcomes she could let go of.

Nadia could stop obsessing over plausible tragedies surrounding her husband's prison sentence and no longer worry about her oldest son's weight problem, obsessing about how her children never studied enough. I don't remember the precise day Nadia called me from Pakistan shedding tears of joy, ecstatic that her husband's name had been cleared. Aabid was finally released from prison. Nadia was sorry that I couldn't be there to celebrate together. I watched her get dressed up and Aabid, practically a stranger, broke her heart again. We didn't need another celebration.

Nadia could begin a newly married life with the husband that went away before they could go on a honeymoon to Muree together. No one cared about Nadia at fancy wedding parties she attended. Upper middle-class relatives of our inner circle only invited Nadia to gossip and feel better about their lives. Hearing the excitement come through in Nadias tone of voice made it all worth it. After the last day I spoke with the youngest sister things got dark. I don't know what her in- laws did to Nadia to put that light out. Maybe happiness wasn't in the cards for any of us.

Out of all the occurrences I watched Nadia fantasize about a euphoric family life and marriage away from her village of Ganish vanished. Daniyal's little sister never moved to the city after Aabid was released from prison. There was more false promises Aabid made about beginning a newly married life in a city where Nadia wouldn't have to worry about her son's getting a quality education.

There were times Nadia's husband, Aabid was so cruel that– she called me back in the United States, hysterical, not knowing if this is what prison did to people or if any of the abuse, she endured from Aabid was her fault. Nadia was trapped in a place far away from a progressive City, hidden in a village of Ganish, being used by her in-laws for their selfish needs. I can't forget the better times we shared, and the way Nadia used to be innocent and kind, the first time we met. There never was a happy ending for my little sister and her two children.

After Nadia's husband returned from prison in Karachi, her days were spent at the village of Ganish without necessities, waiting for daylight, withstanding day long electricity outages. Nadia carried a lantern with her as she made her way through dimly lit hallways. There was nothing left to go back to but bitter-sweet memories.

Agriculture workers tore down Nadia's village home. I listened with intrigue to stories about Nadias oldest brother, Daniyal who went away to the United States. My last memory of the first born of three sisters was sitting around a group of village children. Nadia and I stayed up on chilly nights standing around a fire when the electricity went out. I pictured the house in the city she showed me. I made- believe Nadia danced at all the fancy wedding parties she attended with her husband, Aabid wearing a new shalwar kameez and her finest jewelry.

CHAPTER 9

Karachi, Counter Terrorism Brother-In Law, Ayaan

*B*uildings of outdoor bazaars in Faisalabad were decorated with bright white fairy lights, tied to strings in case of electricity losses. The lively boulevards of Faisalabad and the merriment of people reminded me of festivities and holidays I shared with my family in Louisiana. Since returning to the United States, I recounted joy- filled moments of eating fast food with Ayaan.

Brother-in-law waited outside our house in the city revving up the engine of his motorcycle the next morning, insisting I ride on the back, with two legs on one side, like a real Punjabi. I walked around directionless browsing outdoor bazaars with Ayaan during my first week in Pakistan. I anticipated what region of Pakistan Ayaan, and I would visit next. Once I strolled into a shoe shop at an outdoor store while window shopping with mutual friends drifting into a bazaar, standing below a flashing neon sign outside that read English shoes. I found a pair of bargain priced shoes to wear to a wedding in a hurry.

"Where did you buy those ugly shoes?" Asma asked. I understood very little back then about how to navigate my way around crowded outdoor bazaars in Karachi when shopping or traveling for a special occasion.

I was recovering from a case of food poisoning from a wedding reception I attended the night before. I was ill and couldn't get myself in a mood to get dressed or

54

want to tag along with Ayaan. "All you have to do is wake- up in the morning. You could write fiction novels, relax in the yard and have a garden, a plot of land to call your own. Life could be easy, no more problems. When Daniyal gets his property back, when I get out of the military, my superiors will station me here in Karachi. We'll have a house like this one." Ayaan said.

Ayaan never let on that he knew about my troubled marriage in Louisiana to Daniyal. Ayaan only thought of asking me in the mornings. "Are you crying again?"

The youngest of three brothers was a villager from Ganish inherently proud of his Pakistani lineage and Nadia's little brother. I remembered Ayaan with affection and gratitude for all he did for me during my stay in Faisalabad. Standing side by side with a garland of flowers in hand like the days my in-laws from a village greeted me at the airport, me and Ayaan would welcome Pakistan back again one day.

My brother- in law's dreams of settling in Karachi and proudly serving his people, those ambitions were impossible after my heart was shattered and affection for Pakistani people dismantled. I thought this final time, I would convince Ayaan not to send anymore letters home. Aaliyaa was sure to read every letter her son he wrote home from a military base in Karachi in her best English.

When Ayaan's aspirations of joining the military became a reality, he composed letters to each family member on his days away from Faisalabad. Ayaan's motivation for joining the military was to give me, my children and Aaliyaa a better life than what the village had to offer. The training is rigorous, Ayaan wrote to his mother, Aaliyaa one afternoon. I thought my brother-in-law must have seriously considered quitting the armed services having lost a lot of weight, writing letters to family members while dehydrated and hospitalized.

Ayaan returned home to Ganish but called on breaks and Islamic holidays looking underweight and sickly, reassuring Aaliyaa the training was tough but that his sacrifice would be worth it in the end. Securing a job as a high-ranking officer or UN member of the military was like getting into the United States on a whim as a foreigner, on your first attempt at applying for a visa. Members of the armed forces in Pakistan received free government housing.

Children of military members in Pakistan attended top private schools and lived in well maintained upper middle-class neighborhoods. Government schoolteachers, nurses and laborers lacked job training and resources in most places throughout provinces of Punjab. Government workers were underpaid, given little recognition, respect or accolades, given the tremendous stress of the job and unpleasant work conditions. Ayaan held people of Ganish and native land of Pakistan in high esteem, proud to serve in the Pakistani military. Toward the end of my stay in Faisalabad, I didn't have a heart to tell my brother the truth about my idea of Pakistani people. I wondered where the UN sent Ayaan off to this time. Maybe Ayaan was sent to a mountain region where wealthy foreigners visited, and rich Pakistanis vacationed or the worst places anyone could imagine.

As a member of the Pakistani army, getting family members into gourmet restaurants where I dined with my children nearly free of charge in cities like Peshawar was one of the perks of being a relative of a service member. The outfit called in Urdu- shalwar kameez Aaliyaa made for me fit comfortably like a pair of pajamas. I had to ask Aaliyaa to add more length to the bottom. When I dined out with my extended family at fine dining establishments in Peshawar and Karachi, my in- laws insisted I eat more.

According to concerned family members I was too gaunt and slender compared to full figured new brides. I was considered too thin by family members no matter how much I ate. To make matters worse, I didn't have long hair like most local Punjabi women of Ganish who were considered village beauties. When I first began traveling to Faisalabad, out of rebellion, I cut my hair short. To be considered attractive by Pakistan's beauty standards, I would have to let my hair grow out.

I didn't want to become like Rani, giving up on my life and being devalued by Pakistani in- laws and relatives early in my marriage. At one point I appreciated Ayaan for caring about me and listening when I cried some nights. Ayaan must have taken me to nearly every historical region of Pakistan and driven me around to a place I now considered home at our family's village of Ganish. I was like a village girl at times, simple, caring and aware of each mistake I made while living in a foreign country over a prolonged period. It's not that I wouldn't go back to visit Pakistan again. Ayaan made it a point to tell me I wasn't conventionally attractive as a Pakistani but pretty for an American.

After a few months living in tribal areas of Ganish, I realized that I would never fit in with Daniyal's family. Somewhere throughout my journey to Pakistan I came to care about each member of my immediate family, at least at the start of my travels.

"You've changed," that's what Ayaan said after returning home for a short stint from a random location where the Pakistani military sent him last, all while showing me around a dream, a house in Karachi. On our last trip to Pakistan, Zarah straightened my hair, insisting on buying me new clothes from local bazaars and designer shops nearby. "I'm doing this for us," Ayaan swore. I decided at one point, I was never going to divorce Daniyal. I would end up settling in Karachi for good somewhere, a housewife, picturing myself becoming an accomplished author and publishing novels.

Even the most supportive members that comprised my Pakistani family didn't want to listen when I shared intimate details about my home life in the States with their eldest brother, Daniyal. Everyone claimed to respect and at times pedestalize Daniyal. Ayaan must have carried a photo of me in his wallet somewhere, thinking highly of me for journeying to Faisalabad, wondering when he would meet a woman called gora again. When my brother-in-law complimented me about my dedication and loyalty to Daniyal especially as a Christian, Ayaan would say things like, "In Pakistani culture when you marry one person you are married to everyone in the family."

"We fall in love with you."

Daniyal would go to any measures to fight for his land or the people he cared about and valued as much as his property was worth. No one told me that I would be developing feelings for Ayaan. Maybe it was pregnancy hormones, Indian romance stories I re-watched with our housekeeper Bushra, on quiet afternoons fearing Daniyal's criticisms of me or when he would call to inform me of everything, I did wrong that day. For a while, to cope with living in another country and being away from anything familiar, I would forget about when my husband Daniyal would think to call or inquire about my well-being. It was almost like Daniyal, and I were never married or knew each other before I came to Ganish.

Inaya reminded me of how I made Ayaan cry. My last recollection of Ayaan was one afternoon when he came home gushing to anyone who'd listen about how he aced every test and got into the Pakistani military with flying colors. Like Daniyal, Ayaan, considered running away from the problems he experienced living in his birth country of Pakistan, forgetting all of us, leaving a note behind. I thought of the last time I visited Ayaan's Father in jail and how despite brother's exciting news about joining the armed services, he couldn't hide the anger searing through his voice. Ayaan was like me, unsure if he would return from an army barracks in Karachi to a prison cell in Faisalabad to see his father alive again.

Ayaan insisted I join him on this last visit to see his dad in prison. Before my brother-in-law joined the Pakistani army, I was going over reasons no one bothered to tell Ayaan about what really happened to his father after we saw him last in the emergency room. In my letters to Ayaan, who was living at a military barracks in Karachi, I would be sure to tell Ayaan about how his father was still alive. Aaliyaa and her Farah brought Ayaan's dad home from p, ison after suffering a diabetic seizure, losing feeling in the left side of his body. Half alive, Aaliyaa cared for Ayaan's Father alone, turning him periodically, feeding and changing her husband every couple of hours. I didn't know if I should send this final letter.

I was telling Ayaan about my ambitions of publishing books. Ayaan was no different than Daniyal, promising women who made up our joint family a more prosperous life in Karachi when he completed basic training.

Last I heard, Ayaan was sent to a country in Africa. Years later, I am reminded of my bad habits, knowing I would likely never face my favorite brother-in-law and tell him, I got divorced and I couldn't possibly live out a far-fetched dream of a house in a progressive City like Karachi. Aaliyaa would finally move to a progressive city and no longer cook food for a houseful of guests and family members outside without the convenience of modern appliances to make life easier. Aaliyaa would live a carefree life, like what Ayaan wanted for his mom, spending afternoons drinking tea and cooking food for important guests who arrived that afternoon. Ayaan didn't laugh off my ambitions of publishing books. I would lie about how Ayaan's father's health was improving each day. I didn't think it would take this long to receive another letter from Ayaan, listening with curiosity as Farah, the oldest of three sisters attempted to read each word of Ayaan's letters sent home in English.

I rarely had access to a computer during my days living in Ganish. I thought of handwriting my best work at our village home, along with a treasured book of poems. One memory I replay was of my entire family packed in a compact car, blasting music while circling around Daniyal's childhood home of Ganish knowing no one would hear us for miles.

"You won't miss me there." Daniyal reminded. You will find me in every family member and each person I love." I can still hear Daniyal say, as if he had been there with me in Pakistan all along, yet never really present either.

The sting of every criticism Daniyal yelled at me over the phone hit me at once. I couldn't concentrate on the fun I was supposed to be experiencing in a new country. Laughter and celebration were all around me, at least for a while.

Time raced by; I stopped hearing from Daniyal altogether by phone. I stopped bothering to call friends and family back in Louisiana. Daniyal assumed that I was no different than a Pakistani woman by now, submissive, overly critical of myself, knowing enough Urdu to get by. Daniyal must have stopped thinking about me, his American wife. "There is no need for you to return to Louisiana. You have everything you need right here in Faisalabad," Ayaan reminded. I wondered at times if Ayaan harbored sincere feelings of affection for me. I wasn't sure when I would hear from Daniyal again.

I never knew when Daniyal would return to Pakistan. I didn't have any happiness for myself but to think of another life, starting over and new beginnings with my two children without Daniyal's constant putdowns and daily bouts of anger directed at me.

I created new characters for fiction novels while thinking of ways to escape reality by living not unlike a village girl in a province of Punjab. My joint family seldom knew about late night phone calls I made to Daniyal and moments Daniyal would verbally berate me over the phone, emphasizing how I wasn't doing a good enough job at blending in with his Islamic family. There were nights after Sameer and Asad fell asleep, I wept silently, leaving a place in my fictional stories for Daniyal. To forget life in Pakistan without Daniyal, I turned to making up fictitious characters, falling into fantasies about Daniyal never returning to Pakistan. On this last trip to Karachi, in one of my stories I imagined everything changed for the better.

Ayaan wrote home to all the indigenous kids and me, his mom and three cousins each afternoon at almost the same time, going on about a more abundant life away from the challenges of village life. In reading this final letter home, I imagined Ayaan returned from basic training, a new person. There were no more letters to be written or mailed home. Daniyal reminded me over the telephone of how everyone in the city of Faisalabad knew of our extended family and my in-laws. It was more important than ever that I sit up straight, practice good manners and not speak out of turn. Speaking and writing the native language of Urdu fluently was more important than ever.

Having little idea about why Ayaan insisted he take me along with him to Karachi was now clear. An officer named Hakeem was a duplicate of who Ayaan wanted to emulate, leaving a hard life with limited resources in a village behind. "We can have a house like this in Karachi one day," Ayaan guaranteed enthusiastically after Hakeem showed us around his house and backyard in Karachi. "You and Sameer can live in Karachi with us in a house like Hakeem and his wife have one day." Ayaan was juvenile and, well- intentioned but nothing more at times than a gullible village kid, I thought. Pakistani military officers weren't paid a high salary, but the government gave them and their family a house to live in for free. Children of high-ranking military officers usually attended the best private schools and for their time in the service were given a driver, and guards for protection and security.

On one of our visits to Karachi, Ayaan showed me a house the Pakistani military promised to provide him, and his new family once he settled down and found a suitable wife for marriage, as a reward when he became an officer in years to come. With gratitude, I counted the instances my brother- in-law looked out for me, making sure my life wasn't too difficult but that I wasn't bored either during my stay in Karachi. Ayaan made it a point to tell me I stood out. I didn't need fancy jewelry, heavy face powder or bangles. I was like Aaliyaa sometimes, unbothered about wearing an outdated dress.

Ayaan spoke about a better way of life for my children and Aaliyaa, making sure that I wasn't depressed; knowing everything I did throughout the day. My memory of my brother-in-law Ayaan and the house in Karachi was the last thing Ayaan talked about the day he went away to a dangerous region of Africa. I wondered when Ayaan would return.

Brother -in law's time in the army reminded me of letters my mom wrote to me at basic training in Texas each day in cursive writing, reminding me I had what it took and most importantly, to keep going. Ayaan drove four hours from our city of Faisalabad to Karachi. We ate homemade parathas Aaliyaa packed for our trip and stopped periodically for tea and snacks at service stations along the way. Peering out the car window, while Sameer had already fallen soundly asleep in my lap, Karachi was different than our ancient village home, I thought. I took in all Karachi seemed to offer, upscale restaurants, English speaking foreigners dressed in jeans and kameez tops, not bothering to wear a hijab or debutta.

Karachi was a far stretch from village life. I missed driving through miles of open terrain with Ayaan and devouring freshly made naan bread and fruit in the early mornings when we stayed at Aaliyaa's village. I missed making tea outside and the modesty of village people. Being a guest in Karachi reminded me of life in Louisiana. Nothing was out of the ordinary about Karachi, it was an upkept and alluring city when compared to Ganish. Karachi had newer buildings but was still rural like some modern cities in America. The city of Karachi was idyllic and lush surrounded by greenery, bright lights and wealthy foreigners.

Ayaan appeared both excited and nervous when we arrived in Karachi, insisting that I meet a man introduced as Hakeem and his family. A black Asian man appeared, towering above me, dressed in fatigues waiting to greet me outside of a contemporary designed brick home. My time in the armed forces brought back good and bad memories. Military life and serving your country as a Pakistani must have meant something different to a man who grew up in a village, risking his life every day at the border- fighting against Isis and extremist terrorist groups.

Hakeem and Sara showed me their backyard and pointed out a garden with newly planted vegetables and a flower bed. "Something to remind Sara of life back home at our village. Sara likes planting and growing crops in her pastime- gardening," the officer remarked. "How about I take you on a tour of our backyard. Afterwards Sara and my daughter, Haniya can get you settled inside."

"Sorry I didn't have time to change out of uniform," insisting that me and Sameer sit down and make ourselves comfortable. Hakeem's wife Sara, was busy in the kitchen preparing our favorite dish. "Most foreign guests that come here prefer to eat Chinese food over traditional Pakistani meals. I think your favorite meal is Bryani." Hakeem said.

Hakeem's wife, Sara appeared out of nowhere, a petite woman wearing a comfortable pair of shalwar kameez. Sara covered her long hair with a Debetta, a sheer piece of satin. Sara offered me a medley of different foods, minestrone soup, salad, Chinese egg rolls and a variety of ethnic rice with bread and Bhatti, a type of meat covered in a thick sauce, most foreigners preferred.

Sara was too timid to speak English with me, she stayed in the kitchen busying herself with preparing masala tea or setting the table for her next meal.

"Sara is a housewife," Hakeem announced proudly, taking a puff from his cigarette, blowing smoke away from me. "I can step outside if the smoke is bothering you." Hakeem offered. I secretly hoped this would be Hakeem's last cigarette. I was bothered by the smell of tobacco, afraid that my oldest son, Sameer may have an asthma attack. "Sara doesn't speak any English at all."

"She wants me to tell you that she has heard wonderful things about you and welcome to Pakistan!" Sara says your Muslim name Kasra is an Islamic name that suits you well. Kasra is a modest but elegant traditional Islamic name taken from the Koran. Your in-laws must think a lot of you to call you a name like Kasra," Hakeem complimented, taking another puff of his cigarette.

"We try to copy the American way of life in Karachi. My two daughters tell me they don't want to visit their village."

"My daughters and wife grew up in that same place where your family lives in

Ganish. Tribal areas of Pakistan are not suitable places for foreigners to travel at all. My village home is full of small-minded tribal people."

"My girls tell me all the time; we have every luxury here in Karachi at our finger-tips that life abroad has to offer. My job requirements at the border of Afghanistan are incredibly dangerous. I am given the responsibility of upholding American principals and fighting against terrorist groups like Isis. Isis and the Taliban do not represent our religion of Islam. The Taliban does not speak for Pakistani people, religion or culture, only hate ignorance and the looming threat of violence. Groups like the Taliban have gone against our holy prophet Muhammed, gaining power through fear, intimidation and keeping women uneducated. There are a few honorable people in Pakistan left fighting for freedom against uncivilized people who call themselves true followers of Islam." Hakeem explained.

Sara and Hakeem were courteous, inquiring again about my life In America with my two children and husband. Hakeem wanted to know about my opinions surrounding women's rights and terrorism, asking about my life with Daniyal in Louisiana.

Like Ayaan who spoke about visions for the people of Ganish one day being set free from terrorist groups and building a new future, Hakeem spoke about true followers of Islam and how they should live together in peace in a conversation with me during my stay at his house.

"I see it as my duty to my country to stand up for principles written about in the Koran. I don't think twice about putting my life in danger for my country. I am a proud Pakistani after all."

"You must be hungry."

Like Ayaan, Hakeem was convinced there would be no urgency for me or my sons to return to America. Life in Karachi could be better. There would be no need to travel back to the United States.

During our stay in Karachi, I imagined Daniyal never returning to Faisalabad. I pictured what being a housewife in Karachi would be like. I thought about the possibility that Daniyal, would never return to Pakistan and that Ayaan would complete his training in the army. My days would be spent cooking meals for foreign guests- never thinking of Daniyal again. Brother would stress in each of his letters to family in his down time when brother-in-law wrote home from Africa, that his sacrifice would all be worth it in the end.

During dinner, Hakeem's oldest daughter, Haniya came out of her bedroom to greet me. Haniya made a point to sit next to me at the dinner table. "Assalamu alaikum" Haniya welcomed, offering me a plate of warm roti bread. "You are much different than the picture I kept of you in my mind. I can't believe you are able to live in the village of Ganish without electricity and water as a person who grew up in the United States with every facility available." Haniya wore large, framed glasses and seemed apprehensive about meeting me at first. Haniya was articulate and well mannered, genuinely curious to learn more about my life since living in Pakistan.

Hakeem got up in the middle of dinner, took a phone call and disappeared into another room, joining us again at the dinner table not long after, reaching down to double knot the laces of his boots. During my visit to Karachi, I never saw the officer change out of his fatigues. Hakeem vanished, never offering an explanation as to where he was going.

"She's wonderful, my daughter Haniya is the brightest in her class by far. Haniya says she wants to study abroad and finish medical school in the United States. This one has got a mouth on her. Haniya is very opinionated, not like most Pakistani women who grow up in backward villages. My daughter was excited for weeks to meet you, wanting to know every story from your own mouth about how an American, could survive so long living at a village."

"Enjoy your dinner." Hakeem said before leaving.

Hakeem glanced back at his wife and daughter one more time before closing the door behind him. I wondered if every time Hakeem left for active duty he felt as though he was saying goodbye a final time, not sure if he would see his wife and daughter again. "You have no idea the things I've seen go on in villages."

"I don't know how you can live in Ganish for so long. My mom is here alone since dad is gone much of the time. She is content living as a housewife, spending her afternoons learning cooking new recipes." Haniya shared, slurping down the last of her Chinese noodles, wiping extra sauce on a napkin.

"She isn't educated, my mom. I've tried my best to teach her to speak and write in English, but she feels embarrassed, wasting away afternoons making popular Pakistani recipes instead. My mother worries about dad. I hear her pray namaz at night for my dad's safety. My mom never wants to go back to life in a village. Since Hakeem is away so often, my mom learned to deal with his absence by cooking. She knows how to make almost every different type of dish: Chinese, Italian, Indian and Pakistani recipes. Many foreigners dine at our house in Karachi."

"You should really get some rest," Haniya said in English, offering me a cup of tea.

"You and Sameer have traveled a long way. You will like the way I make tea. Each person who is a guest in our home requests a cup of tea I boiled with the perfect balance of spices," Haniya stated, pouring out a pot of boiled water from a plate of pasta she strained.

After dinner, Haniya complained about intense requirements from private schools in Karachi. Hakeems oldest daughter smiled broadly when speaking about her life before moving to Karachi and spoke apprehensively about her time living at her mother's village home as a girl. "Although Hakeem has a stressful job working near the border in Afghanistan, it is unsafe. I feel the risks are worth it. Our family could never afford to live in a City like Karachi if Hakeem wasn't a high-ranking officer." Haniya was right about making a delicious cup of tea, it was a perfect balance of spices, not too bitter or sweet.

I stayed with Ayaan in Karachi for three days. In the evenings after dinner, we sat outside in the backyard when Hakeem returned home, listening to another story of Hakeem's time working at the border of Afghanistan, stories of hope, heroism and danger. "Look at my daughter, isn't she remarkable?" Hakeem gushed about how his oldest daughter scored high marks on a final exam. "Did I mention, Haniya makes the best cup of tea?"

Insisting I join Hakeem and his wife outside in the yard and talk. "This capable young man has got everything it takes to make it in the Pakistani army, strength, bravery, a well brought up boy from our neighboring village of Ganish," Hakeem said taking another sip of tea.

"Ayaan will make a fine officer one day," Hakeem complimented, grinning at Ayaan proudly, touching the shoulders of my Nadia's little brother-in-law affectionately.

"These are well known, and respectable people," Ayaan reminded, pulling me off to the side during our stay in Karachi while I was in the kitchen or sitting alone. "Make sure you are gracious and offer to help his wife with anything she needs. The eldest daughter enjoys speaking in English with you. Talk to her about school and her interests. Go and change your clothes." Brother- in-law insisted one afternoon during our stay.

"Are you going to wear that?"

"Be a confident American, what I meant to say is, be yourself. You're doing okay so far, everyone seems to like you," Ayaan instructed, nervously.

Although Ayaan was an accommodating host to me and Sameer when we first arrived in Pakistan, getting ready to meet who my brother-in-law referred to as influential people become tiresome after a while. Ayaan asked that I show up and make a good impression on strangers who he referred to as his family's inner circle. I couldn't bring myself to decline each invitation to a city when I understood that Aaliyaa was generous and helpful to my children during our stay in Faisalabad. I was like an obedient housewife -smiling and drinking tea, asking the right questions, being gracious enough.

On my last evening in Karachi, Hakeem never returned to see me, or my children Sameer and Asad off or extend a final goodbye. I thought about dangers at the Afghanistan border and measured safety threats at the border against the possibility that Hakeem never returned home safely to his family again. During my visit to Karachi, I rarely noticed Hakeem change out of his military fatigues. Hakeem's wife and daughter stood outside, seeing me off, waving goodbye. Ayaan drove off, exhausted and searching for our home in our familiar city of Faisalabad. On the three-hour drive, I pretended that years passed, and Ayaan returned from the Pakistani army- as a high-ranking officer.

As we drove away, I turned to look at the family home Sara and Hakeem shared in Karachi with their two daughters. I envisioned myself dressed in fashionable Salwar Kameez- sitting out in the backyard alone on quiet evenings writing or reading cooking recipes of different style dishes, serving foreign guests. My old life as Kasra, Daniyal's wife felt distant and out of reach. When my ability to speak the native language of Urdu improved, I started speaking less English. I was never returning to America, I decided on the drive. In many ways, I became no different than upper middle class Pakistani people envisioning a more prosperous future for myself and two children, rarely thinking of Daniyal or his return to Pakistan any longer.

Before traveling back to our city of Faisalabad, Ayaan insisted I visit a real estate developer and his family in Karachi. The real estate developer was an influential person who I checked off a list of important people I met during my stay in Pakistan. Nothing was realistic about a type of heaven that could exist in a third world country like what the wealthy real estate developer, Ibrahim described. For Ayaan, I mentally checked off a list what I needed to do while visiting places in Pakistan and Karachi, which included insignificant things like: eating food I didn't like, sitting up straight and trying my best to speak the little Urdu I knew. I ran through a list of inappropriate jokes and things not to say to people who Ayaan labeled influential people, also known as the upper-class society of Pakistan.

A description of heaven could be found in forward thinking areas throughout Pakistan and centered around wealthy families who existed in the upper-class bracket of society.

Ayaan insisted that Aaliyaa take me to the best fabric shops in Faisalabad and that I wear stylish outfits. My salwar kameez was not an expensive outfit. Aaliyaa was like other middle-class families in Faisalabad who made clothes taken from fashion magazines for the women of our family. it was important to Ayaan that I look like the embodiment of a native of Pakistan, the version of who influential people wanted to meet.

Ibrahim was a successful real estate developer in Karachi. I felt small and alone standing in the middle of Ibrahim's home compared to the ghettos, a few blocks away.

Ibrahim lived with his family in what most villagers considered a mansion, a newly remodeled three-story bungalow with high ceilings and a glass chandelier. "You look lost, Kasra, do you know your way around?" Ibrahim's daughter Kajol asked sarcastically. Two housekeeper I recognized as poor village workers from Faisalabad talked in nontraditional Punjabi when I walked into the real estate developer's home.

A group of boisterous girls passed by, dressed in fashionable embroidered salwar kameez, dragging long debuttas and decorative scarves behind.

The group of teenagers went back and forth to the restroom primping in the mirror- reapplying make-up. I must have been underdressed and plain looking compared to other girls who were invited frequently to weddings choosing to wear little make- up. Wearing heavy bangles and a bindi made me feel out of place.

When I went to the bathroom there were perfectly categorized baskets of cosmetics and perfume and hand wipes for guests. There were no underground toilets inside the mansion. Jacuzzi bathtubs were built into each remodeled squat toilet. When Kajol gave me a tour of the house, she was hesitant to show me the bathroom.

"There are many people here tonight and luckily, I found you, the American girl standing alone. in Faisalabad if you are quiet or sitting alone too long, we think we are not being good hosts."

"We don't have underground toilets in this house," Kajol joked.

"My Father had our home custom built. This is a self-cleaning toilet, not like squat toilets you use outside in villages like Ganish. My two siblings live abroad, one in Canada and the other in England. You could say although I don't consider Pakistan home, I'm not sure I will settle in my country of origin for good."

"What is the right saying America, nice to meet you?" Kajol asked apprehensively. As the oldest of three daughters, Kajol was well mannered and carried herself with grace, offering to show me around her family home speaking in a diluted British accent that I had trouble understanding.

"I'm home now from a girl's hostel in Pakistan on break. I'm in my last year of medical school. After that I will work as an intern at a children's hospital in Karachi. Sometimes guests venture off on their own and get lost in this house. My Mother, Amera likes to make clothes. She's into interior design and home decorating. Amera, along with an interior decorator designed each of our rooms. Let me give you a tour of every room my mom has designed herself."

When the oldest of three daughters opened the bedroom door to show me the first room, Kajol's Mom, Amera sat on a chair behind a desk closing her laptop computer. Amera sat up quickly putting down a novel she was reading, taking off her reading glasses, startled when she saw me. Amera took a sip of her tea from a decorative mug sitting the mug of tea back on her nightstand table.

Amera got up carefully, as though unsure of how to greet me as a guest from Louisiana. "I've heard so much about you from Ayaan. I'm glad you'll be a guest in our home for the next few days. There is no need to be formal with names, you can call me mother or Amera. You can use the jacuzzi with jets and bathtubs in our bathroom. My husband, Ibraham, must turn on the hot water heater for you first." Kajol informed me, switching off the light. Kajol's mom showed me each bedroom in the home while describing why she carefully went about choosing a suitable color and design for every bedroom. Amera described the high-quality fabric of her sheets and curtains that her oldest daughter Kajol hand selected. "This is my dream home. Our own piece of heaven is right here in Pakistan." Kajol said grinning.

"Here we go, this is your bedroom where you'll be sleeping for the rest of your stay. It's the best room in our house," Amera said. I threw my bag on the bed. Our housekeeper Khala will be right around the corner if you need anything to eat or drink, you only need to ask. Kahla makes the best cup of tea. One more thing, there is a bathroom with a jacuzzi in your room in case you need to bathe," Amera said disappearing to her room, closing the door. I pictured Amera enthralled in the novel that sat on her nightstand table- sipping from her tea, going back to sleep with few worries other less fortunate people in Pakistan faced.

"Tell me all about yourself and life back in America." Kajol inquired, sitting beside me on the sofa in the living room. A Pakistani drama, a popular family sitcom I watched several times over with Sana played in the background. "I was a housewife for a while. I enjoyed staying home with my sons in Louisiana with Daniyal. I write fiction and poetry. I'm working on something now about Pakistan, a fiction book, my first one," I explained enthusiastically.

"Did you have a job back in Louisiana? I'm sure you must have done something." Kajol asked rudely.

"I didn't graduate from college. I have a high school diploma and some college education." I answered hesitantly, surprised at Kajol's obvious judgment of my social and economic standing in America. "You are lucky that your children are intelligent, I hear from people in Faisalabad that Ayaan is also very bright."

"Ayaan says you're our guest for the next few days. Make yourself at home and get some rest."

"Can I offer you something to drink?" Kajol asked politely, closing the bedroom door. Late in the evening, the oldest daughter and a few guests from that morning were still up watching a Pakistani family sitcom when I went to the kitchen to ask Khala to make something us to eat and a cup of tea.

Two housekeepers from our village didn't want to acknowledge me. Khala went back to washing and scrubbing. Two housekeepers who worked for Ibrahim followed through on their instructions of how to keep the rich people comfortable. Upper Class society of Pakistan was worse than any wealthy person I encountered in the United States. Elite classes of Pakistani society considered heaven to be surrounded by piles of garbage, loitered alleyways and areas where kids walked around barefoot, begging for money.

Shacks and mud houses where poor people lived were lined up on almost every block. Thieves waited for the sight of Ibrahim, who poor kids called Sir. Child beggars pointed out the wealthy real – estate developer who lived around the corner. I went along with Ayaan in the beginning of my travels to Pakistan to meet wealthy foreigners before I knew what the upper-class societies of Pakistan thought of worldly women and poor castes.

Ghettos of Pakistan were present all around, even in wealthy neighborhoods.

I walked down to the corner vendor with Kajol to buy snacks from a kid selling calling cards, chips and candies. I was careful to lift my foot over broken pieces of glass and piles of garbage, aware of each time Ibrahim or his daughter, Kajol turned away a poor kid asking for pocket change. I was worse than all of them and should have never come to a place like Pakistan. Knowing my brother-in -law cared about me, at least wanting to make believe Ayaan cared, during my last day at the real estate developers' home, I sat with Ibrahim and Kajol in their backyard, waiting to be served by well-dressed maids from a nearby village. Each housekeeper from the village smiled mechanically carrying trays of food. Surrounding neighborhoods of Ibraimis house sat next to alleyways where poor kids appeared out of nowhere asking for food and money.

Kajol walked with me to a canteen down the road where a child beggar sold me a bag of chips and some chocolates, I recognized the poor kid from our walk earlier that morning. "Poor kids appear out of nowhere, expecting our family to be loaded with cash and saying in Punjabi God will punish the wealthy who look down on us."

"Don't give them any money Kasra. If you give something one time, they will never leave us alone. We are condemned to hell, these awful kids say each time, cursing us. I learned to ignore beggars."

"Dad recently built this house and before that- our cul -de -sac was an area where many poor lived," Kajol said, motioning away another child beggar.

Not giving money to the poor children each time plagued me with a sense of guilt.

"Stop giving them money and they will go away. You will smarten up after living in Pakistan and learn your lesson the hard way like I had to," Kajol said, chugging down the last of her canned soda. "This is our heaven," the real estate developer's wife said, wearing a nice pair of salwar kameez.

I was still hopeful Ayaan would get into the United Nations and build a better future for the women of our family. "Our family is living well in Pakistan. We don't desire to settle in any foreign country," Kajol repeated. I looked at the guests dressed in expensive clothing, their arms adorned with shiny silver bangles. When I peered down at the artificial grass surrounded by colorless landscape, in Ibraham's yard, I realized me and Ayaan were sitting in a stranger's backyard on chairs outside of an exquisite house. Ibrahim's home was no different than a village I visited during my stay in Karachi. There were no trees, plush farm fields or grazing cattle of Ayyan's village around to quiet my mind. I missed my time at Ganish.

An idea of heaven wasn't conceivable in a place like Pakistan. After meeting the real estate developer and his family, I stopped going to places. I turned down each offer of traveling to a new part of Pakistan to meet another important person. After that day of meeting the real estate developer and his daughter Kajol, not even for my most well-liked brother-in-law, Ayaan would I have gone back to Karachi again.

CHAPTER 10

Aaliyaa, The Caretaker

"People take advantage of my mother because she didn't finish elementary school," Ayaan reminded. My earliest memory of meeting Aaliyaa was unpacking a suitcase full of my oldest son, Sameer's belongings. I can remember the way Aaliyaa unpacked my sons' clothes and toys methodically, carefully taking each piece of clothing out of the suitcase and the look of grief that came over her.

Aaliyaa prayed five times a day, waiting for her brother Daniyal's return to Pakistan. Aaliyaa was the appointed caretaker of the family, never bothering to fix herself up or buy new shalwar kameez for herself, aside from weddings or religious celebrations she went to with close family. Aaliyaa applied ointment to Sameer and Asad's' cuts and scrapes, helping get kids ready for school and packing Sameer's lunch some mornings. I thought of reminding the middle sister that her prayers to Allah weren't for nothing. God answered her wishes in one way or another.

"She wants to say something, but Aaliyaa can't talk in English," a translator explained. We had an English translator present, a mutual friend named Asma.

"How do you say in English, you are deeply cared about more than I can express?" That's what Aaliyaa wants to say to you.

"Aaliyaa is emotional because she says your son's clothes are dirty. You struggled a lot in America. We love you and your sons," Asma translated.

Plagued with a nagging feeling I did something wrong or worse yet that I would be viewed as a bad mother by Aaliyaa in Islamic culture, I asked again if everything was alright. Tell Aaliyaa not to be upset with me. I was packing at the last minute and was planning to wash my son's clothes when I arrived in Pakistan. I've traveled all the way from Louisiana, on a sixteen-hour flight with Sameer and Asad. Most of Sameer's things are clean, look inside. Before I could finish explaining, Aaliyaa disappeared to another room. Asma continued in a British accent, "she meant to say, I don't want Kasra to see me hurt."

A few hours later, when I finished unpacking all of Sameer's clothes from America, Aaliyaa reemerged after hand washing a few of my son's clothes.

"Like brand new," Aaliyaa said in English while showing me Sameer's once stained white shirt, now spotlessly clean.

"She isn't educated. Aaliyaa doesn't speak English at all. She's from the village."

"Aaliyaa says she gets emotional because her husband went away. They moved him to the prison far from us in Faisalabad." Asma explained.

"Sister can't go and see her husband right now, the jail they moved him to is not a good facility. There is no nutritious food at the prison in Faisalabad. Aaliyaa can't go and see her husband for a while."

"Aaliyaa is making food for you but first she has to cook meals to be sent to her husband who has low blood sugar," Asma said in English, disappearing to the kitchen.

Aaliyaa was kindest to me when I first arrived in Pakistan, visibly anxious that she may use the wrong english word or phrase. Aaliyaa was by far the most sensitive and compassionate out of three daughters. Ayaan emphasized that Aaliyaa, the middle sibling, was taken advantage of because she wasn't educated. Aaliyaa was the strongest and most spiritual of three girls praying for family members, visiting sick relatives in the emergency room and cooking meals for a houseful of guests on Muslim holidays.

When a group of Ayaan's college-educated, forward-thinking friends showed up to our home in Faisalabad. Aaliyaa acted skirmish and caught off guard. Ayaan asked his mom not to do so much cooking and cleaning up after guests. "These are only my friends from the city. Sit down and relax." Ayaan insisted

Aaliyaa wasn't sure how to sit or talk in front of more educated people. Ayan's Mom disappeared to the kitchen hiding from a noisy crowd of teenagers making a plate of food for herself, sitting and eating alone in the quiet space. After overextending herself to guests, and college friends of Ayaan, I wasn't sure the rowdy group of forward-thinking girls noticed Aaliyaa's discomfort. Ayan's college friends chuckled while sharing stories, scarfing down platefuls of pakoras Aaliyaa fried, seeming not to notice Aaliyaa's discomfort.

"You've done enough. You must be tired," Ayaan said, touching Aaliyaa's shoulders in a gesture that suggested Aaliyaa take a break. When Aaliyaa finally sat down with the group of her sons' college friends and appeared relaxed, I noticed Aaliyaa fidgeting with her clothes, choosing to eat alone on a stool in the kitchen. After a few minutes, Aaliyaa retreated to the kitchen.

"She isn't educated, my mom doesn't know English," Ayaan repeated

"Come sit next to me, so we can talk. I told you I didn't want anything from America." Aaliyaa insisted. It was late in the evening. All the shoe stores in Faisalabad were about to close. I needed to find the right style and size tennis shoes for Aaliyaa.

I stopped waiting for a letter to be read out loud by Aaliyaa, not that I didn't care about my brother-in-law. I didn't think to ask about what country the armed services sent Ayaan off to last. We were family after all. Each member of my Pakistani family who and embraced my sons, Sameer and Asad, that was what I wanted most.

I remember my first-time meeting a housekeeper who Aaliyaa hired to help with my son's needs. Bushra was an attractive girl with a jovial disposition in her 20's who had an obvious crush on Rani's husband. Most of my sisters-in-law didn't want a pretty, scantily dressed housekeeper working for our family. No one went against Aaliyaa's wishes. Bushra spoke English proficiently and could be a useful translator while I was settling into life in Pakistan.

"Every time our new housekeeper, Bushra comes to work, she's wearing a full face of wedding make- up, and a low-cut Kameez. Bushra doesn't work, she watches her favorite television sitcoms all afternoon. Bushra purposely doesn't bother covering herself with a debutta. The new housekeepers I hired always wait until my husband is home in his room to clean in front of him. Housekeepers from Ganish are juvenile and disadvantaged dancing and singing around the house, like this." Rani spun around, silver bangles covering her arms jingled while me and Aaliyaa chuckled, watching from a distance.

I was friends with most of the housekeepers who lived with us in Ganish and Faisalabad. I genuinely found this new housekeeper to be a nice person with an alluring singing voice. Late nights. I stayed up with Bushra talking while the new maid shared stories about growing up in a village. I talked about my life back in Louisiana with my son Sameer and my husband, Daniyal.

Bushra made it a point to emphasize that she only took a job as a housekeeper for fun in her leisure time, and to help Aaliyaa, who she considered family. Bushra didn't necessarily need the passive income and was not poor but middle class. Bushra said her family lived in a comfortable middle-class house at our village of Ganish.

"My little brother works in Dubai at a well-paying job and earns a good salary." Bushra reassured me. Later, I was informed Bushra's brother worked a hard labor job for little money in Dubai. Bushra's family was hardly making enough to survive. The new housekeeper took my hand, smiling, "Bhabhi you should come to my home and meet my family. We live in a big, beautiful house with lots of land. We recently bought a buffalo. I can fix your hair," Bushra said enthusiastically.

"This girl is lying just like other poor agriculture workers who come here to work,", Rani corrected.

"Bushra is trying to impress you. She lives in a cramped house and comes from our village home in Ganish. Don't be fooled. Here, the housekeepers steal everything, from expensive make up to personal items."

"Kasra. can I tell you one thing?"

"Don't get too friendly with the maids. Learn to be stern with them. We are not of the same caste." Rani informed me.

In the mornings on religious holidays, Bushra sang a sacred prayer while the entire family stood around, listening. At her village home, Bushra recited namaz prayers over a loudspeaker. Groups of relatives congregated around in a circle excited to hear Bushra sing.

Bushra's singing voice was tragic and captivating, representing the pain of growing up as a villager. Each time Bushra sang a ballad, I missed home in Louisiana. In the evenings Bushra came into my room, sobbing and whispering about how Rani and other family members were abusing her. Bushra was quitting. Soon my brother will earn enough money for us to be middle class. "I won't have to work here," Bushra exclaimed.

"People say I flirt," Bushra exclaimed, lifting covers over her head, checking the door to see if Inaya found her in my room. "This family is no good, very bad people," Bushra said loudly, muttering something in Punjabi. I couldn't make out in Urdu what else Bushra was whispering when she slammed the door.

All the housekeepers who worked for our family slept on the floor or in separate living quarters. Bushra stressed how she was middle class. Housekeepers from our village were not allowed to use the same bathrooms, sit on the furniture or sleep in shared beds. "This is what happens when you spoil the housekeepers," Aaliyaa said resting a broom by my bedroom door and switching off the hallway light.

Despite how poorly Rani treated Bushra, Aaliyaa consoled Bushra, pleading with the adolescent housekeepers not to quit. "We still have Kasra, the American here and I can't speak English," Aaliyaa said in Urdu persuading Bushra not to leave. Aaliyaa promised to hand sew new salwar kameez for Bushra.

"Next week, I'll make new clothes for you," Aaliyaa said. I could tell Aaliyaa genuinely cared for poor people she took into our home, because of coming from a lower caste, there were lines Aaliyaa couldn't cross.

Bushra returned the next morning wearing a new salwar kameez Aaliyaa designed for her along with new silver bangles and make- up

"How do I look?" Bushra asked, spinning around, feeling like a member of the family. Next week, Bushra got into a fight with Rani again and threatened to quit while running to Aaliyaa for help. Aaliyaa complained about how taxing it was to make bread for so many guests every afternoon, especially on hot days.

When our shared washing machine broke, Bushra hand washed the family's portion of laundry. Aaliyaa demanded that Bushra stay at the job a few more months, reassuring her that she was cared about and a member of the extended family. Any concept of caring about the housekeepers came with the understanding that like anything unfamiliar or different in Pakistani culture, there were boundaries one couldn't cross as a family with a solid reputation who came from a good caste.

When Bushra didn't know I was watching, our new housekeeper danced in a room. Seeing Bushra dance was different than listening to her sing. Bushra's dance brought me feelings of joy and celebration. For a while I was close friends with the new maid. She was thrifty and careful about her appearance. You would never know the juvenile housekeeper was a poor villager working for a middle-class family in Faisalabad.

When the new housekeeper pulled a stained white purse, I purchased it from America out of the trash can, showing up the next morning with the bag I threw away hanging over her arm.

"Is that the bag I threw away?"

"The bag looks brand- new."

"I thought you didn't need to need it anymore," Bushra said blushing, handing me back the bag.

"No, it suits you better, keep it," I insisted.

On the day our newest member of the family left the job, Aaliyaa picked up a few English words and phrases and I learned enough Urdu for us to communicate. On her last day at work, Bushra hugged me sobbing, excited to tell me her brother found a more permanent, better paying job in Dubai. Bushra didn't have to work or return to a job as a housekeeper employed for our family any longer. One thing I missed after the day Bushra left was our housemaid's enthusiasm for life and her passion for music and dance. Sometimes I think about similarities between Bushra and me. Like many women from our village, Bushra would likely never escape poverty. Song and dance, maybe that was Bushra's passion, the thing that made her hopeful again despite life's setbacks.

CHAPTER 11

Rani, *The Forgotten Sister*

$\mathcal{M}$y first-time meeting Rani was at her village home of Ganish, within walking distance of my in-law's property. Rani was a newlywed village girl when we met with silky black hair and fair skin, dressed in a stylish pair of shalwar kameez. Rani's long black hair was soaked in mustard oil.

You would have assumed I was close friends with Rani before living together in Pakistan. Nadia told me that her newest sister-in-law, resembled a Bollywood actress from old black and white films. Rani sat a few feet away from me on a plastic chair, trying to remove a thorn imbedded in her foot. Forgotten sister removed the flats she wore, making her way toward me, limping slightly, extending a hand. A group of village kids circled around. "Forgive me Bhabhi, I don't know English." Rani said shyly.

In the evenings, Rani took walks with her brothers, mentioning that she didn't bother to wear the most comfortable shoes. "You will enjoy visiting my village when you can Kasra, there are fields and green pastures where cattle graze, a few buffalo and cows my oldest brother purchased for a fair price." Rani said in her best English.

Rani was a girl with traditional values who grew up at our village, home of Ganish. As the oldest of three children, she got up early to fight her way through crowded bazaars to select fresh produce she would cook in recipes for large groups of family members and guests. Rani's husband, Malak seemed overly concerned with Rani's beauty, that his village wife be a follower of Islam, light complected and able to conceive sons. I don't know if Rani was always mean and spiteful toward women. My Pakistani in-laws must have influenced Rani.

Rani was considered an exceptional beauty. There was little to no way out of a life back at Ganish for an uneducated village woman except for marrying a wealthy landlord. When I tried to read children's books to my newest family member, I realized Rani gave up on learning at some point in childhood. Rani, called forgotten sister, was afraid to write or speak in English, made self-conscious by my perceived judgements of her intellect. There was little to no hope of Rani acquiring a higher level of education in a modern city.

Staying behind as the oldest of three girls wasn't uncommon. Rani's male family members moved away from life in a rural village in pursuit of higher studies in progressive cities. Rani's oldest brother stayed at his village home helping to run the family business, selling milk and rice to markets. Rani's sister moved hours away from home in Ganish, traveling abroad in pursuit of better job prospects. She accepted her role as the oldest sibling, staying behind, catering to guests, choosing not to further her education. The oldest of three daughters seemed to have given up on her own sense of purpose and happiness before marrying Malak.

Rani was the instigator of the family, spreading rumors about me while pretending to be my closest friend and supporter. Forgotten sister treated me no better than the housekeepers and held stereotypical biases about westernized women and poor people born into lower castes.

On different occasions, my former students from the government school where I taught English classes, showed up to check on me. The downside of living close to Pakistani in laws were misogynistic women who viewed other females as competitors. Powerful men in Pakistani society regarded women as having little value.

Promising marriage to prepubescent daughters before their bodies fully developed wasn't unheard of in impoverished regions of Punjab. In some villages, divorce was forbidden especially if initiated by a woman. If a wealthy man from Ganish was experiencing marital problems, polygamy was an option. Taking a second or third wife to avoid divorce wasn't unheard of.

My favorite brother- in-law, Ayaan informed me that Rani was telling family members I controlled and abused the hired help. I had little access to the maids who worked for us in Faisalabad and couldn't speak the native language of Urdu fluently. I was told by family members no one knew Forgotten sister had this many problems before marriage. Rani was always considered family.

Ayaan talked about growing up with Rani at his village home of Ganish and explained ways in which Rani acted as the sole caretaker for her mother as a child. "You cannot trust Rani."

"You understand nothing about Pakistani culture," Ayaan reminded.

When I lived with Rani, our home was crowded with guests and relatives almost every afternoon at nearly the same time. Rani spent afternoons cooking for people who arrived at our home in Faisalabad. Bringing her hands together to roll out a soft piece of dough in her palm for making bread, Rani placed another handful of dough in the tandoori oven to bake.

I heard about an employee who spilled a tray of scalding hot tea on Rani's daughter, Maya. "You're lucky to have sons. In a place like Pakistan raising a daughter is difficult." Rani told me.

Inaya and Rani worried about Maya's beauty and marriage prospects. Inaya took her Granddaughter, Maya, to a nearby hospital concerned about how burns covering the little girl's face may hinder Maya's chances of marrying into a respectable middle- class family.

Rani mentioned how life before marriage was cheerful. After her last delivery, a daughter, Rani promised not to conceive more children. Rani tried her best to make my life miserable during my stay in Pakistan by doing petty things like purposely uninviting me to weddings or celebrations centered around religious holidays or festivities at the village.

Being American didn't prevent Rani from spreading vicious lies about me to anyone who would listen. Next to no one in Faisalabad had many kind things to say about Rani. I would find a reason to justify Rani's abuses toward me and other family members by remembering stories I heard about Rani's sick Mother, Tabina. Tabina came from our neighboring village of Ganish and passed away after a long battle with tuberculosis. Rani stayed back, caring for her Tabina. Rani was no different than the Pakistani version of a mean girl.

"She's trying to ruin your life so you can't stay in Pakistan." Ayaan warned me. Rani informed anyone who would listen about how I was not a good mother or wife.

I chuckled to myself thinking about Rani's desperation to marry into our family. Someone should have warned forgotten sister about what she was getting herself into. Last I heard, Rani's husband was going to take on a second wife who could adequately care for and educate his primary school age daughter.

Sometimes I wondered what happened to Rani after I left. Aaliyaa wanted to send Rani back to her village where she came from, an invisible place where you couldn't be seen or heard from again. I guess that's what Aaliyaa meant. Rani despised me as a nonnative of Pakistan living abroad and all those unlucky enough to be born female.

According to Aaliyaa, Rani treated her newest sister-in law, Shahida no better than the hired help, talking frequently about how she doesn't owe her new Bhabhi anything because she comes from a poorer caste. When Rani went for a surprise visit to Ganish, Shahida was catering to guests' days after having a c- section. Rani didn't bother to allow Shahida adequate time to recover after giving birth.

Before marriage, Aaliyaa described how Rani arrived at her home in the city for weeks at a time pleading to marry her little brother. Aaliyaa claimed her brother, Malak usually turned down Rani's marriage proposals. "Rani's brothers and Father should be ashamed of themselves, making the women of their family work like the hired help, not allowing female members of the family opportunities to get a higher education, hoarding all the money for themselves."

"When Rani returns to our home in Faisalabad from visiting relatives, Rani finds faults in her newest Bhabhi. According to Rani, this new sister can't cook, doesn't clean."

"She's lazy," Aaliyaa explained.

Despite Aaliyaa's disapproval of Rani marrying into our family, Daniyal mentioned an arranged marriage he never accepted back in Pakistan to a first or second cousin. Rani pretended to care about me while spreading malicious rumors. This had been going on for a while.

It wasn't until Rani found out her first child would be a daughter that I began seeing the extent of her hatred for all women. The twisted mind games Rani played with me began to add up over time.

Punishing a first-born daughter for her own misfortunes and marrying a daughter off before puberty happened commonly in backward villages. Being black or born from a lower caste family meant possibly being punished for simply being born a female or unlucky.

We all felt helpless to do anything. The little Asian girl slept soundly, like a porcelain doll in Aaliyaa's arms. I wondered if Maya recalled being hurt by her own mother, Rani.

Aaliyaa reassured me Rani would no longer be returning as part of the family.

Aaliyaa said Rani would move back to her ancestral village home soon, permanently erased from our lives for good this time.

No one would likely see or hear from Rani again, not after the last time she went too far abusing her first born daughter, drawing blood. Other times, Rani prayed namaz for her first-born daughter, Maya when she was sick or struggling in school. According to Maya's pediatrician Rani's daughter was malnourished and put on supplements to gain weight. Maya never grew in height or weight like other children her age. Farah told me about a breathtaking girl desperate to marry into the family, known as the village beauty years, ago, Rani.

Counting how much pocket change I had left in dollar bills, Malak glanced over at a father dressed in a suit and tie standing in front of us in a long line at the department store. The man's daughter wore a frilly lace dress with a pink bow tied in the back. She must have been around the same age as Malak's daughter Maya. The girl in the department store was twice Maya's size, pudgy but not overweight. The man in the department store line looked like he was buying expensive clothes for his daughter. We left overpriced toys like dolls and cars behind. I looked back at the upscale store in the big city where wealthy businessmen shopped – splurging on privileged family members and daughters. I thought about Rani and how she dressed Maya in old or unwashed shalwar kameez even on special occasions.

Aaliyaa was a disadvantaged woman from Ganish and carried most of the baggage of those around her. Growing up in a village may meant you struggled as a woman, but likely faced abuse too. "I should have never married Rani to my brother, not after she spanked Maya more than a couple of times."

"This was my fault, I brought Rani into our extended family," Aaliyaa exclaimed remorsefully. We shared our sorrows and losses together. Nothing was separate.

Sana told me she shut her eyes to the unimaginable of what was happening. Aaliyaa talked about plans to get her brother, Malak married to someone else, an educated girl with traditional values. Rani had no choice but to return to her village home of Ganish and disappear for good this time.

Sharing space, resources and living quarters with in-laws meant you may be subject to taking on blame for other family member's problems. We laughed and celebrated when good times circled around.

"I liked you better than Rani for my brother," Aaliyaa joked in Urdu. Aaliyaa never understood my marital problems with her brother Daniyal.

Aaliyaa swore that Daniyal would get his share of property and wealth returned to him soon.

I wanted to believe that.

Aaliyaa explained that I would be appalled by the way Rani was living before she showed up to our house in Faisalabad desperate to marry Malak. When we were guests at Rani's village, she acted more like a housekeeper, cooking all the time and not bothering to attend school after five years of formal education. At Rani's village there were extended periods of power and water shortages.

Nadia gossiped about Rani talking about life before marriage how Rani slept most of the afternoons away, wasting time, not bothering to apply make-up or fix herself up. Each time Rani invited us to her village home. The family's shared home was gross.

"Rani's three brothers have more property and land than anyone in Faisalabad."

"Her three brothers are filthy rich." Aaliyaa complained, speaking half in unconventional English.

"Rani's brothers have all that money, but Rani's brothers and Father keep their daughters uneducated."

"She is too busy tending to guests and cooking to bother with books or studying. No time for studies, only time for gossip."

"Let me tell you about Rani, you like her, your friends with her, let me tell you what your friend is up to." Aaliyaa went on.

By now, I understood enough Urdu to get by and Aaliyaa picked up on my American sense of humor enough to make me laugh when she spoke about Rani in English. I watched Aaliyaa double check each room and washroom after our new housekeeper finished cleaning. Aaliyaa was thorough in remembering to spray down soapy tiles of bathroom floors while mimicking Rani in English. I hesitated to ask about when, if ever Rani would be returning from her village.

"Let me tell you what your friend is doing."

"Do you know where Rani disappears off to every weekend or where she goes on Islamic holidays?" Aaliyaa shook her head in disbelief, muttering something in Urdu.

"I bet you don't have a clue," Aaliyaa continued.

CHAPTER 12

Oldest Sister, Farah, Three Daughters and a Dream

On visits to our ancestral village home, I sat with three sisters gathered around an underground imu made by digging a pit to trap heat. Bilal, an agriculture worker Malak hired placed a handful of branches below a pan to keep the fire going. Each time Bilal made tea, he brought his hands together to crush a few more cardamom seeds and stir the pot by blowing on the top when water nearly came to a boil, tilting the deep saucepan from side-to-side mixing in different spices.

Bilal was another poor villager who labored for our family. "You keep forgetting to cover your hair," Bilal reminded, during Islamic prayer times. Early mornings before breakfast, I sat on our terrace while Farah boiled a pot of tea. Quiet mornings sitting on the terrace, drinking tea, watching people from above were better moments I missed.

Nearly every weekend I traveled with Farah to crowded markets by rickshaw to buy fresh vegetables used for preparing family meals for weeks to come. On my first days in Faisalabad, Sana woke me up before sunrise. We walked up the rickety ladder to the third story, all the way to the rooftop, where a flock of pigeons gathered, covering the roof. Sana, the oldest of three daughters, scattered a handful of crumbled breadcrumbs on the ground.

"I thought you would like it up here," Sana gushed, smiling.

Thinking about how fascinating it was in Pakistan and how happy I seemed.

I nodded in agreement, Farah hand-picked damp clothes from the hamper to line- dry on hot days. After school when the weather was pleasant, Sameer and Asad played games of cricket or badminton, a sport like baseball. I was next up to bat; except I couldn't remember the rules of cricket and didn't have great hand –eye coordination when swinging. I would lose the ball in an alleyway below us. Looking down from a rooftop, I watched as a poor man-made roti bread from scratch. I could picture the way Bilal's wrinkled hands moved together with ease. I was soothed by the clapping rhythm Bilal's hands made when shaping bread. The poor man hired by Malak placed each piece of dough in the tandoor oven to bake.

When I failed at a few attempts to publish my novels while living in Pakistan, I decided to try my hand at painting. When I started taking an art class family members made jokes and laughed in the beginning at my juvenile paintings. Most indigenous women had no standards for beauty or criteria for failure or success. Nothing was ugly or not useful. I observed people of Faisalabad go about their daily routines. Sana and I stopped doing yoga on the roof when we realized our neighbors could see us from across the way. Nadia spoke sarcastically about opening a gym for women in the city of Faisalabad.

I knew we were going somewhere special when I opened the bedroom door to find Sana sprawled out on the bed. I spotted a private school uniform, khaki pants and a navy-blue vest and book bag lying half open on the floor. It was too early to be home on a school day. Sana was studying at a local University in hopes of applying to one of the best medical schools in Karachi.

My earliest memory of meeting the oldest of three sisters, Farah, was when she traveled from Saudi Arabia to Pakistan for a visit. After returning from Saudia Arabia on almost every trip back to Faisalabad, Farah brought gifts and necessities she assumed we needed from Saudi Arabia. Sana and Ayaan rushed downstairs eager to see what Farah brought for us from Saudi Arabia. In a large, overstuffed suitcase, Farah distributed random things like appliances she thought were better quality, name brand shampoo and conditioner, not the rip off brands we purchased in Faisalabad.

I asked myself if Farah was the catalyst behind why I left Pakistan last time. During short stints from Saudi Arabia to our village home of Ganish, Farah made it a point not to discuss her marital problems. Farah rarely disclosed anything personal. Reasons behind why she ultimately decided to settle in Pakistan with three teenage daughters were matters Farah never shared. I knew from Farah's three girls, mostly Sana, about Farah's marital troubles in Saudi Arabia. Sana described in detail, the abuse Farah and her daughters tolerated at the hands of their father, Muhammad, a man from Saudi Arabia.

I wonder if Farah cared about me. Sana swore there was no such thing as romance or affection that existed in a country like Pakistan. I lived with Sameer and Asad in the house upstairs from Farah and her three daughters. The oldest of the three sisters, Farah and her three daughters appeared ecstatic at first, to meet me, the American and Daniyal's wife who they must have heard so much about.

Sana was eighteen and had a bright future ahead, except she lived in Faisalabad and was a middle-class girl, raised practically by a single mom and a partially absent father. I would work up the nerve to tell Farah about my divorce from Daniyal, eventually.

Sana was the most nurturing and courteous, especially when it came to bonding with my two children, Sameer and Asad. Sana claimed my sons as her own and I didn't mind that she acted possessive over my little son, Asad, who was most attached to her. When Sana's father, Muhammad arrived from Saudi Arabia, out of nowhere, Sana told me she was sorry she couldn't play with my kids, Asad and Sameer or meet with me for weeks to come. Muhammad was visiting as a respected guest from another country.

Sameer and Asad got into the routine of going downstairs some mornings before I sent them off to school enjoying a hearty breakfast. I would brush off Farah's obvious distrust of me, assuming she was well intended but cautious of accepting of an American family member just yet.

Early mornings after breakfast, I was consoled by watching my son, Asad bond with Sana. It was the same routine after school every afternoon. Sana threw her heavy book bag down and switched on a rerun of a Turkish family drama, we watched together countless times. The plot was about victimized or vengeful family members. I could see real-life family members portrayed on screen. I must have seen this episode a handful of times.

After switching on her favorite family drama, Sana descended downstairs in a hurry to make a cup of tea the same way every time, with a handful of looseleaf tea leaves and a few cardamom seeds thrown in for flavor. Sana waited a few minutes for the pot of water to come to a boil. Before turning down the heat, Sana let the tea simmer before going back to her television program. I rarely saw Farah's middle daughter Kimila, a reserved and creative girl. Kimila was a deep thinker who had an interest in art and poetry. Farrah's teenage daughter stayed mostly to herself except to peek out of her room or look up from her school textbooks and say a friendly hello to Sameer.

In Pakistan women and relatives who made up social networks were much needed support systems most people in Faisalabad relied on, especially during trying times. Visiting Faisalabad again with Sameer and Asad would be worth it. I wanted to return to see Sana, the oldest of Farah's three daughters, graduate college and live an independent life in a modernized city like Karachi or Islamabad. Sana was too ambitious and independent to marry a first cousin.

After this last trip to Faisalabad, I imagined Sana visiting our village of Ganish once more, thinking about what direction her life would take.

When returning from college, Sana made tea for both of us each afternoon, living in a girl's hostel in Karachi was comparable to sharing a college dorm room with a group of female friends or roommates.

Sana discussed new friendships she made at Hamdard college and filled me in on college life at the local government University where she studied to become a doctor. Sana handwrote pages in a notebook filled with diary entrees chronicling life at Hamdard college where Sana spent afternoons hauling a rickshaw to work, writing magazine articles and eating junk food with friends. I thought about my first days in Faisalabad, waiting for the lights to die out when Sana and I struggled to find our way back home in the dark. We climbed over the gate, waiting for a guard to let us inside.

"When are you coming back to Pakistan?" Sana asked on my last trip to Faisalabad.

Farah must be planning her oldest daughter Sana's wedding to a first cousin by now. On another return visit to Faisalabad from Saudia Arabia, Farah unpacked a black hijab dress she brought from Saudi Arabia. I spotted the dress hanging on the back of a chair in Sana's room and reluctantly tried on the hijab, throwing on a light matching black cardigan. I walked upstairs searching for Sana, thinking momentarily about what it would feel like to wear the hijab or burka every day.

The dress requirements for women and standards for covering up for women who traveled alone in countries like Saudia Arabia were much stricter than Pakistan. Women who lived in Saudia Arabia weren't permitted to travel alone to places.

Women from Saudia Arabia were made to cover their bodies in a full-length burka and hijab everywhere.

"You look nice wearing the hijab as an American," Sana complimented. Take off the hijab before my mom sees you, she is picky about who touches religious things she brings over from Saudia Arabia.

Sana explained that according to her mom, Farah, Saudi Arabia was considered a sacred place of worship. I picked up on the fact that to a big sister, I wasn't viewed as Islamic or religious enough to be accepted as a part of my Muslim family. Farah was at times, petty and mean spirited, counting the number of times I bathed in a week while telling other family members details about my personal life in Louisiana with Daniyal, secrets I shared with Sana. Farah spoke the most fluent English of three daughters and told me next time I wasn't to go near the things she brought from Saudi Arabia.

Farah was the most respected of the family. No matter what I did to please Farah, she found reasons to criticize me. The oldest of three girls didn't like the way I disciplined my children. Farah nitpicked how I ate, dressed and failed at trying to learn the native language of Urdu.

I overheard Farah speaking in Urdu to relatives about a girl named Kasra from another country who she couldn't stand. Farah picked apart my looks, the way I ate and even taught Sameer and Asad. Sana filled me in on what life was like growing up in Saudi Arabia revealing details about Farah's abusive arranged marriage and a strained relationship Sana had with their father, Muhammad who came in and out of their lives. After Farah left this last time for Saudia Arabia, I didn't know the truth surrounding why Farah and her daughters returned to Pakistan again. I didn't think to ask when Farah and her girls would be going back to live in Saudia Arabia permanently this time around.

After Farah and her three teenage daughters left for Saudia Arabia, my mother-in-law, Inaya, offered me and Sameer Farah's living space downstairs temporarily. The downstairs portion of the house had a separate kitchen and entryway, bigger rooms, a space that according to Inaya would be more private than upstairs. Before Farah left for Saudia Arabia, I shared the upstairs portion of the house in Faisalabad, with Rani and her daughter, Maya.

Farah returned from Saudi Arabia without warning. Soon after arriving in Faisalabad with her daughters, Farah hired contractors who began painting and renovating downstairs where I stayed with my sons, Sameer and Asad. The contractors

Farah hired looked like skilled laborers from our village. A group of men wearing baggy jeans stained with white paint and sleeveless shirts began ripping out old tile floors, replacing kitchen counters, outdated appliances and moving furniture. I was standing in the middle of a house renovation, struggling to move back and forth between homes to collect the rest of our belongings. I wove around crews of sweaty village men who were too busy applying a final layer of white primer to notice me. I made my way upstairs, leaning up against newly painted walls on my way out.

"I bought this place. This is my house. Find some other place to go!" Farah yelled when I returned a few hours later to collect the last of our things. Farah was the oldest of three children and the most respected.

I had no choice but to leave.

Sameer, Asad and I swiftly packed up and moved out of Farah's living space downstairs. Farah changed out the décor of every room downstairs, ripping apart outdated wallpaper and floors. When we left, the kitchen was brand new. Farah replaced the back door. After Farah remodeled downstairs, the oldest of three girls, never went back to Saudi Arabia, not even for a visit.

I learned from Sana details surrounding what Farah's life in Saudi Arabia was like. I understood by now that emotions like happiness and sadness weren't yours to keep as a Pakistani. Saudi Arabia was a country much like Pakistan, an Islamic country where most went to worship and pray, a country where I wouldn't be welcome.

Farah centered her religious principles around feelings of duty and upholding the family's good name. Ayaan would no longer show up with a mob of kids, uncles and cousins surrounding him, with an offering of flowers welcoming me to his country of Pakistan. Sana and her two sisters would no longer sit anxiously awaiting my arrival to Faisalabad, eager to fill me in on life at a college dorm, living in a girl's hostel. As the oldest, despite being from another country I was obligated to uphold family values, as I listened to Sana, excited to show me the new shalwar kameez she made. Sana offered to take me around to every location in Pakistan. Nothing was the same after that day.

Farah's life in Saudia Arabia frightened me enough to make me realize there was no such thing as satisfying arranged marriages. The more weddings I attended in Pakistan, the more I remembered laughing and dancing at weddings where I was around people who didn't care about me. Farah's story of an abusive arranged marriage made me think of Shaadi, Pakistani weddings and Islamic holidays.

Feelings of excitement surrounding going to an outdoor market to search for an intricately embroidered new shalwar kameez meant I had a couple of days beforehand to shop. Going to fancy wedding parties grew tiresome after a while. I thought about being an unassuming Pakistani bride and wondered if this new bride found happiness.

Farah, whose wish was to educate her three daughters, had the equivalent of a high school diploma. I knew Farah's ambitions to move away and study at the local college and make something more of her life was gone after marriage. Village life came with limited resources and inaccessibility to better quality schools that kept women from furthering their education. At least Farah had ambitions for her three daughters. Aside from cooking meals and serving guests, Farah didn't appear to have hobbies or goals outside of rearing three girls and stitching shalwar kameez for female family members, housekeepers and friends.

CHAPTER 13

A man from Saudi Arabia

arah's arranged marriage to Muhammad was a union that most Pakistanis considered a good match. Farah's husband, Muhammad worked as an engineer in Saudi Arabia and made a decent salary as the sole provider of his family. I was told Muhammad's family was from a poorer caste in Faisalabad and didn't own much property. Sana rarely mentioned their father except on Islamic holidays when he traveled from Saudia Arabia to Faisalabad, Pakistan to stay at Ganish. I later found out Muhammad resented his wife, Farah for not being able to give him sons. Sana told me their father was an alcoholic who psychologically and physically abused, controlled and manipulated them and their mother for years. Farah couldn't take the abuse any longer and fled to Faisalabad, Pakistan with her three daughters with the hope of starting over again in their homeland.

Farah cooked meals for her husband, Muhammad during his travels to Faisalabad from Saudia Arabia. Muhammad's three daughters celebrated their dad's arrival as if he never left. Farah served food to her husband Muhammad, pretending like there were no problems in their marriage. Farah appeared uneasy and sat off to herself drinking tea when there were roomfuls of guests, sitting upright with tense posture, choosing not to speak much when her husband, Muhammad was around. When I was brave enough and spoke coherent Urdu to haul a rickshaw on my own to my favorite spots like shops or bazaars around Faisalabad, I came across Muhammad roaming around busy markets, looking intoxicated and standing beside food vendors striking up conversations with people he encountered but seemed to know well. I hoped Muhammad didn't notice me.

Despite his shortcomings a man from Saudia, called Muhammad had a generous side. During his trips to Pakistan, Muhammad took the whole family on outings to popular coffee shops and malls in Peshawar. Years of listening to Sana reveal secrets about their father and a life of hardship in Saudia Arabia, took me back to the evening I learned of Muhammad's passing.

Before going into surgery, Muhammad made one last phone call, reassuring his wife and teenage daughters that he would return home for dinner. I regretted speaking poorly of the dead, recalling with gratitude nice things Muhammad did for my two sons while I lived in Faisalabad like splurging on Sameer, gifting us cash to spend in rupees and taking us to some of the best restaurants and shopping malls in Peshawar. Muhammad died from a type of cancer that went undetected that night in the emergency room and didn't make it through surgery.

Muhammad sat back grinning, as though pleased to see Sameer and Asad content and settling into life in a foreign country. I wondered how this could be the same man Sana spoke of. We were the keepers of secrets.

Being a woman in Pakistani society meant you had to fight harder for education, independence and pursuing a career after marriage. Little did I know accepting gifts or compassion in Pakistan came with expectations. When saying goodbye and burying their dad in Pakistan, Farah and her girls didn't appear to want me around for the burial. Farah didn't seem to want me present to sit with them and their dad during visits.

To Sana's Father, I wasn't considered Islamic enough. I didn't know enough about Islamic, religious customs to be in Muhammad's presence. Now Muhammad was gone. Part of me was relieved Sana's father would no longer be around to make me feel self-conscious about following religious traditions, smiling at the right moment, and not serving guests. Sana and Kasmir were free to come and go at any hour of the day.

A sacred city in Saudi Arabia known as the holy city of Mecca was a place I heard about where one may go for spiritual enlightenment and to be made new again. On each visit to Faisalabad, Sana and her sisters brought bottles of holy water taken from the city of Mecca. Kasmir spoke of traveling to the city of Mecca and having unanswered prayers miraculously heard and answered.

Before the abuse and belittling began in my marriage to Daniyal, I used to dream about happiness and starting a family. Visiting Mecca one day made me think of an illusionary city in Saudi – that I would go to in my mind each time I wanted to start over or seek forgiveness. In my imagination, I traveled back to the holy city of Mecca asking for another chance.

Getting into a top international University required preparation and hard work. When Sana received high marks on another final exam, we celebrated by eating at a fast-food chain where my children played outside. I walked at least half a mile until I recognized the public school Hamdard University Sana attended and pressed a button on an intercom until a guard let me inside. I wandered through Hamdard college for hours, asking random students loitering hallways if they came across Sana, wondering why she hadn't bothered showing up for any of her classes.

On my way out of the school, I stopped at a nearby family park, a walking trail that reminded me of farm fields. Only men visited family parks during certain daytime hours. I walked closer to what looked like the outline of a girl, her long black hair was covered with a shawl. The girl was dressed out of uniform in a pair of comfortable pair of shalwar kameez she wore when at home.

I noticed Sana in the distance rocking back and forth on a swing where a few men wearing white shalwar kameez sat on grass -like fields or sidewalks eating lunch or chatting nearby. Sana's secret hideout was revealed. A family park near Hamdard school was where Sana journeyed off to on school days when there was an important test to skip out on. Thankfully the oldest of three girls hadn't decided to ditch classes for good, run away to another country and elope with a secret boyfriend.

"How did you find me?"

"I don't want to go to medical school, but I don't have the heart to tell mom. My mom prays namaz for me daily. Her dream is for me to get into a top college in Pakistan." Sana said.

It must be nice, having a secret hideout where you could go to skip out on a biology class and indulge in fantasy. I thought. It was serene at the family park during this hour of day. The oldest of three girls was savvy about waiting to hideout at a family park at just the right hour in the afternoon, when there likely wouldn't be many people around. I'm sure Sana thought carefully about the possibility of insulting her mother or the holy prophet Muhammed, peace be upon him, by daring to sit among strange men as a middle-class girl from a good caste. "You've been out here all afternoon daydreaming, let's go home."

"Please don't do this again," I said. The oldest of the girls nodded in agreement.

I heard the familiar bustle of rowdy neighborhood kids playing cricket on the corner near our house in Faisalabad, recognizing the family's morning load of laundry hanging over the balcony to line- dry. Pakistan became home and Sana was like family. We walked together a few blocks. I never said anything about a secret place where Sana went to skip classes. We were the keepers of secrets. I told myself from now on, I would ignore unkind remarks and insults Farah aimed at me.

My in laws assumed I would convert to Islam eventually. During prayer times and religious holidays in Faisalabad, I chose not to show up to what I now consider cult-like prayer rituals. I wanted to return to anything familiar, like Catholic sermons I attended on Sundays with my mom. Over time, my prolonged absence at religious functions or celebrated Islamic holidays meant I insulted Islam and was unappreciative for all the generous things my in laws did for my children and I during our stay in Pakistan.

I was like Rani, reduced to holding tight to cherished memories of a better time somewhere in childhood before marriage. Pakistani in - laws accepted that I was never going to convert to Islam. More apparent were the sins of Daniyal, stains that could never be washed away, not even by bathing in the holiest waters taken from a city of Mecca. I was doomed to suffer alongside devout Muslim women of our family whose prayer rituals of calling out to God were the only ways to make a clean slate. Somewhere along my journey living in another country, I was treated like a stranger, rather than a celebrated guest, a turning point I didn't see coming.

When Farah began distancing herself from me, I watched on Friday mornings after mosque as sister rolled out a prayer mat depicting an image of the holy city of Mecca on the front. Going through the motions of namaz prayer, Farah held out her open palms, reciting namaz, asking forgiveness for the sins of relatives, and family members. I wanted to insist Farah stop asking God for forgiveness for the burdens of what men of our family handed us. After a while, I couldn't stand listening to Farah recite namaz prayers daily. In that moment I regretted giving any friend or relative false hope for why Islam was a religion I could accept in my heart. The overwhelming affection and support of Pakistani relatives I encountered came with an expectation that I would accept Islam as a Muslim woman somewhere down the line. I was compared to the new daughter in- law, Zarah who was highly educated, a devoted Islamic woman with traditional family values, who grew up in a village.

"Have you recited namaz prayers today?" Inaya asked.

I ignored daily insults spoken in Urdu or comparisons to other female family members or relatives. Constant put downs aimed at me made me understand I was viewed as unlucky or blamed for Daniyal's problems in America.

"My sister in America lives a stable married life with her two children in Texas. Why don't you want to work?" Asma made another snarky comment, knowing I was a stay-at-home Mom for most of my marriage to Daniyal.

Once my dress size increased pregnancy, no shalwar kameez Aaliyaa hemmed fit comfortably. Farah told me she was done listening to demands from the spoiled American and didn't have new Shawar kameez available that would fit. I started living for Sameer and Asad, knowing at least they were well cared for, besides my oldest son's health was improving.

I was no longer invited to Islamic wedding parties or important functions. Family members no longer cared to be associated with me and disinvited me to outings I enjoyed going on when traveling or shopping for new clothes or visiting my favorite outdoor bazaars.

"You're a terrible parent," Farah yelled one afternoon when Sameer returned from playing outside. Bathing was a challenge in Pakistan, especially during prolong electricity outages. Most days I stayed to myself, thankful to be away from relatives or crowds of strangers, finding solace in reading and writing. The keepers of secrets were thieves of sunshine. We were thieves of laughter and joy.

PART 3

Things I Couldn't Say

CHAPTER 14

Territorial Disputes

I was living in another country facing the stigma of an unresolved court case in Karachi over family inheritance and the acquisition of shared property. Aaliyaa assured us that in a couple of months' time, Daniyal and my in- laws still residing in Faisalabad, would no longer be implicated in an ongoing dispute over land, purchased for a fair price. After six months, I waited patiently in Louisiana for the outcome of a pending trial involving the claim of family territory that was delayed. The trial date had since moved to a high circuit court in Islamabad for review. The lives of Sameer and Asad were on hold.

Daniyal waited an additional year, sending large amounts of money overseas to fund crooked lawyers acting on behalf of his defense team. Daniyal swore he was innocent, blaming the dishonest judicial system in Karachi for our financial problems, downplaying money troubles. Nadia's brother summarized issues over undivided assets in Karachi as a family feud that spiraled out of control. For several years, Daniyal sent large quantities of money overseas to fund attorneys.

After an undisclosed amount of time, Daniyal led his three sisters to believe that certainly by the end of the year, our family life in Louisiana would settle down. In less than one year, our financial troubles would be resolved. Nadia vowed that a petty disagreement involving stolen property in Karachi, Pakistan would be sorted out by the end of January, at the start of next year. In one years', time I could focus my attention on raising Sameer and Asad together and building a stable family life in Louisiana, putting our money problems in the past.

For a long time, I thought about what I should tell my parents from Louisiana who raised me with traditional principles. My mom used to stay up nights in a row waiting for me during my adolescence when I came home on a school night, after curfew. During a rebellious phase in my youth when out with school friends or a new boyfriend, I broke curfew. I always came home without the right alibi. On the fence about telling my mother back in Louisiana that some of my husband's property was being disputed in a place most people never heard of before in a tribal area of Pakistan, I stayed quiet. For an extended period, I lived with Sameer and Asad in Ganish, calling home only on Christian holidays.

The English adjective in Urdu pronounced as pagal, was commonly misused. Relatives who talked in nontraditional English referred to a family members perceived misfortunes over stolen land as unlucky. If you were unfortunate enough to be born a female in Pakistan into a poor family or caste, Inaya assumed that it must have been your own karma to suffer. For Pakistani in-laws and relatives, stealing property was a business they invested in. Being born unlucky may be used to describe your value in the eyes of the Islamic community. Not being born attractive, smart and enduring beatings from a male spouse meant you were among the less fortunate, born from a poor caste. Like the stigma of mental illness, most indigenous women were deemed crazy or not marriage material when experiencing mental health issues in Ganish, choosing not to speak out or seek treatment.

Daughters of wealthy landowners usually gifted their entire inheritance, known as dowry or portion of territory, to big brothers who arranged marriages for sisters and daughters. Male family members financed weddings in rural areas of Punjab. Relationships between brothers and women and girls in some territories of Punjab were at times protective and other times, intrusive.

First born brothers carried sole financial responsibilities of providing for women from good castes. In exchange for providing financially, some disadvantaged women handed over all their generational assets, inheritance and their portion of acreage to brothers and fathers. Jealousy, rumors and fights between siblings and females was usually about security, territory and a dependency on senior male figures to provide financially.

Landowners in Pakistan earned their money by managing employees who oversaw family property. Poor laborers hired by Malak took care of profitable farm animals like cattle, cows, and buffalo. Wealthy landowners commonly sold rice, wheat and milk to local markets to sustain their farms, living as agriculture workers or farmers, earning a decent enough livelihood. Some farm workers or government employees even with a college degree had to work several different jobs at a time to meet all their living expenses. Without land, you didn't have much – not as a person living in a village area throughout provinces of Punjab. Without land most were considered a minimum wage earner. What I learned from teaching English classes at a Vocational school in Faisalabad was that employment opportunities in rural areas of Ganish were limited.

Vindictive family members who felt their share of property and family inheritance had been unfairly stolen felt justified in punishing targeted family members. Any chosen blood relative of the accused was a target and not off limits. Greedy relatives and in-laws from tribal areas of Ganish went after the close kin of the alleged guilty party for their rightful share of assets. In regressive areas of Pakistan truth, justice and law was almost never on your side. Wronged family members usually took matters of law into their own hands and sought out their own forms of justice.

Before I understood that fights over acreage happened between relatives in countries with shady governments, I knew little about the inequalities of wealth distribution in Ganish. Living In tribal areas of Punjab meant that having influence, the right connections and family money was all you needed to extract revenge or ruin someone's life or reputation. In Faisalabad, you didn't need lawfulness, facts or evidence to earn money under the table stealing property.

Daniyal's father, Abbas, a man in his seventies was physically tortured in a remote village area of Ganish almost to death by a group of unethical police officers. Immoral officers and court officials hoped to extract a false statement or confession from Abbas. When I asked Daniyal why he didn't go to the police or the courts in Ganish for help, Daniyal explained that most authorities, judges and court officials didn't do much about family quarrels over land. Police officers usually accepted bribes from exploitative lawyers and judges looking for a payday. Government employees cared little about truth, justice or fairness in uncivilized regions of Punjab.

Once respected relatives and close friends comprised of our inner circle spread malicious gossip and rumors about my family. Friends and relatives from Ganish drew negative assumptions about me. I got used to staying to myself during times when I went through bouts of depression, choosing to isolate myself from people, in one room of the house. Close relatives and friends I stayed with in Faisalabad viewed my family with an air of distrust and suspicion. Malak criticized and degraded my cooking, weight and what he considered strange behavior to close relatives. Sameer and Asad started behaving differently toward me.

Daniyal claimed to be a devoutly religious man, who prayed five times a day. Aaliyaa swore her oldest brother was a true follower of Islam who would never condone the use of violence to solve family matters. Daniyal explained that he only wanted his ancestral property passed down and birthright returned to him. In the United States, I was struggling to cope with Sameer's health issues, unsure if we were going to make next months' rent. Daniyal didn't tell me that he had been borrowing money from friends and relatives to cover rent and living expenses for some time now. Years of working night- shifts as a cab driver meant that lawyer's fees and an accumulated debt piled up

I was only trying to keep my head above water. When I questioned Daniyal about an ongoing trial in Karachi that was supposed to have been settled at an earlier date, he didn't go into detail about problems he called personal family matters. Daniyal offered my children and I plane tickets to Pakistan. Nadia's brother presented me with a choice between airline tickets to a foreign country or being faced with the possibility of eviction. I chose the better of two options. I took the plane tickets. Daniyal explained that members of his extended family were true followers of Islam. People from Faisalabad genuinely cared about me and Sameer. Attorney's fees and court costs skyrocketed. Our family was facing eviction back in Louisiana.

Daniyal didn't bother mentioning that he couldn't make next month's rent. Even though we were in debt, Daniyal swore that problems over land and inheritance in Karachi would be resolved soon. In a few months, we could go back to our ordinary day-to-day lives. Daniyal gave his word. In the beginning I didn't regret my decision to take the plane tickets to, Pakistan. I hardly thought about my old life of chaos. The family life I once shared in Louisiana with Daniyal felt distant and far away, like my memory of who Nadia lovingly called the American man.

CHAPTER 15

Beena, a Widowed Woman

"If Daniyal returns to Pakistan we will kill him," Beena threatened, after meeting me at her village home of Ganish for the first time. Beena disappeared for prayer hour. According to the holy Koran, a widowed woman had the right as stated in Islam to seek out revenge against anyone connected to Daniyal, the accused murderer of Beena's husband. On evening walks, Nadia and I stopped on farm fields to pick sunflowers to decorate my curly auburn locs when I was happiest. Each family member who showed up in my life during my stay in Faisalabad was more mysterious than the last stranger.

I never knew your husband, I wanted to answer," the image of Beena, a grieving woman faded. Beena wanted to take away my happiest moments in Pakistan and convince each member of my extended family who took care of Sameer and Asad that I was guilty of making her husband go away.

I didn't know your husband, I wanted to say. Beena was already gone.

Each morning, I saw Beena waiting outside the gate of our home offering gifts of clothes and food, apologizing for not remembering to gift me flowers on each of my visits to Ganish. Now a tranquil village where Nadia and I took quiet walks together, lying in a pool of blood in the middle of a battlefield, I saw images of Beena knelt over her dying husband, cursing Prophet Muhammad in a Muslim prayer. Beena returned every evening during walks to Nadia's village with newly picked sunflowers to place on her dead husband's gravestone.

After reciting Muslim prayers, Beena vanished into a field of sunflowers, singing and dancing in tall wheatfields where no one could find her.

"If Daniyal returns to Pakistan, he's as good as a dead man. Kasra, you murdered my husband!" Beena shouted, following close behind me to each region of Pakistan I went alone, blaming me for her misfortunes.

Beena was like Daniyal, who became invisible but was still present in every region of Pakistan I traveled to alone. I didn't know who Beena was but heard stories about her involvement in a family business with a brother and her deceased husband. Aaliyaa swore Beena, who everyone called widowed woman, and her big brother were dangerous criminals. Some people of Ganish labeled Beena's family domestic terrorists and gang members. Farah told me that Beena and her brothers were responsible for seizing property in the wealthiest territories throughout Provinces of Punjab.

On the mornings before I hauled a rickshaw, got the kids off to school, or arrived early for class to meet with students from the Trade school, I saw Beena draped in white. Her long hair was covered with a shawl. Beena stood outside of our home. Aaliyaa's cousin appeared to be waiting to greet a woman from America who was given the Muslim name Kasra. Beena must have heard outlandish stories about me. Nadia stopped showing me the most breathtaking destinations around Pakistan. After Beena showed up in my life to take away every happiness, I thought about Daniyal. He talked about his country of origin with a nostalgic longing. Daniyal once described Pakistan as an idyllic country where I would find family support and acceptance. "You will never think of returning to America once you visit Pakistan and meet my three sisters." Daniyal swore.

Aaliyaa referred to her now estranged cousin, Beena as a devote Islamic woman who disappeared on religious holidays or prayer times to a Mosque about a mile from Ganish. Beena made sure to remember to ring a prayer bell before reciting namaz again, splashing cold water on her face. Aaliyaa's cousin remembered to give thanks to Allah, pleading for forgiveness for the sins of her brothers and forefathers. The widowed woman named Beena left a Mosque at three o'clock every afternoon, making sure no one noticed her uncovered hair. Aaliyaa told me that Beena was an evil person who was once married to a dangerous gang leader. According to Nadia, Beena's brothers were made up of domestic terrorists who plotted to siege all of Daniyal's generational property and wealth for themselves.

At my lowest points as a guest in Daniyal's homeland, Beena's presence was there like a dark shadow that followed me everywhere. Beena slandered my name to my closest friends and relatives who helped take care of Sameer and Asad. Compared to other Pakistani relatives who gossiped about me in a quiet voice under their breath, Beena was more malicious than Rani. Beena talked down on my appearance, saying that I wasn't nearly as good looking as people claimed. Beena's presence in Ganish caused me mental anguish.

Relatives with close family ties to Beena told people around Ganish and Faisalabad that I was mentally unstable and demanding. Farah labeled me an arrogant westernized woman from America who treated maids and relatives poorly. Friends of Beena told mutual friends I coddled Sameer, describing me as a lazy housewife who refused to get a job. According to Islam I was not a suitable mother or wife. Aaliyaa's cousin told friends and relatives around Ganish that I was the mastermind behind a family feud between Daniyal and Abdullah. Daniyal and his sisters never told me the truth about a pending court case in Karachi.

Beena showed up outside our home at nearly the same time every afternoon during hours of worship. Sometimes Beena left, reemerging again to torment me on better days I shared with family. Widowed women returned to her murdered husband's gravestone with a promise to avenge her husband's death, bowing in the presence of Prophet Muhammad. Aaliyaa's first cousin was sure to give thanks to Prophet Muhammed and recite namaz prayer correctly for fulfilling her request to seek out her own form of justice on each family member connected to Daniyal. Beena returned to her husband's gravesite with a new person to punish, covering her dark hair with a veil.

On a random Islamic holiday, Abdullah traveled back to his village of Ganish from his home state of Minnesota for a short visit. After straightening out creases of a prayer mat, Farah stood over a brightly colored vintage mat displaying a picture of the holy temple in Saudi Arabia on the front, a cherished gift. I remembered thinking while watching Aaliyaa complete a prayer ritual, saying something in Urdu, giving thanks to Prophet Muhammad a final time. "Don't answer the phone." I wanted to urge Aaliyaa.

On the day Abdullah traveled back to his village of Ganish, Beena returned a final time to her slain husband's graveyard reciting a Muslim prayer, placing one single flower off to the side, designated for Abdullah and his family wealth that Beena planned to steal. Abdullah called Malak one day out of the blue like nothing was the matter. Farah had just finished reciting namaz and reached her hand out, as a gesture of thanks in Urdu. I couldn't guess what Farah was asking Prophet Muhammed for this time. Just like that, all of Farah's problems involving stolen property and money were solved.

Malak crammed three more village kids into a small car. I sat next to Aaliyaa in the car, listening to music from the soundtrack of Hindi films. Just like my memory of visiting Ganish for the first time, Malak drove in a circle around Daniyal's piece of land. Malak encircled Daniyal's portion of land again, pointing out a plot of land next to Farh's that belonged to Abdullah. Malak turned down the static noise emitting from the car's radio.

"Abdullah from Minnesota has more land than all of us combined. Abdullah is very respected in our village area of Ganish and incredibly wealthy." Malak told me. According to close relatives from Ganish, Abdullah from Minnesota was callous and self-serving, hoarding generational wealth and property for himself. Abdullah belonged to a caste called Sheikh, a tribe of wealthy landowners that spanned back generations. Aaliyaa told me about Abdullah from America who was once Beena's closest friend and ally. During Abdullah's last trip to Pakistan, his name was written above mine in bold. Abdullah's life was in grave danger.

Before heading back to Faisalabad Malak stopped at a corner store for Kulfi ice-cream, a traditional sweet dessert and Sameer's favorite treat. I thought of the vast stretches of ancestral land Abdullah owned in Ganish. Until now I didn't know what Daniyal's land was worth to him in American dollars.

Malak drove around different areas of Ganish for a while, pointing out Abdullah's piece of property, next to Aaliyaa's property. A trendy Bollywood song played on the radio. We rode back to Faisalabad in silence. The entire family was crammed in a small car. It never dawned on me that Beena may have wanted to exchange Abdullah's life for the life of her murdered husband.

On Abdullah's last visit to Faisalabad, Nadia told me that Abdullah risked his life to travel back to his village home of Ganish because he wanted to tell Beena and the Muslim brotherhood in person that he needed all his property given back. Abdullah came back to Ganish to tell Beena to her face that he wanted out of a life of stealing property. Beena and her brothers were said to have gotten wealthy from a business of stealing generational land deserted by ambitious men seeking a better life abroad.

Abdullah traveled back to Pakistan this last visit with the understanding that he would be risking his safety by asking Beena in person to return his property.

Abdullah risked his life and safety to come back to Faisalabad to demand his generational wealth passed down by landlords, be returned. One random afternoon, Abdullah called Aaliyaa, asking for protection.

"Aaliyaa, I'm in trouble," Abdullah said over the phone. He spoke in the same inaudible Punjabi over the phone, a language that ran together. I always had a difficult time understanding what Abdullah was saying when he spoke in his mother tongue of Punjabi.

"Forgive me Aaliyaa," Abdullah cried out. Aaliyaa remained silent for longer than I can remember.

Aaliyaa was the least educated of three daughters and the easiest to deceive. Aaliyaa set a timer for afternoon prayer time to remind herself to recite namaz five times per day. Down the road from our village of Ganish, Aaliyaa rang a bell during hours of worship. Women of Islamic faith covered their hair with a veil out of respect for Prophet Muhammad. I watched Farah perform the last namaz prayer, bringing her hands back down to her side, breathing out.

Aaliyaa rang the prayer bell a second time. I was reminded to cover my hair with a shawl. "Aaliyaa my life is in danger, I need your help." Abdullah begged.

The Middle daughter was too childlike and innocent to see the worst in people. Abdullah didn't deserve forgiveness after he had the nerve to make a phone call to Aaliyaa, seeking help. I thought of asking Aaliyaa to count the number of days she could no longer get back because of a fight between Daniyal and Abdullah. Abdullah only wanted his portion of land equally distributed and given back without facing any consequences. Don't bother answering the phone, I wanted to say to Aaliyaa.

For a while, life seemed to go back to normal. Daniyal would no longer ask me to wait for a new trial date. There would be no need to send money overseas in US currency. Before Abdullah called one afternoon, Aaliyaa prayed tirelessly while waiting for her husband to be released from prison. In Louisiana, nearly every other week, I was informed of a new trial date in Karachi that was delayed yet again. With each new trial date that was set, Daniyal sent more money in US currency back home to Pakistan to cover legal expenses. From what I knew of Abdullah from Minnesota was that he wasn't afraid to die for what belonged to him. Local People from Ganish considered Abdullah and his children to be master manipulators and criminals

Abdullah and his family owned more territory than anyone in the family. Years later, I realized Abdullah and his family would stop at nothing to seek revenge on anyone linked to Daniyal who he considered an enemy by association. During my stay in Faisalabad, I was told I needed to leave Pakistan for safety reasons. I suspected that Abdullah and his family were responsible for having me stalked and spreading malicious rumors about me to anyone who would listen. Abdullah tried to ruin my reputation in Faisalabad for years over what began as a disputed piece of property in Ganish.

I couldn't stand the sound of Aaliyaa reciting namaz any longer. I was made antsy at the thought of the telephone ringing again, knowing it was probably Abdullah on the other end of the line. After a couple minutes of speaking in Punjabi, Aaliyaa disappeared to another room, chatting with Abdullah. When Aaliyaa appeared a couple hours later, visibly shaken, looking away, I didn't bother asking what the matter was.

Aaliyaa couldn't do anything about pending legal troubles except pray namaz five times a day. I stopped believing in God before receiving a phone call from Abdullah, who wanted to make amends. Relatives told me there was nothing to worry about. Abdullah was calling again with good news. Our misfortunes seemed to be changing for the better.

Aaliyaa must have been the first-person Abdullah thought of calling for advice.

"It's not safe for you to travel to where I am. They will kill both of us." Abdullah said in Urdu

"Beena and her brothers always prayed for your happiness,"

"I only asked for my portion of land back." Abdullah cried.

"Tell me the reason behind why you traveled to Pakistan?" Aaliyaa-spoke in her mother tongue of Punjabi, a language she used when she was frustrated.

"Beena sent her goons after me! I told Beena I wanted out. No more stealing property. Aaliyaa, can you forgive me?" Aaliyaa recited a Muslim prayer to herself. She must have been thinking about what to do next.

"Beena sent her goons after me! Men showed up at my village armed with rifles. I swear Aaliyaa, I told Beena and her thugs before they showed up, pointing a gun to my head, that I wanted out."

Aaliyaa hesitated before offering to save Abdullah's life.

"One of Beena's men pointed a rifle at my head. Beena told me my family house in Ganish wasn't my land or home any longer. Beena and her gang of criminals stole all my land." Uncle exclaimed.

"Are you one of them?" Aaliyaa asked in Punjabi, still reciting a prayer.

"Not anymore, Aaliyaa I told Beena's men years ago that I wanted out of stealing property. I will return all your family's inheritance in due time" Abdullah promised.

Aaliyaa hesitated to say anything before responding to Abdullah's pleas for help. I assumed if it were not for Aaliyaa's interpretation of the holy Koran and her morals about helping family no matter the cost, she would have hung up, not caring about Abdullah's life. Aaliyaa seldom forgot to pray five times a day, devoting her life to Islam.

"I will send my brother and his guards to help you. They will provide you with security for the rest of your stay in Pakistan," Aaliyaa stated.

"We want nothing more from you, but all our property in Karachi to be equally distributed. You can stay at my cousins' house in Faisalabad until my brother, Malak arrives. You will be safe there," Aaliyaa advised, returning to namaz prayers. On the day I left Pakistan, I thought of the oldest sister, Farah.

After my marriage to Daniyal ended, I thought about an idyllic country of Pakistan that Daniyal used to say existed in his dreams.

I saw a younger version of Daniyal back at his village home of Ganish, standing guard over his ancestral land. In my vision, Daniyal was a child at Ganish, sifting through pictures of white people from the contents of a magazine. When they ask me about Daniyal, I'll tell them the truth, that I was married to someone who told me I reminded him of his country of origin, Pakistan. I will tell them I was once married to someone who missed home, and a family he left behind in a remote village of Pakistan. Any reminder of Daniyal's home country of Pakistan meant he needed me around to remember his old life as a villager from Ganish, hidden away from crowded cities and the bustle of people haggling for bargain priced merchandise and produce at bazaars.

When they ask me about Daniyal, I'll tell them the truth, that I was married to someone who kept many secrets; who I once gave my heart to. I came to embrace Daniyal's birth country of Pakistan and carry it with me everywhere.

CHAPTER 16

Gay and Transgender Sovereignty Rights, Pakistan

Aaliyaa straightened out creases of her black hijab while reciting a Muslim prayer in Urdu. Ayaan's school friend, Murad visited my in laws shared residency in Faisalabad to check on, who he affectionately called his American friend with a pocketful of international calling cards, he scratched off with a coin. Murad insisted on checking my cell phone to add calling credit. During breaks from the public-school Murad attended during the week, he sat on a kitchen stool next to me while Farah fixed homemade bread and traditional food for Murad. Ayaan's college friend grinned every time I shot a beaming smile in his direction.

Murad carried a digital camera with him when he was a guest at our home. Brother- in law's friend earned side money while studying by taking photographs of upper middle-class brides at high society weddings. Aaliyaa handed our teenage housekeeper, Rohan, another tray of hot food and drinks to be served to Murad. No one in the family seemed to know anything about Ayaan's photographer friend, a village kid from a lower caste family who took breathtaking pictures and treated me with compassion.

Our frequent houseguest, who Ayaan called his close friend was hired by Farah to take wedding and reception photos of her new daughter in law at Ganish. I decided to tell Daniyal that I suspected his nephew, Ayaan was gay or bisexual. Murad showed me a series of stunning photographs he had taken from a professional work portfolio. When traveling around to different areas of Pakistan on school breaks or holidays, Murad took scenic still photographs of Muree, a chilly region of Pakistan. Ayaan hired his school friend, Murad to take professional looking family photographs of my children. Murad said my youngest son Asad was photogenic and should do catalog work for a trendy clothing magazine for a popular kids store in Lahore.

Being forthcoming and speaking publicly about what Malak called family secrets was considered taboo, especially as a girl from a respectable upper middle-class family living in Ganish. I decided to take a risk and tell Daniyal I believed Ayaan should be free to make his own life choices regarding who he wanted to marry. I don't know what type of response I was expecting from Daniyal. On some level, I was hoping Daniyal would say, you know what are right. I won't plan my nephew's arranged marriage to a second cousin.

Daniyal told me I was lying about his nephews' sexual preferences to create problems within the extended family. According to Nadia's brother from America, this was a phase in a young man's life, a growing adolescent experiencing a fluctuation in hormones. Daniyal told me not to repeat my suspicions about a gay or bisexual family member to people of our community of Ganish or Faisalabad, especially well-known mutual friends or relatives from Ganish. Daniyal promised to recite namaz prayer five times per day for Ayaan until he saw the errors in his way. According to Islam, Ayaan had committed unforgivable sins.

Gay and transgender people lived in hiding, meeting with their partners at family recreational parks. Most high school age dating couples bought time, expressing affection at recreational places, searching for ways to live independently away from villages. Most adolescents from Ganish were desperate to escape the idea of loveless arranged marriages. Aaliyaa still cooked ethnic food for Murad at the same time on his breaks from college.

I stayed silent about my objections to Nadia's arranged marriage to a cousin. Like Ayaan's University friend Murad, who double tipped rickshaw drivers when we went out somewhere, Aaliyaa reminded me of prayers she recited to Allah for a successful married life. I thought of paying in advance for debts I owed. I became an outcast among Pakistani relatives and once supportive friends I met while living in Faisalabad.

Like child brides born to poor village workers who tended fields and cared for livestock, gays in certain tribal communities of Punjab could be sold off for as little as $200 in US currency. A small number of superstitious members of the middle-class Pakistani community believed transgender people were wicked or possessed supernatural abilities of cursing and harming true believers of Islam. Throughout most areas of Pakistan, those who identified as transgender, and bisexual were considered outcasts by members of society and their families. Some gay or trans people residing in provinces of Punjab were employed as farmers, beggars or maids who worked for wealthy upper middle-class families in regions where I lived with extended family in Faisalabad. Trans-teens were sometimes considered shameful and unlovable.

The worst-case scenarios I heard of were transgenders, trans- teens and bisexuals in Pakistan being disowned by immediate family, friends and the Pakistani community. Select members of society who defied tradition by openly share their preferences, disobediently turned against Islam and could be forced to work manual labor jobs to survive. Pagal in Urdu could be used to describe anyone having an off day, in a bad mood or suffering from a serious mental health issue requiring treatment.

I heard rumors of middle-class people from tribal communities and poor castes who were labeled as mentally unstable. Some middle-class Pakistani people threw trash on gays, bisexuals or trans people. Coming out or openly expressing your sexual orientation meant being subjected to bullying and harassing minority groups. Fears of being physically attacked, shunned by peers, disinherited or going against Islam, are among reasons I found explaining why most gay or transgender people living in rural areas of Pakistan chose to not speak about their sexual orientation or preferences to strict Muslim families

Positive change for transgender people and those who identified as gay happened in 2009, when after protests and appeals, the supreme court recognized transgender people in Pakistan, categorizing transgenders as a third identity, issuing them identification cards. The transgender community of Pakistan were able to vote and receive voter cards distributed by the political legislation. Employment opportunities for gays and transgenders in Pakistan were still scarce, following the supreme court's decision in 2009 that allowed trans people to be employed by bureaucratic agencies under the tax recovery act. After the tax recovery act went into effect, there were still few prospects for the LGBT community of Punjab of securing jobs and equal pay without facing danger.

Aaliyaa prayed namaz every day for me and my marriage to her brother, Daniyal who was still working in America, sending money back to Faisalabad in the form of US currency. Like Ayaan and his life choices that went against Islam and its teachings, I couldn't be truthful with supportive relatives and friends about how unhappy I was in my marriage. I knew what it felt like to have no family support and what it was like living as a struggling Mom with Sameer and another child on the way to raise. When Sameer was born, we had little money and lived in a one-bedroom apartment, in unsafe neighborhoods. Our family only seemed to be scraping by.

I should have known better than to be blunt as a woman living in a gender biased society like Pakistan. Sharing feelings about Ayaan and his photographer friend, Murad, who I suspected were more than friends was none of my business. Forbidden affection was a concept like love marriages, hand holding and physical touch that I only saw displayed by youthful couples when I went to family parks or small caffes with Mahnoor. Speaking about the confidences of family members could have gotten me in trouble. Each time one member of my extended family prayed namaz for me, I wanted to tell Aaliyaa why I traveled to Pakistan like a single Mother with Sameer and Asad searching for answers.

Farah sliced fresh vegetables on a wooden cutting board she used for rolling out dough for making bread. Women of our family cooked organic food, mostly vegan meals in large pots to feed congregations of relatives, family members and friends who were guests at our village home in Ganish. Through an open-door Aaliyaa propped open one evening when the breeze was pleasant, a group of transgenders walked into our home, appearing as men dressed- in women's salwar kameez, sewn from a fabric shop to save money.

I wasn't skilled at blending in with my Pakistani family who spoke fluent Urdu and Punjabi. I was a recognizable western woman, from America who understood little of the native language. The group of street beggars pointed me out right away as a foreigner, visiting from another country. The group of transgenders were standing in our living room for a while and must have caught me looking at them with curiosity. I observed the group of transgenders for a while, who appeared to have distinguishable masculine features like broad shoulders and a muscular build. One transgender removed his shawl and spoke in a raspy voice to Aaliyaa. I recognized one of the transgenders as a street beggar looking for money, a job or a place to stay. One of the transgenders wore a bright shalwar kameez with a cloth shawl thrown over his shoulders, some had visible facial hair.

"She's from Louisiana," one of the transgenders shouted from outside the gate of our home. I looked at them from the third story terrace.

Thinking that I must be a wealthy foreigner, or at the least comfortable, one trans walked up to Aaliyaa demanding money, refusing to leave unless we paid them.

Pakistani people rarely called the police over what Aaliyaa considered non-threatening personal matters in rural parts of Punjab. Farah was a tough, no-nonsense Pakistani woman embarrassed and outraged at the group of unin-vited guests who walked right into our home. Aaliyaa decided to take matters into her own hands. Farah gave the beggars who showed up dressed in female clothing walking right into our home without warning, a piece of her mind. "Whose house do you think this is? Farah scolded in her thick Punjabi accent. "Find somewhere else to go!" Farah yelled.

"You have money. She's from America," one transgender pointed out, deter-mined to get some cash from us.

"I said get out!" Farah scolded again, her stern tone of voice echoed through the entire house, frightening me.

The ringleader of the group was wearing a colorful wig and seemed to take great pleasure in banishing our entire family to hell. "Crooks, liars, thieves," one trans-gender shouted. The other cross dresser looked like he was going to cry and break down right in front of us. I thought the transgender would get into a screaming match with Aaliyaa, if we didn't comply and give them something.

The group of transgenders stormed out of our home, in a hostile protest, calling each of my family members filthy names in Urdu on their way out. I was later told by Farah that some beggars were harmless poor men dressed up as women to get pity and deceive middle class family out of money.

The middle daughter, Aaliyaa blushed timidly, laughing off our encounter with who she labeled paupers, I would likely find in every part of Pakistan where for-eigners visited, especially cities like Karachi and Lahore. Ayaan swore to me that the group of transgenders who walked right into our home weren't dangerous and didn't intend to physically harm us. The ringleader of the group wore a bright wig, sending one final look of disgust my way before storming out of our home. Another, looked suspiciously at the grey-haired Punjabi woman who had been sleeping on our living room floor for months.

I had no clue who the old woman sleeping in the middle of our living room floor was or what village she originated from. The grey-haired woman looked like a poor farm worker. She hardly spoke to me, only looked quizzically over at me sometimes and prayed an eerie chant that kept me up most nights. Aaliyaa said she was a poor villager who had some of her property stolen. Aaliyaa took the grey-haired woman in after she had no place to go, thinking Allah would look favorably on her.

After the same group of whom Aaliyaa label poor and lower caste people left our home through the same propped door they entered, I noticed the same transgenders on our neighborhood street. I snuck out the back door, handing the transgenders pocket money that consisted of cash in the US currency I saved from a birthday card from Louisiana. My pocket change totaled a week's allowance I kept on hand for food and outings with my children. A few of my students from the Trade school refused to take my English class if they found out I was Christian or what they considered to be a non-follower of Islam. Being different or unique, made most people residing in rural areas of Punjab consider you a target.

"Keep this money and don't come back," I yelled, handing the transgenders money through a gate. If Malak sees you, he will call the police." One of the transgenders smiled graciously, while reciting namaz prayer.

I wondered if I would come across the group of beggars again. I must have scared them off in my meek, non-threatening voice. They would be back, I said to myself. I secretively hoped they had a safe place to call home and someone who looked after them. Remembering Aaliyaa's prayers of protection for me, I prayed for you, I whispered, into thin air. The group transgenders who Farah referred to as lowly poor men dressed in womans clothing looking for a handout, disappeared from eye view.

CHAPTER 17

Healthcare in Pakistan: Visiting Government Hospitals

Faisalabad, Pakistan

To avoid visiting facilities in the public domain, most middle-class families living in provinces of Punjab who could afford it preferred seeing private doctors and specialists. Many regulatory medical centers I visited in less forward-thinking areas of Punjab were in deplorable conditions. Private clinics in Faisalabad required patients to pay out of pocket for an appointment.

High out of pocket copays were required upfront to see a private physician, which meant cash payments were collected before seeing a primary doctor. A negotiated rate for those who couldn't afford cash payments was usually more cash in rupees than most middle-class families from Ganish could afford. A select number of private healthcare facilities were only available at a Physician's home residence. Physicians and specialists who ran in- home businesses only saw patients who could pay high out of pocket co fees. Specialist I took Sameer to were open during limited hours, closing frequently in recognition of Muslim holidays.

Legislative officials I watched in Urdu on international news channels talked about their efforts to make real positive changes to Pakistan's declining healthcare system. Public hospitals would soon provide Pakistani citizens with health insurance cards. Future medical insurance would offer some coverage for Pakistani citizens who would not be able to spend money on medical care in the future.

Going to a government-funded medical facility in Faisalabad was a second option for middle class people living in Ganish who could not see private doctors. Most public medical facilities in Faisalabad were poorly maintained, crowded, and understaffed. Walk-in clinics that did not require an appointment and emergency rooms that I took Sameer to at erratic hours in Faisalabad were almost always busy, overflowing with people suffering from life threatening emergencies. Sick people waited for hours in line- ahead of Sameer and Aaliyaa to be seen. There is still no available health insurance coverage issued by the Pakistani government. Last I heard, the former prime minister of Pakistan spoke at a rally on an international news channel when I listened to a political leader refer to Pakistan as a welfare dependent country that he wanted to reform.

On my first couple of visits to Faisalabad, I came down with severe cases of food poisoning. Aaliyaa insisted on visiting a public clinic a few miles down the road. I was a special guest at a friend's wedding party the week before, enjoying my fill of fried food. After two days of diarrhea and vomiting, I was too weak to stand or get out of bed. When my fever shot up, Aaliyaa kept doubling checking on me. The middle sister didn't want to take her chances on waiting for an appointment with a private physician.

Most private hospitals in our city of Faisalabad were closed off to the public during hours designated to namaz, Islamic holidays or hours of worship. As a last resort, Nadia told me about the filthy conditions of most government facilities in Faisalabad before we hauled a rickshaw in the middle of the night when my fever shot up again and Sameer wasn't feeling well. Any time Aaliyaa determined that a family member was extremely ill, our only option was walking into a local medical center without an appointment. Nadia advised me before visiting a public emergency room in our city of Faisalabad to shut my eyes and expect the worst. Pharmacies were attached to local emergency rooms. Patients could buy insulin, aerosol or asthma inhalers without prescriptions.

Aaliyaa decided that with her American sister there, she would take our last visit to an emergency room in Faisalabad as an opportunity to give the team of staff workers, doctors, and nurses on duty that night a piece of her mind. "You should be ashamed of yourselves!"

"Look at the condition of this place!" Aaliyaa scolded in Punjabi. Calling out overworked and underpaid hospital workers may not have been the best choice considering my need for immediate medical care.

I was forced to use the only bathroom available, an underground squat toilet. There was no running water. The underground toilet was gross and leaking water. A nurse on duty that evening, looked unbothered by Aaliyaa's emotional outburst. "Call the Pakistani government and voice your concerns," the nurse on duty coldly suggested, while simultaneously directing a long line of patients flooding in.

Aaliyaa took my hand. We made our way to the front of a line. Aaliyaa left me standing in the line while she went to check on an available hospital bed for me. A man on a stretcher stood in front of me at the patient check- in counter, letting out soft whimpers. A giant cockroach skirted across the tile floor of the waiting room, catching Aaliyaa's attention. She covered her mouth with a shawl, looking at me anxiously, as if she was hoping I didn't see the giant insect.

Concerned about my fever spiking up again, the middle sister explained that there was no other emergency room open at this late hour. Aaliyaa dabbed a cold towel on my forehead every other hour. "A tiny bug," Aaliyaa remarked, trying not to laugh. Out of sheer embarrassment, the middle sister must have realized by now that I got a good look at the large cockroach.

No one visiting the medical facility in Faisalabad cared that I was a foreigner visiting with Sameer and Asad from Louisiana. As a guest from a more modernized part of the world, it didn't mean I was given preferential treatment. Aaliyaa guided me through crowded hallways. We sat on benches in the waiting rooms. We waited for medical staff on duty to call out our patient numbers to be seen.

"This is Kasra, my sister from Louisiana."

"She's very ill." Aaliyaa-informed medical staff on duty that night. In hopes that Nurses' aides and administrators would allow us to be seen ahead of a long line pouring in, looking at me with concern, an administrator jotted something on a prescription slip, misdirecting us to the wrong room. Aaliyaa guided me down a narrow hallway until I felt too nauseous to stand. Aaliyaa's hand felt clammy.

Another administrator and nurses on duty that night handed us a slip, I sensed Aaliyaa's growing fear about my fever spiking up again. Aaliyaa led me down an-other long hallway. We sat on benches until our number was called.

Ayaan showed up at the public hospital in Faisalabad out of nowhere, getting into a fight with his mother Aaliyaa, talking in his native language of Punjabi too fast for me to make out what he was saying. Aaliyaa's youngest son was visibly agitated, concerned after Aaliyaa disappeared for hours and still hadn't returned home, without bothering to call. Ayaan lectured his mother sternly until I noticed other people in the waiting room, staring and whispering at the three of us.

Ayaan's former schoolteacher who taught a history class walked up to me and asked in English if everything was alright. Ayaan stopped arguing with his mother immediately, caught off guard and embarrassed when he realized that his college professor from last semester had been there all along, masked in a crowd of sick patients waiting on benches for their numbers to be called.

Ayaan apologized profusely to his teacher, who scolded him for fighting in public with Aaliyaa, citing examples of how Ayaan never took lessons she taught seriously, misbehaving with friends in her history class.

Ayaan sat off to himself, unusually quiet, too embarrassed by his college teacher's abrupt appearance to utter another word to me or Aaliyaa. A few hours passed. I realized that it was already early morning. Ayaan was exhausted, sitting next to us on benches outside of the waiting room, fast asleep. Aaliyaa must have realized after so many hours passed that administrators forgot to call our number. I fell asleep next to Aaliyaa on a waiting room bench, hours before, too dizzy and nauseous to wake up. In a dreamy state, I could still see Ayaan's old schoolteacher walk down a busy hallway across from us, still lecturing him under her breath.

Most government run clinics in Faisalabad didn't provide enough beds to accommodate every patient who walked into the emergency room without an appointment. I thought back to Aaliyaa's warnings about unsanitary conditions of most public funded medical centers in Faisalabad. Patients admitted to the emergency room without an appointment, some in critical condition, were forced to share beds with other patients. Aaliyaa screeched in a high-pitched voice, in Punjabi at anyone trying to take a hospital bed she reserved for me, frightening sick people in need of unclaimed beds away.

A nurse on duty that evening struck me a couple times, struggling to draw a blood sample. A nurse on duty scribbled something on a notepad, hooking me up to an IV, standing over my bed, Aaliyaa. was reciting namaz in Urdu

Each time I traveled with my extended family by rickshaw to go anyplace new in Pakistan, Aaliyaa recited prayers of protection for immediate friends and family. Aaliyaa was the appointed caretaker of the family, praying Islamic prayers for family and children when leaving our home in the city. Male family members went to Aaliyaa first when they needed a positive outcome for an important test, when applying for a new job or when they wanted to recover swiftly from an illness. I felt like a family member years ago when I first began traveling to Faisalabad, cared for and looked after by paternal relatives and friends.

When I finally returned from the medical center, I was too tired to get around for days. Aaliyaa made boiled rice with lentils for anyone recovering from stomach pain, diarrhea or vomiting. Sameer told me not to get out of bed. I shouldn't think about making a plate of food for myself or boiling a pot of tea in the kitchen. Sameer would remind me lovingly, that I wasn't well enough to be up and walking around. Rohan brought me herbal tea with lemon every morning until I recovered, a natural remedy Aaliyaa swore by, made with a mixture of spices and lemon water that tasted bitter and hard to swallow.

I don't know if it was because of Aaliyaa's concern for my health or the herbal remedies she made for family members experiencing health problems. I got well much faster after her quick fixes, herbal remedies and Muslim prayers.

On the car ride back to Faisalabad, I noticed Ayaans eyes glazed over from lack of sleep. He was still scolding his mom about acting weird around his school friends who came by the house for a hot meal. Aaliyaa fixed. traditional meals for important Islamic holidays and parties. She still shied away from meeting girlfriends or friends of Ayaan who spoke fluent English or lived in modern cities. Ayaan told me that although women of our family were disadvantaged, my in-laws were widely recognized in the Pakistani community for being great cooks, and welcoming hosts to people who showed up all the time to our home in Faisalabad and Ganish.

I ruminated over what it must have been like for Aaliyaa to live as a subservient housewife from Ganish, tasked with looking after a large extended family. In rural parts of Punjab, women from villages took care of entire families and communities without questioning the motives of men around them. Senior male figures of Ganish assigned Aaliyaa, Nadia and Farah gender biased roles. Aaliyaa took on the burdens and pleasurable moments experienced by each family member.

Aaliyaa barely expressed her own needs, or interests outside of family matters. I wondered if Aaliyaa desired a life outside of being the appointed caretaker. Ayaan's Mom was considered uneducated, she was a highly respected person that made up our extended family. Aaliyaa was called on to take care of sick family members, marking another day off the Islamic calendar until her husband came home from jail.

PART 4

Bad Parts

CHAPTER 18

Rock Bottom

Like the chill of Pakistan's unpredictable winters and brutally hot summers, the bad days came out of nowhere. I was content holding onto the good days. In Pakistani culture, no one tells you about the bad parts, women who begin to see you as the same. There was no longer an understanding that being a citizen of the United States made me safer or any better than a Punjabi woman born on the soil of every place I visited. Things had gotten bad at home

At my lowest moments, Zarah consoled me, sectioning off pieces of my long wavy hair, twisting a silky portion into a clip. Zarah gently combed out the rest of my knotted auburn hair with a detangling brush. I felt like an adolescent who needed to be soothed and listened to. When I was brave enough to tell Zarah about Daniyal's disinterest in our oldest son, Sameer, who he once adored. I was surprised at her apathetic reply, "My sister from Virginia, has been a faithful Islamic bride, married to a Pakistani from Ganish for several years. They share three sons and live a stable home life in a large house in Virginia. When Daniyal gets his land back, you won't have to worry, things will go back to normal for you and your family."

When I close my eyes, I revisit my darkest days, like the morning at the clinic in Pakistan. You should have known something was wrong, I should have told you. No one would have believed me. I could still see nurses cloaked in white, standing around, rushing to check in on the next patient. I was hysterical. Aaliyaa couldn't quiet me down.

I could still hear what the nurse said that night at the medical center. I knew what happened and chose not to tell anyone. Before the day at the clinic in Pakistan, in laws from Ganish gave me every happiness and stole every flower on my behalf. My darkest day along with a humiliating secret, remained hidden. A bad memory of my last appointment at a medical center in Faisalabad, I didn't want that to be all that was left of my time in Ganish.

"Nothing can be done about anything now." Zarah said, shifting blame onto me about my chaotic home life in Louisiana with Daniyal. An ongoing case over land in Karachi was delayed and moved to a higher court in another district. When I told Zarah about Daniyal's infidelity and alcoholism, she brushed off the oldest brother's horrible abuse and neglect to bad habits and coping mechanisms related to family problems over inheritance. Virtues like forgiveness when it came to shouldering the problems of male family members was written somewhere in the holy Koran.

I was becoming most like Rani, who select family members discarded. Farah helped Malak cover– up an extramarital affair he was having in Karachi. Malak drove into the city for business, going on dates like a single man with a more educated girl from a lower caste. Ranis' husband, Malak, later promised to take the girl he was sleeping with on as a second wife.

I blamed myself for problems in my marriage to Nadia's brother. In-laws held me responsible for Daniyal's financial troubles and debts surrounding a disagreement over family property and shared assets. According to Farah's interpretation of the Koran, I was guilty of not learning to pray namaz correctly. Rock bottom was comprised of my worst moments in Pakistan.

Farah assumed I understood by now that it was my duty as a good Muslim to speak fluent Urdu and accept my role as a subservient housewife and nothing more. Asking intrusive questions about the teachings of Islam was considered disrespectful. The worst parts about my time living at a village in Pakistan I wanted to leave out. Being born a woman in Pakistani society must have been the most humiliating experience.

On this last trip to Faisalabad, I had my share of fun and entertainment, browsing outdoor bazaars in my down time and visiting places of enjoyment and shopping malls while in Peshawar with friends. I had more freedom and independence while living in Faisalabad as a US citizen than my extended family assumed I should ask for.

No longer considered a guest according to Pakistani customs, months ago, I wore out my welcome and was now treated no differently than a true Pakistani wife and follower of Islam. I was more isolated, ignored and ostracized. On my last trip to Pakistan, Farah was there to greet me with a new pair of salwar kameez and a collection of things she must have noticed I liked but didn't buy for myself when we traveled to the city. We sat together in the room I shared with Sameer and Asad. Zarah styled my hair. I felt safe enough to tell Zarah why I traveled to Pakistan with Sameer.

As a faithful follower of Islam, Aaliyaa told me I needed to seek out forgiveness, stop asking questions and move on. Zarah knew of unconventional ways Malak kept his wife Rani in line but didn't say anything. Women from Ganish were no longer phased by abusive male figures and were told to remain quiet and stop creating conflict. To my Pakistani in laws marriage was a sacred oath I took and a promise to Allah to stay together through tough times, a spiritual bond I shouldn't abandon. Constant humiliation stemming from the years I tolerated Daniyal's infidelity, addictions and erratic behavior were summed up by members of the immediate family to sacrificing for marriage as an obedient Islamic wife. Aaliyaa considered it a married womans obligation to care for her husband in his time of suffering. In some social circles I was considered unlucky.

Women from Ganish who befriended me, in the same breath criticized me for Daniyal's problems over family inheritance. A handful of women with college degrees who claimed to respect me for converting to Islam and living in a place like Pakistan, lied for the most esteemed brother, Daniyal. No one cared to listen when I told my most dedicated sources of support about the outrageous psychological and physical abuse I tolerated from Daniyal for years.

I was unsure of what I got myself into by agreeing to travel to Pakistan with Sameer in an attempt at blending in with Daniyal's family. When I arrived at Idris's home, I was visibly shaken and highly emotional, pleading with Sadiya that I should return to Louisiana. Idris's mother, Sadiya was a light- hearted woman, I remembered meeting when I first arrived as a guest to Pakistan. Sadiya had a three-story bungalow style home a couple of blocks away.

I had enough of my in- laws persecuting me for failing in my marriage and at motherhood. I was no longer willing to remain complacent. After months of hearing malicious gossip and rumors about myself repeated, I left my in- law's shared residency in Faisalabad.

Sadiya peered out of a kitchen window, shouting down to the maid to let me inside. Sadiya's housekeeper Zohra waved down to me, rushing to open the gate. The cheerful housekeeper embraced me with a hug and a warm smile. Standing outside the gate of a stranger's home too long, wearing outdated shalwar kameez and no head scarf, meant I brought shame and dishonor onto the family's name. According to Aaliyaa, I irreparably damaged my in laws reputation in the community when I left my in laws home without warning.

The ultimate sign of defiance was showing up uninvited as a married middle-class woman, standing unveiled outside the gate of a stranger's home. I stayed longer than I should have, bringing dishonor to the family's name. Tamanna was right. I still knew little about Pakistani culture.

The adolescent housemaid let me inside without hesitation. "I'll do your hair and make-up," Zohra said, flipping through a teen magazine showing me a picture of a popular American singer on the front cover. "I like this one," Zohra said excitedly, speaking in Urdu, referencing a photograph of a western performer I recognized with wavy, sun kissed blonde hair and side bangs.

Zohra disappeared to the kitchen fixing me something to eat. The maid returned later with a full plate of rice biryani and a cup of tea. My smallest son, Asad wasn't eating well and struggling to gain back his appetite. His pediatrician put him on medicine. After finding out about viscous rumors Rani was spreading, I had enough and wanted to return to America. Sadiya offered me the spare bedroom downstairs. I closed the door and let myself fall apart without thinking about who might be listening. No one knew what was wrong with me or why I couldn't calm down.

Sadiya showed up a couple hours later, setting a plate of hot food on a table outside my room, a vegan dish she made from scratch along with a piece of bread made from dough Sadiya rolled out and cooked on a large frying pan. Sadiya knew I wasn't doing well. I wasn't ready to discuss why I showed up at Sadiya's home without calling first. Sadiya didn't say anything. She left me alone to finish dinner.

My little son, Asad grew attached to Sadiya and her granddaughter, Tamanna. Tamanna came home after school at the same time every afternoon to give Asad a stack of miscellaneous toys and books she bought from a bazaar, a collection of things she found for a deal. Sadiya's granddaughter sat on the floor reading and playing with Asad. All I could seem to do was sleep in the spare bedroom. Asad ran back to my room periodically to see if I was alright. Sometimes the hardest moments were not letting my children see me stressed or fall apart in front of them. Women who were intentionally spiteful toward me was something I didn't see coming. I had many good days before the day I left our city home of Faisalabad.

After dinner, Tamanna walked into my room, intent on cheering me up. Tamanna was an optimistic teenager who seemed to enjoy my company. She told me that I served as a reminder of her biological Mother who died of tuberculosis, when she was in primary school. Tuberculosis was a deadly disease, still prevalent in rural villages like Ganish. Tamanna shared her ambitions of settling abroad in Germany. Sadiya's granddaughter discussed her plans of getting out of Pakistan for good. "I pray all the time for my education and that God show me another way." The teenager explained, standing over a prayer mat, reciting namaz. Meeting Tamanna and seeing pictures of her youthful Mother who died after a long battle with tuberculosis was the most agonizing part of staying as a guest in Idris's family home.

"You remind me a lot of my mom from Ganish," Tamanna remarked, closing an old photo album filled with better childhood memories, depicting an upbringing Tamanna must have shared with her mom at the village before her death.

Early mornings before school, when getting ready for a wedding reception, I styled Tamanna's hair and make-up, copying western fashions from magazine clippings she saved of celebrities. Tamanna made a collage from magazine clippings featuring some of her favorite western, Indian and Pakistani female celebrities and models. Tamanna pinned a series of pictures to a bulletin board that told a story of a short-lived childhood she shared with her mom growing up in the village. In some pictures, I noticed happier memories of Tamanna, smiling broadly, dressed in a school uniform, shown having a good time with school friends.

Sadiya agreed that I could stay as a guest in her home until things settled down. I made Tamanna food when she returned from school. We watched popular afternoon sitcoms in Urdu and English. Tamanna shared stories of her day at an all-girls private school. In the evenings, I tagged along with Tamanna on trips by rickshaw to purchase groceries, cosmetics and new clothes at outdoor markets where Tamanna bargained for the cheapest price. It was comforting to have family and close relatives who were there for me during my lowest moments as a foreign guest in Pakistan. For a while, you could say I was elated, at least hopeful again about my future and the lives of Sameer and Asad.

In Pakistani culture, long standing traditions were at times, burdensome and other times confusing. "You know nothing about Pakistani culture." Tamanna emphasized, when I still couldn't wrap a head scarf or hijab, I wore out to public places the right way "We respect you, Kasra because you came to Pakistan and faced every problem for your husband."

Tamanna was forced to navigate a frightening world in a country like Pakistan after losing a parent at a tender age. Tamanna was a head strong adolescent girl who needed a parental figure around. Sadiya's granddaughter was at an age where she was going through bodily changes and needed more than a grandmother around to act as a maternal figure. Sadiya's health was in decline. According to Tamanna, Sadiya could be moody and at times didn't seem to want anyone around. I overstayed my welcome as a guest in Sadiya's home. In Pakistani society, it was considered rude to break cultural norms and traditions. At the very least staying this long at a relative's home was an insult to Daniyal's family. I wasn't ready to go back.

Three Weeks later, I was almost a permanent resident at Sadiya's house. I missed life in Louisiana, thankful that my kids didn't see me lose my composure. I stayed at Sadiya's home for three weeks. Sadiya's granddaughter asked if I wanted to work as a teacher at her school. Tamanna and her grandma, Sadiya helped with the care of Sameer and Asad.

Shortly after arriving as a guest in Tamanna's home, I met Jamila who stayed in a spare bedroom. Jamila still had not finished unpacking all her children's clothes. Jamila had two little sons of her own. After picking her kids up from a private school down the road, Jamila confided to me about her lawyer husband who still couldn't find work. Everyday Jamila prayed namaz desperate for a visa to Germany.

Jamila took daily beatings from her husband, Salman, who struck his wife in front of their small children. Tamanna told me Salman hit Jamila to keep her in line. Months later, Salman was still unable to find steady employment as a lawyer. I thought about similar circumstances I went through with Daniyal in Louisiana. Violence toward women was common throughout rural areas of Pakistan. Abuse toward women wasn't taken seriously. Considered a privileged foreigner, most people from Faisalabad assumed I could easily leave my marriage to Daniyal. I worried about Sameer and Asad.

After Jamila left Idris's home in Faisalabad where I stayed for almost one month, I worried about Jamila, hoping she settled in Germany with her kids by now and found safety, family support and a more prosperous life in Germany. I Prayed that Tamanna's aunt got away from her unemployed lawyer husband who brutalized her in front of two little kids.

I heard from Tamanna that her aunt, Jamila was granted a visa to Germany a couple weeks later. Jamila left with her two kids, not long after we met, leaving her husband behind in Faisalabad still looking for work. Like most maternal figures I met while in Pakistan, Jamila cared about getting her sons educated, finding safety and new opportunities in another country above her own peace of mind and happiness. I never thought to ask Tamanna about her aunt again. I wondered if I would see Jamila or her children in Pakistan. This time around, I knew better than to speak freely about Daniyal.

Ayaan showed up to Sadiya's house on a motorbike, informing me of juvenile stories Rani repeated to family members. The longer I stayed in Pakistan, the more I became no different than a villager, subject to daily abuse, slander and character assassinations by women around me. Rani spent afternoons rotating between two different homes, one home at her village and back a few weeks later to my in-law's house spreading vicious rumors about me. Rani filled her downtime with abusing her little daughter and going on weekend visits to Ganish nitpicking her brother's new wife.

"This letter from your in laws came for you," Rohan said in Urdu, handing me a manila envelope. On the front page my name was written as Kasra. Our housekeeper, Rohan, sped away. My joint family most likely wanted to apologize for how they treated me and ask that I return home. Wondering if I should open the envelope or throw it in the trash, I held the manila envelope in my hand, there was nothing to worry about. It was probably good news.

Rohan's messy handwriting was written at the top of the page in a letter format addressed as, Dear Kasra. I counted each page of loose-leaf paper, totaling an eight-page character assassination brimming with hate-filled rhetoric about my own shortcomings in English. After reading slanderous accusations about myself, I refused to return to Faisalabad or see my in-laws for a long time.

The eight-page smear campaign cited examples of how I was a terrible parent to Sameer and Asad and the worst person in the world. Everyone in the family suddenly hated me. I asked myself who would have dedicated so much time to writing an anonymous, accusatory letter about me, handing off an envelope to Rohan in a rush.

Abbas gave me a Muslim name that represented beauty and modesty when I first came to Faisalabad with Sameer and Asad. I broke another cultural norm that made me guilty of something. The eight-page letter listed specific reasons explaining why I didn't deserve to be a part of the family. I would no longer be welcome back to my in laws native land of Pakistan.

I called Daniyal in Louisiana after sharing the contents of the letter, reading the eight-page letter back word for word. "I'll call you later," Daniyal said hanging up.

Tamanna returned from class, throwing her backpack on the ground, tired and sweaty. Tamanna was listening in on my phone conversation to Daniyal. She knew writing a slanderous letter addressed to me wasn't okay. I didn't deserve to be spoken about in that way. Tamanna was an incredibly empathetic and mature fifteen-year-old.

"Stay here, I like having you around. You don't have to go back home right away. This is your house. Live here as long as you want. You should apply for a job at my private school as a teacher if you decide to hideout here longer. We can visit my school next week if you are still here." Tamanna offered.

Years before traveling to Pakistan, I carried the weight of my husband's problems and secrets. "Everything is going to be okay," Tamanna consoled me. I couldn't stop the teenage girl from seeing me lose my composure in front of her. Being comforted by a fifteen-year-old who had already faced a great deal of loss and tragedy made me feel guilty.

I envisioned Tamanna as a little girl consoling her sick Mother. "Please don't cry, you are none of the things written in a silly letter. Cheer up and get ready so we can go someplace."

"For all the times I prayed and missed my mom. Your presence in Pakistan was a blessing. You can stay here and apply to jobs until you're ready to go back to America. We enjoy having you as a guest. Since you came to live with us, everything has been good for me." Tamanna said

Days later, Nadia showed up remorseful and sobbing, asking for forgiveness. Nadia's presence at Sadiya's house wasn't an admission of guilt. I could sense that she felt terrible and had been crying. Everyone in the family got together believing rumors incited by problems they faced over inheritance to write a hateful letter about me.

Nadia mentioned perceived mistakes I made while living in Faisalabad. In the letter my in-laws swore that I was no longer considered a member of the family, trashing me in every way imaginable. "Sorry," Nadia apologized in English, with tears in her eyes. I couldn't face Nadia again after that day. Daniyal used to tell his family in Pakistan when we started dating that he was only using me. In the next breath, Daniyal proclaimed his marriage vows and dying commitment to me.

"Hang out here as long as you want. I like having you here, I swear." Tamanna insisted.

After a few weeks, different family members stopped by the house buying me gifts, asking for forgiveness. After I read the contents of the letter out loud, Daniyal persuaded each family member involved in smearing my name to apologize to me in person. Family members who once celebrated my arrival to Faisalabad suddenly despised me.

After retiring from a life of hard work, Daniyal spoke about his plans to permanently settle down in Pakistan where we could live an ordinary existence in a quiet village away from noise, technology and the stress of working thankless jobs. Daniyal described his native land as his forever home, a place he cherished. Daniyal swore we would end up traveling to Pakistan together, this last time we would settle in Faisalabad with Sameer and Asad for good. Our family would live a modest existence in a village of Ganish. There would be no more problems pertaining to the division of family property and assets to be sorted out.

Pakistan was a country where mobs f relatives didn't allow you to sit by yourself for too long or grieve alone. Falling in love and marrying an immigrant from Pakistan turned into something different than what I imagined, a tragic story about meeting an unconventional community of people who I would eventually call family.

Last I heard, the most educated of three sisters asked about me. Zarah told relatives she wanted me to travel from Louisiana to Faisalabad again for the birth of her daughter saying things like, "You were the one I admired most for your struggles to come to a country like Pakistan. You did your best to live without the comforts and resources you were accustomed to in Louisiana." Religious customs were still an integral part of Pakistani culture especially when it came to blessings bestowed to a first-born child of a newly married Muslim bride.

Insisting that I travel back to Faisalabad for the birth of a first-born daughter meant Zarah admired me. It was too late to assume Zarah genuinely cared about me or fully accepted me as a member of the family. Zarah and more conventional family members were opposed to love marriages, skeptical about welcoming a person born of a different caste into the family. After falling out of touch, Zarah held onto hope that my unconventional marriage to Daniyal would still work out.

"Your sacrifice for Daniyal won't be forgotten by anyone in Pakistan." Zarah remarked.

I wasn't in the delivery room to be the first to hold or feed Zarah's' newborn daughter. Even if I returned to Faisalabad to welcome the birth of a first born, my presence in Pakistan wouldn't change anything.

I thought about my new sister-in-law, Zarah with admiration, remembering challenges and setbacks she faced while trying to get a college degree, after the death of her father. I missed Zarah and Ayaan the most when I returned to Louisiana this last visit.

My last memory of Zarah was giving her an expensive foundation I bought at an airport during my three-hour flight layover in a foreign country. On my first week in Pakistan, Zarah came into my room with the broadest smile on her face, carrying armfuls of shopping bags, excited to show me new shalwar kameez she designed. I remembered exactly what she said,

"I found a pair of brightly colored violet shalwar Kameez at a popular store in Pakistan and thought the hues of the purple dress would bring out your auburn hair. You almost never wear color. Wearing vibrant colored shalwar kameez signifies happiness as a married woman. I picked these out for you to wear tomorrow to a wedding. The family is considered rich. I already took your measurements. Hopefully your dress size is the same as last time. These clothes should fit you now because these shalwar kameez are expensive. I must return this dress once I hand-make this same design and size for you." Zarah carefully placed the newly pressed pair of shalwar kameez wrapped in a plastic cover over my chair.

Zarah told me about the death of her Father when she was a little girl.

Zarah praised her biological mother and two sisters who encouraged and funded her ambitions to move to Islamabad in pursuit of a college education. Zarah told me that her mom tutored kids at Ganish to cover household expenses after the death of their father. The new sister spoke about her two sisters and Mother, who raised her alone, characterizing the women of her family as her greatest sense of support, and strength. Zarah was head strong and at times a fearlessly independent woman, who was like other female members of her family, always looking out for one another.

"My dad passed away when I was too small to have many pleasant childhood memories of him," Zarah explained, unpacking salwar kameez, cosmetics and bangles she wanted me to wear to her rich friend's wedding. I reminded Zarah not to refer to me by my Islamic name, Kasra.

Zarah combed and straightened my wavy auburn hair, that I let grow out. The most educated sister went out of her way to purchase some essential things for me like cosmetics that were better quality in Karachi and jeans that fit tightly. I wore new clothes Zarah bought me around her rich friends, over large kameez tops she bought me. Zarah got pregnant with a second daughter months later.

Finding our way through congested alleyways on humid summer afternoons, Zarah hauled a rickshaw for fun. We visited bazaars and stopped for snacks and food bought from a food vendor. Zarah pointed out which fabric shops to visit and how to select the best quality material for clothes she made to wear on the next wedding party or Islamic holiday. My instincts told me Zarah wouldn't continue our friendship with me after my divorce and separation from Daniyal. I was sorry that we could no longer be friends. After she learned about my divorce, I was right to assume that after marriage and giving up a career, Zarah was too attached to old traditions and religious beliefs, meaning that the two of us wouldn't speak again. Long-held traditions hung over her and applied to me as well.

I was no longer like sunflowers Rohan handed me during initial visits to Ganish, pure hearted and childlike going on an exploration to a country like Pakistan. I understood nothing would be the same after the birth of Zarah's second daughter. I was no longer considered a part of my Pakistani family after divorcing Daniyal. During the worst moments of my life with Daniyal, my three brothers would advise Zarah not to sit alone in a room chatting for too long with me. I was no different than Rani, no longer a worthy or useful family member. I was someone who could no longer be trusted, easily thrown away and replaced.

We drifted apart, like we never knew each other before I lived in Ganish.

I was suffering in my marriage and failing at fitting in with my in-laws. In Pakistani culture, being born female meant you couldn't strive for your aspirations and dreams like you could as a woman in a country like the United States. In my imagination, I returned to Faisalabad one final time for the birth of Zarah's daughter. Tradition in Pakistan stated that the first person who holds or feeds a newborn is the individual they will become most like. I was the only one who got out of my cult-like family system. I was the only individual who defiantly turned away from the religious teachings of Islam and my Pakistani family. Zarah once welcomed me with sincerity. I chose to move on with my life.

Zarah no longer thought of settling abroad. She stopped working after marriage and gave up on pursuing furthering her education and a career when more children came along. Years passed since Zarah discussed applying for a visa to Canada or the US. She hardly mentioned leaving Pakistan for good any longer.

The most educated of three sisters became weighed down by her marriage, accepting her role as a housewife, and caretaker. For all the generous things Zarah did for me during my stay in Pakistan, I saw a different version of her wearing the same jeans and large size kameez blouse she bought for me, leaving on a one-way trip to America. When sitting alone, I saw a different image of Zarah walking away from protective in laws and etching out a new beginning for herself. The most educated of three sisters used to talk with enthusiasm about working as a nurse at a busy hospital, caring for sick kids.

Desiring a more prosperous future for Zarah meant I saw her moving away from members of the extended family who held her back. I wanted to encourage Zarah's' ambitions by urging her to apply for a visa to the United States or Canada again. This time, there would be no more rejections.

A better life waited for Zarah in a foreign country, who I pictured succeeding as a nurse in a busy emergency room, where patients and children benefited from the kindness, she gave effortlessly to family members who were suffering, without asking for anything back. I secretly wished Zarah would start her life over in another country where she could live far from domineering male figures who dictated her life's choices after marriage. When I traveled to Louisiana, I found Zarah in every person who welcomed me with a bouquet of flowers.

Through her struggles to get a college degree in Karachi, Zarah used to tell me about her plans of applying for a visa to Pennsylvania, swearing she had close relatives from Ganish who offered her family a place to stay. I halfheartedly laughed off Zarah's attempts at applying for a visa to the United States. My new sister-in-law's ambitions of moving away reminded me of novels I handwrote and my attempts at publishing books. Rejection letters from publishers piled up in a junk drawer where I collected things I didn't want. I wanted to believe that something great could come from failures. After this latest rejection I never got around to completing my latest romance novel.

Zarah listed all the ways I would find lasting fulfillment in my marriage to Daniyal, eventually. Being a middle-class Islamic woman in Pakistan meant that marital life was about ignoring insults and tolerating mistreatment, disguised as acceptance from in-laws. Staying faithful to an abusive Islamic husband was expected from women in our family. According to Zarah, I should waste more years of my life waiting for a man to fulfill his marriage vows. Like Aaliyaa, Zarah prayed for the unattainable success of my family.

Words of caution spoken by family about being a listless dreamer meant that I didn't want to hear about Zarah's goals not working out. Although I doubted that Zarah would be given a visa to the United States, I encouraged her to apply for a passport one more time. I listened when Zarah told me about her plans to work at a clinic caring for sick children. There would be no more rejections.

Early life before marriage was designated for fun and celebration, when Islamic women from Ganish went on shopping sprees with friends and traveled around by rickshaw to cities like Peshawar. Life after marriage for women of Ganish meant a loss of freedom and independence. There was little privacy in our home.

Male relatives were nosy and eavesdropped on my conversations with Zarah. The bungalow style shared family home was roomy with five bedrooms and two full- size walk in kitchens. Bedrooms and rooms were double the size of the small apartment I shared with Daniyal and my kids back in Louisiana. Beds and rooms that made up our family home in Faisalabad were considered communal living quarters of the house and shared with countless guests, relatives and mutual friends who came to our house every day. Malak asked that I keep my bedroom door open all of the time. Close guests and relatives came in and out of a room I shared with Sameer and Asad. Notions of independence and career success weren't realistic for Rani, a housewife with little girls to raise.

With this last rejection letter, I put away my latest concept for a novel. Overbearing in laws wouldn't let Zarah move away to a country like America and live a life separate from their own.

I was isolated from outsiders and people who Malak labeled not good enough to be a part of our inner circle. Living at Ganish with limited resources meant I learned how to be content with my solitude. I saw life at Ganish without resources and frequent power outages as down- time spent with in laws. Ayaan assured me that I had plenty of time to learn Urdu.

Malak assumed I understood Pakistani traditions like wearing a burka and re- membering to cover my hair during prayer hours. Learning how to pray namaz were religious practices that meant as a new follower of Islam and a foreign guest, that I showed respect for Pakistani culture. I could understand the spoken language of Urdu well. Guests showed up on Muslim holidays in large groups offering traditional food and gifts giving money in rupees to myself and Sameer.

After my second pregnancy, strangers had no inhibitions about commenting on my body type and weight gain. After my second pregnancy, Farah pointed out how many pounds I gained since living in Ganish. Farah reminded me of how many times she had to re-size my original form -fitting outfit.

Farah went with me to medical appointments. At the start of my third trimester, I stood on a scale so a nurse could record my weight. Farah remembered how much I weighed, telling close friends and relatives the exact number of pounds I gained since the start of my pregnancy. Farah often compared me to her brother's new wife who just had a newborn daughter, making it a point to emphasize how this new daughter-in law lost the baby weight so soon after delivery. According to Farah this new daughter-in-law was a natural beauty. Daniyal was right, most people from Ganish knew of our family. I had little privacy.

Residents of Faisalabad knew personal things I chose not to share with anyone. Relatives who I never met before from Ganish knew how I spent my downtime and gossiped about how I parented Sameer and Asad.

I had a better grasp of Pakistani culture than at the start of my travels.

I reminded myself living in Pakistan was a part of my children's heritage and culture. Living abroad would be good for them in the long term. Sameer and Asad were as intrigued as I was to learn about their heritage and Daniyal's country of origin.

Sameer and Asad enjoyed being part of an extended family, I convinced myself.

Sameer and Asad didn't laugh and play freely in the same carefree way they did with me in Louisiana, when it was only the three of us. Daniyal was never around.

In the future, my hope is that Sameer and Asad measure our time together by the adventure- filled days we experienced while living in Pakistan, when everything was new and exciting. My happiness revolved around Sameer and Asad for so long. My first experiences of love and better memories in Pakistan faded like my hysteria that night at the emergency room. I stopped believing in change and progress for Pakistani people. You didn't have to be a true Pakistani to feel that way. In my imagination, I meet Daniyal in another lifetime, if you believe in that sort of thing.

CHAPTER 19

Earthquakes and Natural Disasters Faisalabad, Pakistan

*A*aliyaa double layered an extra bed sheet she bought from a local bazaar to place over an old bedcover, sure to choose the most vibrant shade to accentuate a room. The bright color bed sheet was meant to offset a dreary tone of white primer chipping from walls that needed to be painted over. Farah already renovated downstairs, replacing old appliances and painting over several layers of cracks in the walls where peeling white primer was still noticeable.

Aaliyaa had a knack for cleanliness. Each room of our city home of Faisalabad was meticulously decorated. Aaliyaa followed close behind our newest housekeeper, Suda a soft-spoken black girl from our village of Ganish who barely said anything accept to nod a yes or no in response to a question Aaliyaa asked in Urdu. Our new maid, Suda was a peculiarly introverted girl who fooled with her debutta and acted skittish around me. Aaliyaa oversaw hiring, recruiting and training of candidates from villages, checking the cleanliness of squat toilets and washrooms after Suda finished mopping. The middle sister sprayed down soapy tiles of bathroom floors, finding dusty corners or dirt smudges and fingerprints left on mirrors and floors that needed to be redone.

Aaliyaa straightened a row of picture frames that were carefully situated along the top of an antique dresser. Like a brief memory of an agonizing childhood with my mom, the ground shook beneath me. Glass picture frames and the reminder of a dancing ballerina globe, my mother gifted me in childhood was all I could think about. I listened to the song of the dancing ballerina girl play over again. Everything went still.

I couldn't steady my body and held onto a wooden bed frame to balance myself. The dancing ballerina globe I held in my hand as a child, shattered. The room swayed around me until all I could do was shut my eyes and call out.

The tragedies of my real-life upbringing spun me into a dizzying panic. For a minute, I couldn't think clearly. The family house in Faisalabad trembled around me. Broken pieces of glass and picture frames were scattered on the tile floor. I held the dancing ballerina globe in my hand and watched it shatter to pieces, like shards of glass leading up to our village home of Ganish. Contagious laughter of village children made me long for home in the United States.

"Daniyal called numerous times to ask if you were okay. We lost electricity and water when the earthquake hit. "Sorry Kasra, there's no internet connection," Nadia exclaimed, trying to hide the fear coming through in her voice. When the earthquake struck out of nowhere, in my imagination, I drifted back to the strangest moments of my past, like a memory of the ballerina dancer globe my mother gifted me. I was still a girl who came from the middle of nowhere, who enjoyed daydreaming and writing stories, once married to a man who harbored long kept secrets and lied about what he did for work. I was once a girl from a village who waited for Daniyal and members of my extended family in Ganish to tell me the truth about why I traveled to Pakistan with Sameer and Asad. When the earthquake hit out of nowhere, in my mind, I retraced the worst tragedies of my early life.

Standing on the third story building, I was sweeping up remaining pieces of debris and broken shards of glass, straightening and re-hanging pictures and family heirlooms from our village of Ganish. Most of the family's belongings were knocked over and destroyed after the earthquake struck, a few hours ago. I looked around at our possessions, some valuable antiques. Tempered glass coverings of our coffee table were scattered on the ground. Light weight pieces of furniture were turned over lying on the floor of Sameer's bedroom. The home I shared with my in-laws in Faisalabad was in tatters.

The rest of my relatives were downstairs looking at me from the ground floor, standing on a boulevard of our neighborhood in Faisalabad. My children along with a group of Asad's school friends played games of cricket, badminton and soccer on the road. Asad was testing out his remote powered bike, that he bought with money in rupees he saved up from Muslim Eid holidays.

On the morning before the earthquake hit, it was the first week of a brand-new school year. I sent my oldest son, Sameer off to school in a rush by rickshaw, checking to make sure he remembered his lunchbox and school supplies. The new housemaid, Sudra was around to help early on mornings when I had to get the kids up before 7:00 AM, showered and dressed, a daunting task. Sudra was an additional pair of hands that helped alleviate much of the work involved in polishing school shoes, double knotting laces and ironing Sameer's uniform.

Private schools in Faisalabad expected that children attending their schools looked clean and polished. From a list of supplies, I marked off almost every item. I stood in a long line at a packed bazaar the day before along with Nadia where we bought each item on the list separately. I marked off a school supply checklist of things I already purchased that included; a white-collar shirt, navy-blue vest, and a pair of khaki pants still wrapped in a plastic covering. Nadia bought a belt and black shoes from a salesman who sold shoes at the shop next door, shouting at a man above him to throw down a bigger size and style the customer requested.

I packed Sameer's favorite sandwich made with a mixture of yogurt, garlic sauce and boneless chicken along with sliced apples in a lunchbox that morning. I saw myself standing high above Sameer on the third story balcony waving down to my children as they entered a rickshaw and drove off. Looking back, I felt gigantic when peering down at my family from the third story balcony. I was back getting Sameer ready for his first week of school, that's what I first thought of when the earthquake hit out of nowhere. My head pounded. Trees, cars and children still playing on the pavement below, appeared blurry and out of focus.

Never knowing when the most serene moments of village life in Ganish could take a turn for the worse, Nadia yelled for us to come downstairs, to ground level, where we would be safe. Steadying myself against a nightstand by our bedroom door, I turned the knob of the music box my mother gifted me in childhood until I heard it click, replaying the melody of the dancing ballerina girl until I finally slept

Nadia held me for a while. I shut my eyes. Thinking about the most mundane things, like returning to another place in time. I could see myself before boarding an airplane to Pakistan when friends and family still called me Samantha. When packing at the last minute for Sameer and our trip to Faisalabad, I saw myself frantic the night before our flight, throwing things together at the last minute for our journey. On our first visit to Faisalabad or to a village meeting with relatives that I never met before; I imagined what it would be like to see Pakistan again. I left the apartment I shared with Daniyal back in Louisiana a mess. Daniyal was nowhere around. He left our plane tickets, money and itinerary on the dining table. Humza was there to drive me and Sameer to the airport in Washington DC.

Pedestrians, rickshaws and tall buildings of Faisalabad looked blurry and out of focus. The world around me quieted down. Like a snapshot of a picture or a moment frozen in time, kids, onlookers and neighbors went about their lives, unfazed, like nothing happened. Citizens of Ganish were used to tragedies and setbacks, enduring weeklong water and electricity outages. The same group of kids played cricket on nearby sidewalks. I placed both hands on my head, dizzy and nauseous. Aaliyaa steadied me, pulling me up from the floor. I opened my eyes.

The pavement shook around me. I couldn't think straight. Nadia said earthquakes in Faisalabad were rare, but only last a few minutes in total.

"Not to worry Kasra, I told you the earthquake would be over soon." Like the character of the brave Lion in a kids story I read to Nadia for her English lessons, every member of Daniyal's' family seemed stronger and more resilient than me.

Sameer and Asad, who considered themselves full-fledged Pakistanis were typically tougher than me when facing weeklong electricity losses and abrupt school closings. "Life in Faisalabad will go back to normal soon. Close your eyes for a little while longer," Nadia told me. My mind replayed old memories of former years when I lived in Louisiana with Daniyal and Sameer.

No one in my extended family panicked when we lost electricity this time, for longer than anyone could anticipate.

Tragic memories of my life before coming to Pakistan, before the earthquake was about not letting on that there were problems in my marriage to Daniyal. At the very least, I didn't want Sameer to see the worst of what comprised of my most challenging times in Pakistan. I squinted my eyes shut until everything quieted back down. My mind wouldn't stop retracing my worst moments in Pakistan up until the earthquake hit. Nadia was right, the earthquake didn't last long.

When I walked up the ladder to the third story floor, the house was a mess; old pictures and glass frames were smashed. Asad's toys were scattered around the room. My hands trembled when I stepped over broken glass. After the earthquake we lost power and water for weeks.

When I walked around our bedroom, stepping over shards of glass, Nadia took my hand and steadied me.

Nadia and our new maid Sudra helped sweep up pieces of glass around the living room. "Daniyal called again, but there is still no electricity or water." Nadia informed me in her best English. We were together through both good and bad times "Tomorrow everything will go back to normal Kasra."

"You really should get some sleep. It's been a long day," Nadia said putting on a clean pillowcase and sweeping the room, straightening the bed, tucking in bed sheets and folding newly washed blankets.

"Please Kasra, don't worry. Go to sleep. You must be worn out. Tomorrow morning everything will be better; a new day. We can start again." I slept for longer than I can remember. The room spun around in circles. My head pounded for days after.

C H A P T E R *20*

My Most Frightening Experience

Malak took the turbulent backroads that night. Our driver was about an hour away from the most state-of-the-art medical center in Karachi, Pakistan. Aaliyaa recited a Muslim prayer on the way to the clinic

Listening to Aaliyaa repeat a Muslim prayer of protection, made me sure I was going to lose the pregnancy. I was in my third trimester and woke up hours earlier complaining of heavy abdominal pain and spotting. There was a pile of mail, plane tickets and some cash sitting on a coffee table back in Louisiana where I lived at the time with Daniyal. Daniyal sent me, his heavily pregnant wife on a one-way trip to Faisalabad, Pakistan.

There was no new crib bought at an expensive department store in Pakistan, no streamers hung, or gifts bestowed to me at a baby shower, not this time around. I didn't bother telling Daniyal that he had another son on the way when I found out the gender of the baby on a visit to the obstetrician with Nadia.

Daniyal did not seem to want me or another child around. Before I knew about Daniyal's infidelity during both my pregnancies and about countless affairs, I couldn't stop thinking about an ongoing court case over land and inheritance that Daniyal brought into my life and the lives of my children. Problems over the division of land were still being settled in a high circuit court in Karachi. Our lives were permanently on hold.

With each jolt of the steering wheel, I became more nauseous. Every time the driver accelerated the gas pedal to slow down or speed up, darting through traffic moving from a bumpy village road to a busy highway in no time, I was more light-headed. I thought about asking our driver to pull over.

My worst fears seemed plausible. Nadia rushed me to the front of the line saying, "Sir, it's an emergency, she's pregnant and very ill." The hospital in Faisalabad was crowded and eerie. I thought I was going into early labor. I was seen quickly by a female nurse on duty that night wearing a headscarf and white medical scrubs. The nurse's dark, beady eyes were all I saw of her features.

A nurse on duty that evening guided me by the arm to a more private room in another section of the clinic, closing the curtains. I looked back at my in-laws. Nadia was sitting in a noisy room outside where she waited in anticipation for the arrival of my second son. A combination of injections and series of medications the nurses put me on, upon arrival at the clinic in Faisalabad, made me feel lethargic and dissociative. The next morning, I woke up feeling like I had been drugged, covered in a sheer blanket Sana brought from home.

The blanket Sana covered me with belonged to Sameer and smelled of soap, reminding me briefly of my childhood. I thought back to when me and Sameer first moved to Pakistan, staying up late in the mornings watching his favorite cartoons. I started seeing and hearing lifelike flashbacks of what happened that morning upon my arrival at the medical center in Karachi. My memory of what took place when I was admitted to the emergency room left me in a state that Nadia described as out of my mind with hysteria.

Dialing Daniyal's number, I woke up from a nightmare, still in a dreamy state. My room was chilly and lacked privacy except for curtains, that were left partially open. Hospital Staff and nurse's aides rarely came to check on me. I redialed Daniyal's phone number. I waited a few minutes before saying anything, making sure it was him on the other end of the line. I don't remember exactly what I told Daniyal about what happened. I screamed and cried out to him, pleading for someone to hear or believe me. Hate and rage came through in Daniyal's tone of voice when he told me not in so many words that I could stay in Pakistan with the baby." No one will believe you. You're crazy." Daniyal hung up, in a fit of rage. I went back to sleep.

No – one in my family knew what was wrong with me or how to calm me down. I felt momentarily, like I was in a dreamy state, drifting in and out of consciousness.

Hours after waking up, I couldn't remember where I was or why I had been admitted to the medical center in Karachi. At first glance, I didn't recognize close relatives.

A group of noisy mutual relatives from Ganish stood around my hospital bed carrying food wrapped in aluminum foil while chatting animatedly in Urdu, as if expecting to welcome a newborn boy to the family. Malak sat beside me on a hospital bed offering me a cup of tea, brought from Ganish. My arms were lined with bruises from where nurses on duty stuck me. Hooked up to an IV, cold, disoriented and sobbing, I got up gradually to find the bathroom. I began having flashes of what happened after the doctors and nurses admitted me as a patient. Nadia pointed out that I was rude to guests by weeping in front of strangers and refusing to engage in friendly banter in Urdu or force *a smile*. I couldn't worry about Pakistani customs.

Instead of going back to my bed, getting a hold of myself and telling Nadia what I was sure took place after I was heavily medicated and admitted as a patient to the emergency room, I decided not to say anything. I was sure that Nadia would blame my loud emotional episodes on the medication and my state of confusion. When I stayed in the bathroom wailing for too long, Aaliyaa came in to console me. In the same breath Nadia criticized me for not sitting with guests who made traditional food and drove all the way from Peshawar to see me, wanting to talk.

Nadia said that my crying constantly made her worry that I would lose the pregnancy. I chose not to tell anyone what I believe in my heart took place that morning in the emergency room. I carry the shame of all the ways I believe the female nurse on duty violated me. No one would possibly listen, not now.

On the car ride home, I wept quietly. Nadia said a prayer of protection on the hour-long drive back to Faisalabad from Karachi, trying her best to comfort me. I wanted to tell Nadia everything. I tried my best to block out explicit images of what I believe took place the night before. My body felt heavy and sore.

My mind was filled with frantic thoughts of escaping the confinement of a hospital room and graphic images of the female nurse on duty that morning, dressed in white scrubs repeating vulgar things to me in another language. The way I believed the female nurse violated me and the nasty things she said, was all I could see and hear in a series of nightmares and flashbacks that wouldn't subside. I remain like a child, falling back to sleep, drowning out muffled noises. Unable to prevent what followed, I thought I shrieked out loud enough for help.

When I woke up the next morning, I recalled in detail how the nurse on duty that night, dressed in white scrubs, called me names and medicated me without my consent or knowledge. Hours later, I had flashbacks of a dark figure dressed in white molesting me. I tried to drown out the conversation I overheard of my newly engaged sister-in-law- who out of concern, came to visit me at the emergency room that evening. My newest sister-in-law, Nyla, was hopeful about the new beginning she would make with her soon to be husband.

Nyla spent ample time cooking what she called my favorite ethnic cuisines. Nyla took time to pack, make and hand deliver food from Ganish while I was hospitalized. A table full of carefully wrapped homemade food, packed in decorative paper cloths was placed on a table in front of my hospital bed. Nyla made tea and carrot halwa she brought from the village. Nadia made biryani and bread. Rohan brought fresh fruit he picked up from a market down the road from our home. I sat up, still groggy and sipped the hot tea slowly, trying to drown out what I believed happened the night before I was admitted to the ER. Nyla smiled affectionately while passing me a hot plate of food. It was ironic how each time there was a devastating moment, roomfuls of relatives showed up with homemade cultural food. The chattering group of Pakistani relatives amplified my worst nightmares. Mutual Friends and family didn't show up to support me, but in mockery of my most pronounced instances of grief and loss.

Zarah talked about my sacrifice for Daniyal as a subservient Muslim woman, living in Pakistan as an American. Zarah's feelings of admiration for me as a foreigner living in Faisalabad now repulsed me because of the ways I tolerated abuse from Daniyal and his in laws for so long. When I finally broke down and told Nadia about the years of psychological, emotional and physical abuse at the hands of her oldest brother, Nadia heartlessly replied, "I pray every day for your family and for the happiness of your marriage."

I thought about new beginnings, married life and starting over as a deceiveable woman with the yearning of being a mother for a second time and raising a family. The happiness of celebrating the birth of my second son, Asad turned into a reality that I was no longer excited about having a son. For the first time in my life, I didn't find joy at the prospect of becoming a new parent. New beginnings along with the thought of starting over again without Daniyal weren't possible. The evening I was admitted to a medical center in Karachi, I called Daniyal in Louisiana speaking incoherently through my delirium. I described in detail to Daniyal what I thought happened the day before. Mentioning to Nadia that her phone balance ran out. I recall dropping a cell phone Nadia let me borrow.

Still hearing Daniyal's harsh words echo from the other end of the line, swearing that what I described at the hospital was a fabrication, I hung up.

Welcoming the birth of my second son was no longer something I looked forward to. My in-laws went out of their way to cheer me up, offering to take me shopping in Islamabad and help pick -out outfits for the newborn. Farah designed stylish maternity clothes, casual salwar kameez she made of the best quality fabric she could afford. Zarah's affection for me could be measured by the amount of effort she put into sewing new maternity clothes for me. Zarah designed large shalwar kameez from trendy fashion magazines when I got heavier toward the end of my pregnancy.

My in-laws made their way through narrow spaces of crowded bazaars, haggling for the best deals during weekends when kids had time off from school. When my delivery date approached, Aaliyaa decorated my room and bought a new crib and care package of necessities I would need for a newborn. On important family engagements and religious celebrations, I was absent, sat alone or stayed to myself, no longer enthusiastic about experiencing culture and life in Pakistan.

Weeks later, after I gave birth to my second son, Nadia kept double checking on me. It was like I returned to that dark place again; drifting in and out of consciousness, remembering fragments of the violation I experienced at the medical center in Pakistan. During the first months of Asad's life, I kept thinking of death and dying, not of living and taking care of a newborn.

I wasn't the same person I was before; thinking about motherhood as an exciting new beginning since childhood. After the birth of Asad. I was sad and distant. No one knew what was wrong or why everything that was once full of vibrancy and color – now appeared dull, and flat, without laughter.

My recollection of concerned family members from Ganish turned into cryptic images that stood around my hospital bed in Karachi. After the birth of Asad, I stopped seeing family who claimed to love me in color. Historic cities I wrote fiction stories about appeared in black and white. I slept until I couldn't feel the pain any longer or remember the day in the emergency room months before. I didn't want a baby and refused to tell Daniyal that I no longer desired to be a wife and Mother. I stopped wanting to live.

I raised Sameer in Louisiana practically alone. When traveling to Faisalabad, years later. I was relieved to have the support of my three sisters. The ending to my real life- romance story about meeting Daniyal's family in Pakistan needed to be at the very least hopeful.

When I was admitted to a hospital in Karachi, complaining of premature labor pains, a nurse ripped out a series of prescription medications scribbled on a notepad. Malak was billed an outrageous fee for my emergency room stay. My in laws were required to pay an enormous bill in full when I was a patient at the emergency room in Karachi. "We can't afford this, why are you charging us so much money? "This is more than the cost of a delivery," Malak yelled at the discharge nurse. not wanting to face the people who I believed violated me. I looked away, wanting my memory of visiting a clinic in Karachi to go away.

All I could think about was going home to Louisiana and sleeping, never returning to a place like the medical center I visited in Karachi again. When I finally went into labor weeks later- choosing not to return to the emergency room in Karachi where I was abused, I remembered what the nurse on duty did to me. Every happiness was taken away.

Pakistani people regarded the former Prime Minister as a leader who would finally win the fight against corruption and stand tall beside Pakistani citizens who wanted desperately to see change and progress. I thought I would put true stories I told about a life I lived with Sameer in a village area of Ganish away for the time being.

I relish in the memory of my first time traveling to Pakistan with Sameer and meeting my Pakistani in laws from a secluded village most have never heard of before Faisalabad. Pakistan. I wanted to wait for the right moment to tell each member of Daniyal's family who waited for change and progress for Pakistani citizens that there would one day be fairness. When I travel the next time to a village or worldly city, Like the Pakistan I once came to appreciate as a US citizen, Ganish was home for now.

Pakistan would welcome my family again someday when times were better and my future brighter, filled with happier memories.

Pakistani people fought like no other for fairness, loyality to family and community above setbacks, political uncertainties and senseless killings. You didn't have to be non-white, a gora or anti- American to feel the sting of that pain too. Like a faded picture of dusty village roads and stillness, a yearning to live, the kids of our village stayed the same. I wrote fiction stories for my own sense of happiness

I wished each child of Ganish well, telling them about my wishes for their lives. Faisalabad could exist in my memory no matter what tragedy struck, welcoming me back one more time. My final visit to Pakistan could be different than I ever imagined, a land of dreams.

PART 5

Travel Diaries

CHAPTER 21

Teaching at A Government
School: Faisalabad, Pakistan

At the start of summer, Sana waited until produce was in season to pick the ripest fruit for her birthday party. Sana insisted the entire family sat around a bucket of cold mangoes and eat as many as we could stand. Like waiting to pick the ripest mangoes at the start of summers, students from the Vocational school waited for happiness that never came.

I was standing in the middle of a road in our city home of Faisalabad without a head scarf, exposed to eavesdropping neighbors. My rickshaw driver sped off leaving me to fend for myself. A heavy fog concealed our city of Faisalabad.

Hamdard training school was a government funded vocational school my friend Asma attended in our city of Faisalabad, years ago. Asma signed up for cooking classes in her spare time, as a hobby while waiting for a visa to come through. My children were old enough to attend school. I had more than adequate family support and help at home for my kid's academics. A few weeks prior, I convinced my in-laws that I wanted to find work in Faisalabad. I found a job sooner than I expected at a government school in Faisalabad teaching English lessons. I gave myself ample time to get ready for work most mornings because I liked to sit on the balcony before sunrise.

"You cannot teach poor kids," Farah informed me when I tried to tutor two housekeepers from our village in English.

My memory of taking a rickshaw to work every morning and teaching at a run-down government school was like going on an exploration. Because I knew Ayaan prepaid, I asked my rickshaw driver to escort me around places in Faisalabad I knew well, so I could watch people who filled up congested markets where vendors bargained for the best deals.

When visiting local bazaars in Faisalabad, mobs of people pushed their way through cramped alleyways. Customers from Faisalabad bought bargain priced clothing or produce and haggled with food sellers for the best deals on merchandise. On the way back from Hamdard vocational school, our rickshaw driver made another stop to buy fruit in season.

Asma married a successful British Pakistani who lived abroad in Luton, England and worked as an entrepreneur, sending monthly allowances back to Pakistan for his soon to be bride. Asma instructed our driver to stop at a local bakery in Faisalabad to buy an assortment of sweet desserts and pastries. We made another visit to a fish market where I shared lunches with my friend on my work breaks. Traveling by rickshaw with Asma to my favorite bazaars and shops around the city were some of my most enjoyable moments of being a foreigner and standing out as a gora, from America.

I looked away, giving spare pocket change to food sellers, poor farm workers and child beggars who made almost nothing for the afternoons they spent in the sun, making scarcely enough to survive or feed their families.

When I didn't return on time from teaching English classes at the vocational school, my mother-in law, Inaya waited at home questioning where I disappeared off to in the evenings after work. I told Inaya I shared meals with English students at local coffee shops. Some nights after work, I traveled around alone by rickshaw to my favorite outdoor bazaars and shops. Ayaan paid our rickshaw driver a month's fare in advance. Our rickshaw driver could have pocketed the extra money and never returned to the job. Poor farm workers employed by my in-laws were surprisingly honest. I wondered why Ayaan paid in advance.

Ayaan scolded me every time I went somewhere alone that it was unsafe for me as a US citizen to walk on foot or take public transportation anywhere in Pakistan. It was too late to shout down to my rickshaw driver. I had fifteen minutes before my rickshaw drove off.

At nearly the same time every morning, I watched the Punjabi woman across the way line dry clothes. I could make-out her long dark hair and thin silhouette.

Considering the load shedding problem and workload expected from students attending government schools in Faisalabad, it was impressive that my student's showed up to take English classes. I knew most of my students from the government school came from poor backgrounds. Girls and adolescent girls who took vocational courses came from villages and lived cheaply. Their clothes were hand sewn by a family member to save money like most middle-class families.

Malak's rickshaw driver waited another five minutes. Hiding myself in my shawl, I didn't bother fixing myself up, knowing my appearance didn't matter. I didn't have a degree in education but liked to use my creative ideas to discuss issues facing Pakistani women. Poetry writing. was my favorite part of teaching ESL. With little resources, frequent power shortages and no guidance or formal instruction about how to begin teaching English lessons, I saw teaching like my journey to Faisalabad, an unpredictable adventure. I would have to improvise.

My intention for going with Asma to the Vocational Training School was not to apply for a job, but to sign up for art classes. I was offered a job teaching English classes on the spot with no training or experience. After accepting the position, my enthusiasm for the job subsided when I realized I would be on my own planning the curriculum and managing thirty-five students, women of different ages, from varying backgrounds and income levels. The art teacher who hired me, swore that all I had to do was speak in English with the girls who signed up for my class. He was right, there was no pressure, and nothing to lose. Only a handful of teachers who worked at Hamdard Vocational school bothered putting effort into planning materials, assigning homework or following a structured lesson plan.

Students who attended Hamdard Vocational Training School were left to their own devices, with little guidance or formal instruction from teachers who worked there. I think back to the art class I took at an earlier date. The art class was about self-expression. I don't remember completing any of my artwork or assignments. Women from Punjab used their time at Hamdard Vocational school to share real life accounts of their problematic home lives.

My class gathered in one area of the classroom to discuss newspaper articles and popular English novels I bought from bookstores in Pakistan. I instructed my class to choose from current newspaper articles highlighting what was going on in different areas of Pakistan and surrounding provinces of Punjab. My students kept one notebook for journal writing, and another notebook for writing poetry and short stories. Novels I purchased with Ayaan at a popular bookstore were used to teach English lessons when assembling reading groups.

Because this was a career course, my one rule for attending vocational training was that my students only speak English, not their native language of Urdu or Punjabi. I referenced newspaper articles and encouraged my students to speak candidly about issues facing women in Faisalabad. Although some of my students lived in poor conditions and struggled for basic needs, their enthusiasm for showing up to my class each day was inspirational. I wanted to understand more about what the girls enrolled in ESL class knew about American women and learn about their reasons for taking ESL classes.

Hussain hired me as a teacher at Hamdard Vocational school on the spot. Hussain served the academy under the semblance of different roles. On certain days, Hussain worked as a graphic designer and contributing editor for the school's website and newspaper. On other days, my boss posted updates on schedule changes, pictures of the girls in uniform and artist of the week on the school's website. Husain included in weekly newspaper articles, a piece of artwork or clothing designed by students that stood out most. On the remaining weekdays, my boss was known by his previous title of art teacher. When the school's principal was absent, Hussain filled in for her acting as the supervisor, meeting with parents to discuss student's progress, enrolling new students and collecting school tuition from parents.

CHAPTER 22

Unforeseen Challenges as An ESL Teacher in Faisalabad, Pakistan

The art teacher who hired me with no experience or college degree was there to greet me and my friend Asma, waiting in the office next to the school's principal. In rural areas of, Faisalabad it was considered good manners to wear a headscarf or veil in front of strange men or house guests outside of immediate family. Being modest, covering up and wearing a head scarf meant you were either married or didn't welcome wandering eyes or advances from strange men.

Asma pointed out flirtatious glances the art teacher sent in my direction during our first meeting. "You were flirting with him," Asma scolded me as if I had done something more. I brushed off my boss's advances toward me because I enjoyed teaching at the government school and liked the idea of having something to look forward to. I explained to Asma that I didn't intend to give off the wrong impression as a foreigner, I was only trying to get a job. "This isn't America, you don't send the wrong messages here to get a job. Do you know what you did in Pakistani culture and what it means? You're lucky, I won't mention this to Daniyal or anyone else," Asma lectured in punjabi.

I learned later from the school's principal that my boss Hussain was having an affair with another teacher down the hall who he trained and recruited himself. Asma was right, I innocently flirted to get a job.

I understood little about Pakistani customs, especially working-class men in Faisalabad who appeared to have a hidden agenda. Asma was right, I didn't know what it meant to be a conservative Islamic woman from a good family and uphold tradition. After working at the government school for several months, I found out several of my students and female colleagues, some married, were having affairs, trying to hide romantic relationships from their strict, Muslim families. As more time passed, I was content with my days working at the Vocational training school teaching. Eventually, I was unaffected by the toxic work environment.

After my first couple months of working as an English teacher, I learned that the Vocational training school wasn't an academy where students came to improve their English. The school in Faisalabad was more like a community center for abused women who were being controlled and manipulated by male family members. In days to come, I discovered many of the teenage girls enrolled in my class weren't motivated to learn English or work hard toward goals for taking classes. Teenage girls who took different courses at the vocational school were more interested in sneaking off with their boyfriends during lunch hours or in their free time, loitering hallways. I ran into my students skipping my English class brushing by her, making out with her boyfriend, near the same canteen, I passed dozens of times.

CHAPTER 23

Hussain, The Art Teacher

When I arrived late for work some days, my boss waited impatiently for me in his classroom. Hussain told me I was cluttering his office space with English books and magazines I bought for students. Hussain gave me his word that he would clean out a room he assigned for my class down the hall once he fixed it up. My boss assured me that he would eventually get the air conditioner repaired. A few of my students encircled Hassain, whispering and laughing to themselves on days when I arrived late to class. One of my students informed me that some of her classmates got a kick out of making jokes at my expense. I was known after that by students and staff as the serious lady who carried around an out of style bag. Each morning, I brought a bag full of English newspapers and books, from home.

My boss was right, I took things too seriously, putting in long hours. I arrived in the morning with what some of my students and staff called an expensive bag. Girls from poorer castes considered my shalwar kameez to be expensive clothing gifted to me by in-laws. My handbag was filled with English newspapers and novels I purchased at a bookstore in the city with Ayaan. Ayaan told me to purchase as many books as I wanted during my first weeks in Pakistan.

I wasn't earning a high salary, but I had grown accustomed to my daily routine of getting up before everyone in my extended family and riding a rickshaw a few miles down the way to the Government funded trade school. I was having fun teaching English at the government school, learning about Pakistani culture and my students who I had befriended.

Ayaan showed up out of nowhere on his motorcycle at the same time every afternoon to the vocational school to check on me. Ayaan asked staff and coworkers about how my time teaching at the vocational school was going. I told Ayaan that I was waiting on a bigger room with air conditioning to be set up before I could move out of the art teacher's room.

I was willing to accommodate my elementary school age student, Kiran an introverted thirteen-year-old from an upper middle-class family, who recently joined my English class. I thought about compiling together age-appropriate reading material for Kiran's lessons. When the teenager stopped showing up to my English classes, Asma told me the principal of the Vocational training school had a serious discussion with Kiran's parents telling her mom the truth about the government school.

According to my friend Asma, the school's principal spoke to Kiran's family members like a concerned parental figure, warning her parents about predators at the vocational school. Asma explained that it would be unwise to expose a child to a toxic environment. Hamdard's principal suggested Kiran's father think twice about enrolling her impressionable thirteen-year-old daughter in English classes. Measuring by Asma standards, the art teacher was of poor character.

I must have been one of the few teachers employed at the trade school not participating in extra marital affairs. Nadia forewarned me about poor castes in impoverished areas that were, according to Nadia, uncultured people who came from disgraceful families and slept around a lot.

No one cared enough about girls from poorer castes to bother teaching them anything. I must've been one of the only teachers who put in long hours and cared about my students who came to school to improve their English. Most of my students didn't enjoy learning or reading. tried every method I could to get my students to enjoy reading in English, including purchasing novels from a bookstore in Karachi.

Students from the vocational school enjoyed riding a rickshaw to the local library in Faisalabad as a break from sitting in a classroom all day. A bunch of teenage girls sat in the back of a rickshaw with their friends the entire ride to the library, laughing the whole way, like we were all going to a wedding party. Our field trips to the only library in Faisalabad where books in English were limited was a waste of time. Applying for a library card meant you had to pay a fee up front and have a co-signer present.

One of my students explained that she was fearful of reading all the time because she didn't want to be labeled a nerd. Asma told me that staff who worked at the library in Faisalabad were hesitant to issue library cards to locals because books are irreplaceable. Most people don't bother returning books to libraries in Pakistan, Asma explained.

My students from the government school laughed off my efforts of getting them interested in reading English novels. Some of my students did well on exams and assignments to win my approval. Most of the college age women who took my English class never met an American before. Muslim girls from different backgrounds probably had no idea what to think about my time living in Pakistan as a US citizen.

Some girls enrolled in my English class, paid the fee upfront and never showed up to any of their scheduled classes. Their only agenda was signing up for the class to conduct an interview, asking personal questions about my life. Most of my students wanted to know things like how many years I was married to Daniyal and if I was a true Muslim and fully accepted Islam. I was annoyed when my students loitered in the hallways, skipping out on my class to take selfies or meet with their boyfriends, in hiding.

Coming out as gay, transgender or bisexual made some people living in Faisalabad a target to more influential members of society. There was little acceptance of personal choices or self-expression for girls from poorer castes in Faisalabad. After class, my students took me to local coffee shops or recreational parks where I saw gay or bisexual couples hiding from their strict religious family members. Parks, diners and modern cities were the only places where some people could express affection away from domineering brothers or Fathers.

When I brought home a portrait Hussain painted of me, Ayaan asked that I resign from my teaching job immediately. Asma told me about women from village areas of Punjab, describing what it meant to work outside the home as a Muslim woman who married into a respectable caste, carrying the family's honor and good name.

Spending my free time at the government school down the road from our house in Faisalabad wasn't a healthy work environment. I cared about my students. I enjoyed having a place to go outside of social gatherings with extended family and wedding parties, where I rarely socialized with friends and relatives who extended me an invitation. One of my most challenging days in Pakistan was resigning from the government school where I taught English classes. I was proud of my students and wanted them to succeed, especially because I understood the challenges I experienced as an outsider from an upper middle-class family living in Faisalabad. I'm not sure I would have the strength to wake up every morning, looking forward to an English class.

After resigning from the government school, I woke- up at the same time each morning as though expecting my rickshaw driver to be waiting outside for me. Another five minutes, I shouted down to my driver, from the third story balcony. I was never on time.

I no longer had teaching classes at the vocational school to look forward to. My students called my cell phone asking me when I would be coming back to work. Hussain offered me a pay raise and a new contract. Written according to the contract, I would be paid double what I was earning previously as an English teacher at the Vocational training school, if I decided to return.

The main incentive stated in this new employment contract would be earning a higher salary and getting away from my protective brother, Ayaan. Much like the hours after work I spent riding around to familiar areas in Faisalabad, I needed a job outside of the house to take a break from the groups of guests and relatives who showed up to our home in the city and spoke loudly in Urdu. Earning a higher wage meant I could look forward to taking my kids and friends out to places on weekends. Earning more money meant I could dine at nicer places than what luxurious restaurants and bazaars near Ganish offered.

Earning a higher salary meant I could take my children out to amusement parks and their favorite dining establishments found in Cities like Karachi. My son's favorite spots to eat were overpriced fast-food chains we found in Lahore and Karachi. Sameer usually ordered the same thing every time, a zinger burger with fries and soda. To see my kids satisfied and having fun meant my paychecks were well spent. After my experience with dining out at restaurants in Faisalabad and coming down with food poisoning, I was reluctant to order from food menus when I ate out with relatives, friends or extended family. I lost a tremendous amount of weight while living abroad.

Luxury fast-food establishments in Pakistan were usually busy, packed with college students and upper-class families. Food variety was limited at popular westernized duplicate food chains in cities. When I asked for extra sauce, to substitute a topping or take back a meal, relatives and friends I dined out with spoke later with me about appropriate customs in Pakistan. My behavior was considered impolite or too direct when ordering at cafes in Karachi.

With a new contract and pay raise, I would be able to take the kids to amusement parks and recreational places in cities like Karachi. Sameer and Asad rode amusement park rides until they were worn out, enjoying their fill of cotton candy and popcorn. After Hussain from the Vocational training school offered to double my salary, I wouldn't have been able to earn a decent livelihood on a single income.

After resigning from the vocational school, I considered applying to better schools in forward-thinking cities that had more to offer than a village area of Ganish. A student I taught at the Vocational training school offered to help me apply to better paying positions at private universities. I planned my next move carefully. After applying to and getting a better paying teaching job in Karachi, I would inform my in-laws of my career plans. Working as a teacher in Karachi would be a better working environment and a significant pay increase compared to my salary as a government teacher in Faisalabad. My extended family would eventually understand.

I thought about my old boss from the Vocational school, Hussain who showed me pictures of his wife and kids vacationing together in Murree, a mountain area and a region of Pakistan, I recognized as a popular tourist site.

An attractive, well dressed Punjabi woman, Naeema, employed at the vocational school where I taught openly discussed her marital problems with co-workers and students. Naeema was having an affair with the man who hired me. Hussain was a married, working-class man with three small children. Picturing co-workers intimate at work made my stomach turn. I was thankful for the reasons I wouldn't be returning to teach at the Vocational training school. I thought about challenges I faced while living in Pakistan with my in laws. I missed America.

My students from the government school cheered for me when I needed emotional support. Hauling a rickshaw every morning to my job made me understand that Pakistan, was a strange world of its own. Living and working in Faisalabad was an unpredictable journey filled with memories of the hospitality strangers showed to me. I wanted to reassure students from the government school where I taught of all the reasons, they did nothing wrong. I left my teaching job on my own accord, citing personal reasons, whatever that meant at the time.

Chandra was an energetic nineteen-year-old who called almost every day after I left the job. Chandra stopped by the family home in Faisalabad practically every afternoon after coming home from the University, offering to help with household chores and my children's homework. I was struggling along with immediate family to cope and manage Sameer's health problems. Sameer was having seizures and more frequent asthma attacks and was in and out of the emergency room. My extended family prayed namaz for my oldest son, Sameer's health, searching for a specialist who could better guide us. I stayed busy at home, helping Rani with the care of her new baby.

After I left the government school, Chandra showed up at my house in the city to check on me. I didn't have the heart to tell Chandra that after I resigned from my teaching position, coming to my home every day in the city was unprofessional. The truth was that I needed a friend during my stay in Pakistan and enjoyed the teenager's company. I didn't say anything. We dined out or cooked meals together at home.

Chandra filled me in on the girls who took my English class and the latest petty fights or disagreements. According to Chandra, the principal hired a replacement teacher, but the girls were given little structure and guidance as far as implementing lesson plans and assigning homework. Students still weren't being productive.

When Chandra stopped showing up at my home in the city, I asked classmates and friends at the Vocational school if anyone had seen or spoken with Chandra. Despite my best efforts to find her, no one heard from my student or her sister for a while. Out of nowhere, the two girls contacted Ayaan, explaining that my former student Chandra attempted suicide.

Chandra's sister, Nura found her locked in a bedroom. Chandra slit both her wrists, nearly bleeding to death. Luckily, Chandra's family drove the teenager to a medical center before she lost her life. When I got the courage to visit Chandra in the hospital, two girls told me about their friend who was involved with a man from an upper-class family. Chandra was a girl from a poor caste.

The upper-class man Chandra was dating must have assumed he could use her body, as a man from a wealthy family and mislead the teenager into believing he would marry her without facing consequences from society, family or friends. According to Nura, the upper-class man promised to meet Chandra's father, asking for permission to marry his daughter. To a village girl from a lower caste, marrying abroad or into an upper-class family was a Cinderella story. Chandra's plan to marry an upper-class man was a way out of a life of hard work and suffering as a girl from a poor village.

Nura tried to make Chandra understand the ways that she was being used as an object. Most wealthy men had no intention of marrying girls from poor families or lower castes. Chandra believed she was going to live a different lifestyle with a con man who claimed to provide for Chandra and her family.

The upper-class man promised Chandra's father that she would be provided for financially. At the last minute, without informing students from the Vocational training school or her family, the upper-class man married a different girl from a middle-class family. Soon after learning of his marriage and discarding Chandra, he stopped contacting my student and friend. A few days later, Chandra 'attempted suicide.

When I went to visit Chandra in the emergency room, I wanted to promise there would be hope for her life. After I visited this last time at a medical center in Pakistan, I wanted to reassure my student that the system was fair. I wanted to promise Chandra and her family that she would be able to start over again someplace else, away from the tragedy of her past and any reminder of a country like Pakistan. Chandra would find a man worthy of her one day and her desires of a fulfilling married life would come to pass. I would convince Chandra of all the things she had to look forward to, not sure I believed in successful arranged marriages myself. For girls born into poverty there was little to no way out.

I guaranteed Chandra that I would visit her in Pakistan whenever she needed because I didn't want to see something terrible happen again. When I returned to America, my student from the trade school called me at late hours of the night and early mornings. I wondered if I would see Chandra again at a better place in life, married or unmarried, successful and thriving. I wanted good things for my students because I knew I would never have to be hopeless in a place like America. There was always a chance for a more prosperous life in the United States, someone who came along offering a better opportunity. My hope is that I will see Chandra again, happy.

CHAPTER 24

Village Living verses Life
in a Progressive City

I stepped over shards of glass leading to a string of mud houses where teenage girls employed by my in-laws in Faisalabad lived. Shawls and decorative fabric covered windows and doors carved out of mud houses found on the outskirts of ghettos. Kids of Ganish never seemed to grow or evolve after I left Nadia's house in the country and returned months later. A rowdy group of children still played games of cricket outside Nadia's home, running around barefoot and grinning, as though waiting to meet a girl from America for the first-time.

High-priced cattle and buffalo roamed.

In the worst areas that made up ghettos of Punjab, I was certain to encounter a barefoot and shirtless child beggar, asking for spare pocket change. Despite every setback of village life, the kids of Ganish found a reason to dance in rain showers.

During major holidays in Louisiana, Nadia invited me for weeklong- visits to her village, so I wouldn't feel alone during Christian holidays. As a thank you for making delicious food and accommodating my kids and I during weeklong trips to her house in the country, I used children's books my mom sent to teach Nadia how to read in English. A story I read to Nadia one afternoon we spent at her village, was a children's book about a brave lion.

When I looked over at Nadia, I concluded that all she must have learned growing up in Ganish was how to settle for less. Village life was tranquil and majestic, but tragic at the same time, especially for women who found it difficult to pursue a higher education. Middle class women who lived in rural areas of Punjab drove hours into the city to purchase groceries, clothing, school supplies and necessities for their children.

On frequent visits to Nadia's village, poor kids reached out their hands, asking pedestrians for spare change. Gravel roads leading up to Idris's home in the country was once overrun with high spirited kids employed for middle-class families, now a deserted road. Nadia extended week-long invitations to me and my children to stay at her village some weekends, a two-hour drive from Faisalabad to Ganish. Every boulevard or local bazaar appeared empty. Familiar roads around Faisalabad were oddly quiet during Christian birthdays and holidays I celebrated with family in the United States.

Some villages I visited in Ganish were more polluted and littered than ghettos where Daniyal picked up his best paying customers, as a taxicab driver in Washington DC. During outings to popular bazaars and shops, Zarah guided me on what not to buy at bazaars. Zarah offered well-meaning advice about staying safe when traveling alone around in rural areas of Ganish. Beggars who sold merchandise at outdoor markets were no different than paupers or thieves in training for higher stakes crimes.

My new sister-in-law, Zarah, a special education teacher, told me about being cautious when shopping at outdoor bazaars. Zarah opened a jar of skin lightening cream, tightly placing the cap back on. "Don't purchase cosmetics at this bazaar," Zarah scolded.

"Look for yourself, this brand of skin cream has been used, a village kid already switched overpriced skin cream to a rip -off brand," Zarah explained, scolding a poor kid who sold face moisturizer for double the original price.

"I'm sorry Baaji," the kid answered, staring blankly at me, a foreigner from America who innocently gave money in US currency to beggars.

Beggars hung their heads down in shame, whispering "sorry," not hesitating to ask for spare change again from the American when I traveled with family to markets.

When going to wealthy and impoverished regions of Pakistan with family, I had little understanding of social norms and divides between different caste systems. I couldn't understand why adolescent housekeepers from poor castes slept with men from wealthy families so easily, without the promise of marriage or commitment. Girls from lower castes brought dishonor to their brothers and fathers. Maids from Ganish wouldn't think twice about ripping off a middle-class family who employed them. As a foreigner from America, I was easy prey to beggars disguised as unassuming villagers. One piece of advice I disregarded from my family were cautions about being too forthcoming with housekeepers employed to work in our home. Poor kids who worked as vendors couldn't be trusted.

Former students who I befriended from the Government school lived in poorly ventilated farmhouses, cramped with family members. Inaya insulted one of my students, Chandra from the trade school who showed up at our house wanting to show me around her rural community before I returned to the United States. When Chandra asked to have her picture taken with me, I thought nothing of warnings given to me by in laws about poorer castes, beggars and advice about staying safe while living in different regions of Pakistan. I remembered Bushra, a housekeeper I befriended, who worked for Ayaan. Aaliyaa swore Bushra was sleeping with Rani's husband for money.

When my student, Chandra abruptly showed up at my home early most mornings to check on me, Malak offered my student from the Vocational training school a job in our home, employed as a tutor and maid for his school age daughter. Visibly shaken and clearly hurt, Chandra handed back Rani's newborn baby, turning down Malak's offer of employment. Chandra made an excuse about something that came up last minute with her family.

Chandra later pulled me off to the side confiding to me that every time she came to my in laws house in Faisalabad, my mother-in-law, Inaya insulted her clothes and family. Inaya questioned why Chandra still wanted to be friends with me after I resigned from my teaching job.

"You know nothing about people from lower castes and their mindset about worldly women. You can't be so trusting with people from Ganish. The poor here in Pakistan are nothing like us." Zarah informed me. I was beginning to understand differences between the wealthy and poor classes in rural areas of Ganish, at least I thought so.

I ignored Inaya's advice about poor students from the Vocational training school showing up at our family house in the city all the time. I couldn't see anything wrong with posing for a few harmless photographs with students. Chandra showed up on the back of her oldest brother's motorcycle offering me a ride to her farm- house.

Well- intentioned relatives and friends cautioned me about hanging out all the time with girls from poor castes. I knew instinctively it wasn't safe for me to travel to my students' home and should have turned down Chandra's insistence that we take photographs together.

"These people are not of our same caste. They don't think like us," Zarah lectured in Punjabi.

Inaya thought associating frequently with girls from lower castes made our upper middle-class family look bad. I brushed off Inaya's judgments of girls from poorer castes. Inaya looked stoney faced at my friend, and former student from the Vocational school when Chandra extended me an invitation to go out somewhere.

Two college age girls from my English class insisted that I visit their community at least one time before traveling back to the states with my children. Despite being born into poverty, students from the government school knew how to celebrate. After class, Chandra invited me to her home and showed me how to dance to trending Hindi movies, showing off her choreographed moves.

CHAPTER 25

Chandra, My Most Enthusiastic Student

Chandra insisted I go along with her to a Catholic church service. Christians throughout provinces of Punjab were considered a minority group of poor people who turned their backs on their Islamic faith. Practicing Christians were shunned by a predominately Muslim society. I heard about a group of practicing Christians living in rural areas of Punjab who faced prosecution or even death if caught publicly rejecting Islam. The catholic church I visited was no different than church sermons I attended on Sundays in Louisiana. I sat on the floor with friends and prayed namaz for longer than I remember. The bishop read from a biblical text from a bible in Urdu.

There were traditions about holidays back in Louisiana I missed. After resigning from the Vocational school, Chandra looked for me, asking in laws when I would be returning to Pakistan. Chandra stopped by my home in Faisalabad every day to make sure I wasn't sitting alone for too long or depressed. Before I left the government school, I should have tried harder to convince my in–laws of all the reasons I needed to continue teaching at the Trade School in Faisalabad

"When will you be returning to your teaching job?" Chandra asked when she visited my in laws home. I didn't know what to answer.

Members of my extended family stood on the third story balcony, hanging damp clothes out to dry on a hot afternoon, when Chandra and her brother showed up. Chandra waited outside the gate of our home to pick me up, insisting I visit their home not far from us in Ganish, a couple miles down the road.

"Don't worry Kasra, my brother will drive carefully."

Chandra said. I hopped on the back of the motor bike, sitting with two legs on one side.

We darted through narrow country roads, swerving through traffic. Rickshaws, cars and other modes of transportation whizzed by. To my astonishment, I looked over at another motorcycle that sped by, with an entire family hitched on the back. We ended up in the middle of a busy highway. Chandra's brother pumped the brakes when we approached Chandra's home; an old farmhouse with a tire swing in the front yard.

Poor laborers who worked on remote farms took pride in owning livestock that could earn them a decent livelihood. Agriculture workers sold produce and milk to busy markets.

"We have two baby goats that my father recently bought for a fair price, a few chickens, and two good size goats that produce milk. "Chandra gushed proudly, petting a baby goat who nudged my stomach in the form of a friendly greeting. "He must be hungry already, "Chandra said, petting the baby goat. offering to show me inside. My student from the government school wasn't considered middle class but she wasn't nearly as poor as two housekeepers employed by Ayaan who lived in mud houses at Ganish.

"My brother is ecstatic to meet you," Chandra said, pouring a pitcher of cold water into a large pot of rice she boiled outside.

"We are not very poor," Chandra explained, waiting for the pot of rice to come to a boil.

"My oldest brother, the one who drove us by motorbike, gave me a ride to the Government school, Hamdard. Ali drives me to work daily. I walk by foot to take your English classes. The Trade school where you taught English is not far from here," Chandra said, stirring the pot of rice with a wooden spoon periodically.

"Ali doesn't have a job right now. I must work hard."

"I'm making your favorite, rice and vegetables."

Chandra cooked roti bread for me, rolling out dough on a small wooden cutting board while simultaneously heating a flat iron pan on a second burner, telling me about the struggles of being a villager girl from a lower caste, saying things like;

"I told you a while ago about a job I worked at a clothing shop doing sales. My boss still asks about you, Kasra. The boss always wanted to get his photograph taken with my American friend before you left for good this time. I was fired yesterday, the boss said he couldn't afford to keep me. I wasn't meeting the company's sales goals."

"Who cares about that horrible place anyway. I was barely making enough on commission to get by."

"You ought to get some food in your stomach."

I sat across from my former student from the Vocational school watching her make a plate of chicken and vegetable rice she boiled in one large pot. My student grabbed the hot bread from the stove, burning her fingertips, blowing on the bread quickly.

"Eat something," Chandra insisted setting a plate of hot food in front of me, while clearing out a cluttered room full of old textbooks and clothes. My student must've read English textbooks for her assignments and classes at the public school she attended.

Chandra insisted that I hurry up and finish my dinner so I could try on a pair of salwar kameez she bought for me. My former student insisted I stay at her house in the country and try on wedding clothes before returning to Faisalabad. Chandra emphasized how the maroon-color salwar kameez would flatter my slender physique. Chandra couldn't wait for me to finish eating so I could try on each shalwar kameez she wanted me to wear to her cousin's wedding before leaving.

"My in- laws must be worried." I said, after trying on the last pair of salwar kameez from a bag of clothes. "It's getting late."

"You can't leave yet. Have a seat. Don't worry about the time. There is someone I would like you to meet."

"My brother, Ali won't be here to drive you home to Faisalabad for a few more hours."

CHAPTER 26

Meeting Umar

A man with a long greying beard dressed in solid white salwar kameez called Umar who resembled my father-in-law, extended a hand to greet me. Umar brushed off dirt from his kameez. Umar's face was flushed. He looked like he had just come inside from working in the sun.

"It's a Pleasure to meet you," Umar greeted in English, visibly nervous.

"Have a seat and make yourself at home. My daughter, Chandra left for a minute to make a cup of tea for you."

Chandra's Father took a seat next to me on the sofa. A dance sequence to an old Hindi movie broke out. I watched a popular Bollywood re-run countless times with Sana, that played on the television screen in front of me.

"My first-born daughter, Chandra is the strength of our family. Chandra tells me about her favorite English teacher from America all the time. Chandra brags about how she is your best student."

"Pakistan is a diverse country. Chandra tells me all the time about her favorite English teacher, Kasra who works at the government school down the road. We are not poor. My family is not considered very rich either." The teenager's father said proudly, looking around at the cluttered space. I am planning on getting my first-born daughter married soon.

Before I could express my discomfort in being there alone with a stranger, I decided that as a guest at Chandra's home for the first time, I should be polite and finish my cup of tea before finding Chandra and leaving. My student's father, Umar pulled out a cell phone, snapping pictures of me before I could protest, like I was some kind of celebrity.

"Please Kasra, smile once, so I can get a good picture of you. It is not every day that an American citizen travels to Pakistan. You look very pretty in this picture," the girl's father pointed out, showing me a photograph of myself sitting awkwardly on the sofa, trying my best to fake a smile, thinking about making any excuse now to leave.

"I should be heading home, it's already late and the streetlights always flicker out before I can make my way back to Faisalabad by foot." I said, getting up to leave.

"My daughter told me about how you could help her get a visa to America."

"You can't leave yet," Umar insisted.

I got up quickly to leave looking for my former student who was nowhere to be found. I finally located Chandra in another room rummaging through bags of clothing. The teenager held up a pair of new salwar kameez she wanted to give me.

"You only invited me to your home because you thought I could get you a visa to America. It's not that easy, you must first apply on the Embassy's website, pay a fee and wait for an appointment, like everyone else." I explained angrily, questioning why Chandra invited me to her house in the country in the first place.

Chandra was silent for a minute, caught off guard by my rant, pulling fistfuls of clothes out of plastic bags, before emptying the contents of the bag on the floor, sobbing. Chandra looked at the new shalwar kameez lying on a sofa she picked out for me to wear to a cousin's wedding she was invited to later that evening.

"I wanted to give this shalwar kameez to my favorite English teacher as a gift. I bought these clothes for you with the money I saved. You can wear this red dress to a wedding my cousin invited us to. You don't have to worry about buying anything expensive. I already told my friend you would be attending the wedding with Nura. She is excited to meet my friend, Kasra from America." Chandra looked stoney faced. I thought Chandra understood that I was no longer interested in accepting clothes or wedding invitations from her.

"Since you are an American citizen, I thought that it would be easy for me to get into the United States. My brother doesn't have a job. Joseph is forcing me to marry my cousin in a few months. "I'm sorry, I even thought of inviting you to my first cousins wedding," Chandra said, stuffing the fancy red shalwar kameez she picked out for me back inside the plastic bag

"I'm leaving right away. Tell your brother it's urgent. He needs to drive me back to Faisalabad right away."

"Stop showing up at my house, insisting on taking pictures with me," I shouted, leaving the bag of clothes and the brand-new red shalwar kameez Chandra bought for me at the foot of her door.

There was an old tire swing tied to a tree, dead grass and gravel roads surrounding Nadia's home in Ganish, leaving limited space for little children to run and play. I sat with Nadia, watching our children ride bicycles on a circular, cement sidewalk in the front yard until I was dizzy. On chilly nights, I sat with Nadia and a group of kids from Ganish, warming my hands by a fire. The two of us were hidden away from the modern world behind plush fields. The smell of country air and homecooked food made me miss home and my life in Louisiana with Daniyal. Neighboring village homes surrounded us. I thought Nadia and I must have been the only people who stayed up at night talking.

The smallest of three sisters never deviated from her role as a loyal housewife and mother. Nadia's main responsibilities centered around making sure every member of the extended family was cared for. The nights I spent at the third born daughter's village were what I enjoyed most of all. In the evenings, we sat together outside on hand made charpais. Dinners were shared with kids from our village. Nadia finally came outside to eat with me after the fire died down and all the guests went home. Nadia smiled while cutting fruit into a bowl to make a sweet dessert. Sameer's laughter faded.

Nadia lived most of her life at her village home that was falling apart and in need of repairs, with two little kids. Nadia did her best to cope with frequent electricity and water shortages, traveling miles into the city where she could shop for food and school supplies. The smallest sibling cooked meals got her children dressed in the mornings and helped new housekeepers with chores. Little sister stayed back at her village home, watching female family members pursue an education in a city.

For senior siblings from tribal areas, staying behind and watching junior family members pursue an education in places like Lahore or Karachi wasn't uncommon. Cities like Karachi, Lahore and Islamabad were westernized parts of Pakistan where a person who grew up in a country- side could only dream of living. The Oldest daughters born of educated middle class families dressed well in pricey Salwar kameez

Few defiant women from Ganish could be found in western parts of Pakistan pursuing higher studies, choosing to live away from strict Muslim families and brothers. Lahore was a popular tourist destination where you might find name brand clothes and merchandise at wholesale warehouse chains where rich foreigners bought food, appliances and clothes in large quantities for a cheaper price. When going to cities like Lahore, I visited busy shopping malls with Zarah to buy a new pair of jeans or a big size kameez top.

Compared to browsing at local bazaars in Ganish, I was enthusiastic about going to Lahore with Asma to malls to look for better quality merchandise. When Asma found a buy in bulk store in Lahore, we filled our shopping card with necessities like toilet paper, dish soap and cosmetics in large quantities. A popular warehouse store where Asma and I browsed around for hours, buying name brand clothes and shoes was the only retail chain selling products in large quantities I came across in Pakistan. After returning to America, my excitement for scoping out a buy in bulk chain in Lahore, seems laughable now

In most communities of Faisalabad, advanced areas of Punjab were off limits to girls by their protective brothers or strict Muslim Fathers. Overbearing male family members informed their impressionable daughters about what living in a modern city, in pursuit of a better-quality education was all about.

Male family members of middle-class girls said that forward thinking women who lived and studied in places like Lahore and Karachi were loose women who slept around and brought shame onto their middle-class families. Females from middle class families who studied at Universities in Lahore and Karachi insulted their culture by leaving home to better their own lives. Karachi and Lahore were materialistic cities where residents experienced less frequent power outages. Streetlights in Lahore rarely died out before me and Ayaan made it home in the dark by motorbike or Rickshaw.

Foreign tourists visiting Pakistan dressed in western clothing, jeans and baggy shirts. College students who lived in girl's hostels, like dorm rooms, were labeled uncultured by some villagers. Female college students pursuing a better education in modernized cities were said to have few good marriage prospects and many boyfriends. Rebellious upper-class girls who lived in Lahore pursuing an education reminded me of movie themes I watched with Sana about village girls who eloped, fleeing arranged marriages to a first cousin at the last minute, marrying a rich foreigner from an upper-class family instead.

Village life was illusive and magical. Lahore was an ever-changing city where independent career women, and the ambitious of Pakistan went in pursuit of education. In Lahore, I came across foreign tourists from Canada, and the UK who taught ESL classes or worked for the US embassy in Islamabad, some native English speakers befriended me, inviting me out places. Ayaan would not allow me to travel alone to Lahore, for safety reasons.

Commuting alone into a city without the protection of a male family member, was forbidden for girls from respectable middle-class families I knew who lived in Ganish or Faisalabad. Like my students from the Trade School in Faisalabad, a few girls from educated middle class families were allowed more freedom and independence to go places solo by rickshaw or public transportation. Some educated women from middle class families drove themselves to school or appointments rather than rely on a paid driver or male family member to escort them around.

Girls from middle class families with a college degree lived a more independent life before marriage, depending on rules middle class families set for their educated daughters. After marriage, wealthy husbands gave their college-educated counterparts more freedom by allowing wives and daughters to go to local coffee shops alone or with school friends. More intelligent wives of affluent husbands were given permission to broaden their social network of friends, post pictures on the internet and social media and study abroad in places like England, Canada or the US. Most groups of disadvantaged women from Ganish, stayed home, cooking for male family members and guests, caring for children. Uneducated middle-class women from Ganish never traveled alone anywhere outside of Faisalabad.

On my last trip to Pakistan with Asma I thought about what it would be like for me as a US citizen to be a middle-class girl who grew up at Nadia's home in the country.

Tuberculosis was a deadly virus common in regions throughout Ganish and provinces of Punjab that lacked resources. Nadia told stories about poor girls from her village of Ganish, destroyed by wealthy landlords. Rich Pakistani men living abroad used and discarded juvenile women who worked for them. Poor village girls employed for middle class families in Ganish slept with wealthy landowners for money. Most rich men never fulfilled their promises of marriage to impoverished women of Ganish who worked on fields or as housekeepers. Poverty-stricken girls were left dreaming of a better life, away from problems they experienced in a rural field of Pakistan.

Nadia told a story about a black girl from her village, only thirteen, who was promised marriage to a wealthy Pakistani entrepreneur living in Saudi Arabia. After sleeping with the girl employed by home, the Saudi man made a joke of her, making it a point to slander the lower caste girl to his family and male friends. Dishonored, that was the word Nadia was thinking of in English. For fun, the Saudi Man dishonored Nadia's house maids publicly. Worse than parading a poor village girl naked through her village community, what rich men did to poor people who worked for them was worse.

I heard horror stories told by Nadia about women from poor castes, tasked with caring for children of middle-class families, who toiled on fields so often that I was no longer fazed by listening to what happened to girls who worked on farmlands near Aaliyaa's property. Teenagers used for their bodies by wealthy men and branded shameless harlots were no longer marriage material. Wealthy men who used teenage girls for their gain, happened in rural communities where education, stores and resources were limited, or unavailable.

The invisible faces of poor agriculture workers who lived on Nadia's property came to mind during each one of my visits to Ganish. Nadia told nightmarish accounts of suicide cases involving prepubescent child brides sold off before their thirteenth birthday to wealthy landlords of middle upper-class families.

On lengthy visits to Nadia's house in the country we stayed up late hours, after our kids fell asleep talking about life at a village. Nadia desperately wanted to move to a city when her husband returned from prison in Faisalabad. Nadia told me about her brother who came home from working in the fields to discover the body of a housekeeper he hired to help with the care of her sons. Nadia's new housekeeper hung herself in the guest bedroom.

Another poor farm worker employed by Nadia's in-laws was married off before turning twelve. The girl's father and big brothers were laborers who raised livestock and toiled on fields in the summers. The family only just made ends meet and agreed to their first-born daughter's arranged marriage when she hit puberty, before her twelfth birthday.

Village life was challenging for most middle-class Punjabi women. Staying too long at Nadia's home in the country made people numb to the realities of any world existing outside, an insulation of poverty and hopelessness. To be a woman from a lower caste family was a death sentence. Looking at me, a picture of a white woman, meant my little sister must have found someone with auburn hair and fair skin in a magazine. Nadia may have formed an opinion about life in the US from a photograph of a western women from a magazine.

Nadia and the rest of the family got together in their best attempts to emulate Christmas in Pakistan. "Happy Christmas," my fourth grade educated sister-in law said, trying her best to force a smile, having practiced her best English.

The smallest of three daughters checked on me when I sat for hours alone when visiting her home, writing stories or painting. Nadia thought she failed in her attempts to keep me occupied and entertained during my visits to Ganish. My little sister always said, "I love you," like a child.

When Nadia asked incessantly if I was comfortable and settled into my life in Pakistan, I answered yes, making sure to lie every time I was sad or missed home.

In the evenings after the kids fell asleep, I sat on a charpai watching the full moon. The moon felt close, like I could reach out and touch it. I sat on the third story balcony, feeling momentarily like I was invincible. Like the brave lion from the kids book I read to Nadia, I felt unreachable, but mighty and far away. Some nights, I felt like I arrived out of nowhere to Nadia's tragic village home.

CHAPTER 27

Friendships, Hired Help
and Electricity Shortages

"You don't have to be afraid. It's a delightful bird, probably a bluebird. Harmless birds won't bother you," Daniyal explained.

When we shared an apartment in Louisiana, Daniyal opened our patio door like it was no big deal, "Watch this," Daniyal said, letting the bluebird sour freely outside. I asked myself how I couldn't have known the truth about the double life Daniyal lived all those years ago. I wanted to be free to start my life over without Daniyal, not knowing if starting again with my two children, Sameer and Asad, was possible.

I pictured Farah hand wringing wet clothes, muttering something in Punjabi, waving her hands at the crows, while quietly laughing to herself. "Shoo, shoo," Farah yelled at the pesky crows, stomping her feet.

"Crows around Ganish only steal your egg sandwiches in the mornings because you are a foreigner, "Nadia said, chuckling under her breath.

"Everything is going to be alright" A mutual friend, Mahnoor reassured, when I watched my son playing soccer on a field of brown grass with other kids his age in Ganish. I was always afraid Sameer would get out of breath when attempting to run too fast. Mahnoor hugged me, reassuring that Pakistan was a welcoming place I could turn to for support and help when I needed.

"Your kids, have a lot of help from family here in Faisalabad. Many people care for you and your children. Sameer and Asad are content."

"It's a good thing that you came to Pakistan," Mahnoor said grinning, shooting me a look of concern.

In the evenings before sunset, I walked with Mahnoor to a local family park. "You should really get out more. Look around, there's fresh air, people and trees," Mahnoor joked.

Many nights on our walks together, a thick layer of fog set in, hiding the walkway in front of us. I could hardly make out road signs, people or which part of the walking path we ended up on.

"Don't worry," Mahnoor said, the smog comes and goes. Sometimes heavy smog in Faisalabad can be blinding but not too worrisome."

"Are you girls still out here this late?" Aaliyaa questioned in Punjabi. Me and Sana were craving junk food.

"This is the block for thieves and robbers, where you find bad people," Aaliyaa scolded.

"Get on, it's too late for you to be out here at this late hour," Ayaan insisted, revving up the engine of his new motorcycle. That evening, I was aware of the dangers nearby. Rabid dogs and deadly lizards waited for me around the next corner. I walked home alone on some nights when it got too dark for me to make out a clear way back to Nadia's home of Ganish.

Brothers were at times overbearing but appeared on nights when it grew dark, and the poorly lit sidewalks left me lost and searching for home.

On our way home, to Ganish, the remaining streetlights went out. Halfway back to the house in Faisalabad me and Mahnoor were sure we could hear a pack of barking dogs, moving closer. Mahnoor began sprinting home, jumping the fence and climbing over a locked gate of our house. My friend ran directionless in the dark from a pack of rabid dogs we thought were chasing us. We spotted Mahnoor's sister, Asma's neighborhood in Faisalabad. Asma's house was not far, within walking distance.

Mahnoor fell into the upper- middle class income bracket of Pakistani society. She was spoiled and lived comfortably in a three – story bungalow with two housekeepers she hired from her village. I was surprised to learn that Mahnoor had no desire to travel or live abroad in the US or Canada like most upper middle-class families I met in Faisalabad.

Mahnoor told me that she recently changed her major from physician to fashion designer. "My heart wasn't in it anymore," she remarked. My friend's family was outraged at the money wasted on their daughter's plan to become a doctor. Mahnoor was a brilliant student and according to her older sibling, Asma, Mahnoor was wasting her talent on chasing far-fetched ideas of making clothes. Ayaan told me that working as a clothes maker was not considered a respectable profession for a woman from a middle-class family in Faisalabad.

I sat with Mahnoor during my visits to her house in Faisalabad, skimming through fashion magazines of the latest trends and runway models. Mahnoor had ambitions of making a name for herself in Pakistan as a recognized and high paid stylist and clothes maker. My friend lived in a girl's hostel, like a college dorm room and was home on break. Asma's big sister pointed out the shalwar kameez she designed herself, excitedly showing me sketch books she filled up. Mahnoor drew outlines of college students and friends at the university she attended, where she drew pictures of her friends in different styles of clothing. She knew the names of well-known female fashion designers in Pakistan by heart.

My friend pulled up pictures and articles of foreign models and designers on-line. One article was about upper class, Pakistani designers living alone, choosing to stay in Lahore and empower women. Female entrepreneurs of Pakistani descent were shown sipping exotic drinks and reclining next to swimming pools. A maid or village worker catered to their needs. Mahnoor was a dreamer and encouraged me to write or blog about my time living in a village of Ganish.

Mahnoor's father scolded his third born daughter, reminding her that she was never going to make an honest salary designing clothes, a factory workers job. My friend said that her dad never encouraged her dreams. Mahnoor struggled to get her father to fulfill what she called his cultural responsibility of financing her college education. Like Mahnoor's little sister Asma, if all else failed, Mahnoor could always marry a wealthy man and receive monthly allowances to Faisalabad while waiting on a visa. Asma chose a wealthy Pakistani from an elite dating website, listing his requirements for seeking a new bride, in an ad that sought out pretty brides from respectable middle-class families from different areas of Pakistan. Mahnoor had long black hair that cascaded over her shoulders and a pudgy face. Dimples appeared on each corner of her mouth when she smiled.

Asma was visiting Pakistan on a visa. She was engaged to a wealthy Pakistani residing in Luton, England. Mahnoor's big sister wanted to give me some of her nighties she never wore. Mahnoor shyly pulled me away, changing the subject, insisting we go someplace for dinner. We shared in our hobby of reading novels.

From my time teaching English at the government school, I learned most girls from poor or middle-class families around Faisalabad could only think of settling in America, England or Germany. When I asked Mahnoor why she never thought of leaving her city of Faisalabad, her response struck me as out of the ordinary. "When you have everything here you need, why go anywhere else?"

During summers, I slept with Sameer and Asad under the only working air conditioner, in one room when we stayed during humid months at Mahnoor's home in Faisalabad. I was struggling to cope with the load shedding problem in Pakistan. Loss of water and electricity happened more commonly in hot seasons. When I experienced frequent power outages at my in laws house in Faisalabad, I stayed for weeks at a time at Mahnoor's home in Faisalabad with my two kids, Sameer and Asad. I stayed up late with Mahnoor and Asma watching her favorite sitcoms. When at home, Mahnoor wore pajamas and baggy t-shirts. Asma and Mahnoor wore jeans and large shirts, complemented with a light scarf when going out some place.

Only college students and upper-middle class girls from Faisalabad dressed in jeans, and kameez tops. Women from Ganish and Faisalabad wore a full- length burka or shalwar kameez with their hair covered in a veil, when going someplace. Mahnoor seldom wore a debutta or head scarf except at traditional weddings or on special occasions. "When you traveled to Pakistan as a foreigner, I changed my opinion of American women," Mahnoor claimed.

"What exactly do you mean by American? "I asked sarcastically, wondering if Mahnoor knew that she changed my idea of middle-class college students living in Faisalabad. "You were different than I imagined, quiet and sincere," I guess. Don't take this the wrong way, I thought most American women drank alcohol, hung out in bars and slept around. You are more Pakistani than I thought," Mahnoor complemented, smiling

Mahnoor snatched two wedding invitations addressed to her. Mahnoor's name was written in cursive lettering on the front of a white envelope, sitting on her coffee table. When my friend opened the decorative envelope, she was suddenly triggered. "These shameless families, I don't know why they keep sending me invitations to their wedding!"

Asma's sister was a popular guest at weddings and considered a favorite among elites and her upper-class friend groups and relatives. "You don't know the first thing about middle class families in Faisalabad," Mahnoor exclaimed, tossing two wedding invitations in the garbage. The fights and drama that take place behind closed doors between women from good castes, you don't know the half of it."

"Sister in laws do their best to create friction between female relatives, stemming from jealousy and rivalry. Women who thrive off conflict, start fights over inheritance and family money. Envious siblings can't stand losing control over a newly married or engaged brother who is more like a boyfriend or father- figure. Females that make up large extended family members will go to any lengths to ruin a new daughter- in laws reputation. You have no idea the backstabbing, rumors and sibling rivalry that happen between women from Ganish. This family Asma is close to from Ganish aren't good people, I know them well. I hope they don't send anymore wedding invitations because I won't go." Mahnoor explained.

Newly married brides from Ganish who gave up careers to cook for masses of guests and relatives, was another Pakistani custom Mahnoor didn't accept. Mahnoor made my favorite meal, biryani, when I stayed for long periods at her house in Faisalabad. During breaks from the school she attended, my friend followed new cooking recipes online. Mahnoor made instant coffee and blended drinks at home for us when we sat talking, watching television programs together in Urdu. Mahnoor shared her personal experiences about dating and college life at a college she attended in Lahore. Asma's sister revealed problems she experienced related to a strained relationship with her dad. Mahnoor explained sorrowfully that her father never accepted her career or life choices.

My closest friend in Pakistan, Mahnoor was an expert at making the gourmet restaurant version of almost any recipe. Sameer's favorite snack was a breaded chicken sandwich, Mahnoor made, found at popular fast-food chains around Faisalabad, that tasted better homemade. Mahnoor and I frequented local coffee shops where I saw one of my students from the Trade school dining with her boyfriend, hoping I didn't recognize her.

When I first arrived to Faisalabad as a foreign guest, Farah introduced me to a long-time acquaintance, Asma. Farah said Asma reminded her of a poised flight attendant. Asma was a frequent guest at my in laws home. She was always polite and dressed well in new kameez shirts Mahnoor made. Asma was learning to speak and write in German in her spare time, taking costly English classes in Lahore. Mahnoor told me that Asma's English teacher was a foreigner from London who used sarcasm as a method for teaching English classes. Like Nadia who told humorous stories about a childhood she spent with Daniyal in Ganish, Asma told intriguing stories about her life in England.

Asma finished her burger and fries, practicing speaking in nontraditional German with us through a series of witty stories and mishaps. Asma spoke in German about cultural differences she experienced as a foreigner while living abroad in Luton, England. When Aaliyaa half-jokingly suggested Asma apply for a job as a flight attendant, Asma responded by saying sarcastically,

"I would like to work a high-paying job that is not too stressful." Asma and Mahnoor were close siblings who shared a family residency in Faisalabad. Mahnoor traveled back and forth to a university she attended during the week and was home from school on a break. Mahnoor liked to dress me in trendy salwar kameez they copied from fashion magazines, material Mahnoor hand sewed from a fabric shop nearby. Every time Mahnoor took my measurements, she treated me like one of her models, "you gained weight again," Mahnoor said. When I stayed for long periods at Asma's house in Faisalabad, she made a new outfit for me.

Country Roads in rural areas of Pakistan were unsafe, poorly maintained and unregulated. Locals from Ganish chose to travel by motorbike or haul a rickshaw as a way of getting around. Wealthy landlords from Ganish and Faisalabad hired personal drivers. I rarely came across a woman in rural parts of Faisalabad who drove themselves places or who owned vehicles. In the morning, Mahnoor boiled a pot of tea for us. We watched re-runs of popular sitcoms. Reality stars depicted in the popular television drama were actors playing stereotypical roles. Even popular actors playing male and female housemates living together was looked down on by Muslim families in Faisalabad. The Stigma of college students sharing living space with men, was shunned by most conservative middle-class families. Mahnoor was unbiased and open minded in her opinions of American women saying things like; "I don't understand why Islamic girls can't wear what they want. Mahnoor remarked about outdated traditions.

"What's wrong with pursuing a career after marriage? There is nothing the matter with waiting until after marriage and being a successful, career woman." We talked about arranged marriages and progress in Pakistan toward women's rights and self- expression.

"The family park is down the road from my house, I walk there every evening with my little sister, Asma." Mahnoor told me. Families congregated in groups walking together at recreational parks in Pakistan where children played badminton and soccer in lush fields, by a walking trail I went to with Asma and Mahnoor every night. The family park near Mahnoor's house was cleaner and bigger than recreational facilities near my in laws house. I found newly built swing sets, slides and tunnels at a playground where my kids could run. A group of men and children played soccer on green fields. Mahnoor chuckled to herself when I pointed out gay couples cozied up next to each other, making out. Most gay couples went to family parks in rebellion, hiding from controlling, Muslim families.

My friend Mahnoor pulled me off to the side blushing through her embarrassment saying things like;

"Why do you look surprised? My brother hides his girlfriends; we never know where he is meeting in secret."

"These birds are not dangerous."

Arranged marriages were still common in villages. There was no concept of open affection but fear of traditional religious Islamic families finding out and a need to escape to places like family parks where dating couples could openly express affection. Mahnoor was right, Pakistan could be a welcoming place. The crows weren't as frightening as the layer of smog blinding us. The path laid out in front of me was blurry.

CHAPTER 28

Rohan

The new housekeeper Aaliyaa hired was a teenager from Ganish. I brought our new housekeeper, Rohan, along with me almost everywhere I traveled around Faisalabad and Ganish. We took frequent walks to a local convenience store less than a mile from our city of Faisalabad. Rohan bonded with me right away and was a close friend of Sameer's. During my stay in Faisalabad, Rohan stayed up nights before my flight landed, anxiously pacing back and forth. When I arrived at my in laws home in Ganish, Rohan was insistent that he sit next to me and practice speaking with me using new English words and phrases he learned while I was away. I made sure to buy Rohan's favorite flavor ice-cream and snacks, ensuring he finished his treats instead of letting the chocolate candy bar melt in his bag on the walk home. When our new housekeeper Rohan wasn't working as a helper at Ganish, he sold snacks at a food booth, calling cards and chocolates on the corner as a vendor.

Inaya set aside leftovers from dinner, separating flour for making bread into different plastic containers. Inaya made fresh bread and food for house maids that worked for our family in Ganish to take home. Inaya believed that allowing the hired help to use shared utensils or drink from communal glasses or cups was bad hygiene. Despite beliefs that kids from Ganish lacked manners or good hygiene practices, Inaya was considered generous when it came to feeding and clothing the hired help employed to work for our family.

Bilal, a worker hired by Malak demanded a higher wage, swearing my in laws

were wealthy based on antiques taken from our house in Ganish. Farah bought a
new furniture set for guests who would stay at our home after their wedding reception. Because there was little guidance and structure at home, poor village kids
watched television all afternoon refusing to go to school or learn.

Rohan shied away from accepting anything additional my in laws did for him.
I wanted Rohan to know he was cared about and considered a part of the family.
Like most poor children, Rohan struggled for food, clothing and basic needs. The
teenage maid lived in a mud house cramped with family members. Instead of going
to school, Rohan spent afternoons working for our family doing hard labor jobs at
Ganish, milking cattle and selling rice and wheat to market. The teenager worked
as a vendor outside our home where I passed by him during outings to shops and
bazaars. Rohan cooked meals for the family and guests in Faisalabad. The new
housekeeper played with our children and helped Aaliyaa with the family's laundry.

Rohan was twelve years old but still couldn't read or write. The teenager was
Sameer's best friend and around the same age. Rohan had no interest in studying or enrolling in school. Child labor was largely ignored by people in Ganish
and Faisalabad. Middle class families who hired housekeepers viewed cheap labor as a way of helping poor families financially. In some provinces of Punjab,
some middle-class families abused village kids. Other middle-class families from
Faisalabad and Ganish cared for impoverished kids like their own family. Rohan
was a reserved adolescent. On hot summer afternoons Rohan and other kids of our
village danced in rain showers; laughing and splashing in puddles.

Rohan followed close behind me nearly every place I went, looking out for me,
respectful and eager to help around the house. When I left Pakistan for Louisiana
this last visit, Nadia said Sameer's best friend stayed up several nights in a row,
restless, waiting impatiently for my arrival to Ganish. Rohan asked that he sit next
to me and be the first person to welcome me to his homeland of Pakistan.

I used to collect random things I bought at a convenience store with Rohan like
children's books, nail polish and toys for new hires who came from Ganish to work
for my in laws. Last time Rohan's mother came for a visit from Ganish, she welcomed
a newborn son, the eleventh of ten children she gave birth to in total. High -priced
merchandise like shampoo, infant clothes and Rohan's favorite snacks, I bought
from a local convenience store, storing things away for poor kids who came to live
with us.

We passed an old man with bone thin hands, a food vendor selling juice and fruit. On hot summer days the same vendor stood on the next block, like he was waiting for a modern woman from America to purchase a glass of orange juice from him. The food vendor appeared the same way every time I bought something from his pushcart, like no time passed. The familiar vendor waited for me at the same time every afternoon, sure not to overcharge me. I paid him double in the equivalency of rupees, equal to fifty cents in US currency for a glass of juice.

Ayaan showed up unannounced when it grew dark, speeding by on his motor-cycle, with his mom hitched, on the back. I remembered Daniyal's story about being bitten by a rabid dog at Ganish while walking home alone, late at night.

Aaliyaa's stern tone of voice vibrated through the walls, when she shrieked from downstairs. Aaliyaa's Punjabi slang ran together. Aaliyaa knew how to frighten any-one into telling the truth. I never told poor farm workers or hired help from Ganish about financial struggles I experienced in the United States with Sameer and Asad. Most poor kids looked at upper middle-class families in Faisalabad as privileged. Children born of upper middle-class families usually went to private schools and wore new clothes. Kids born of middle-class families were fortunate enough to have plenty of food, extra money to spend on activities outside of school and more than enough family support.

"The maid who worked for me at the time ripped off all my expensive wedding jewelry, never returning to the job. I never thought to ask for my mom's jewelry back. In Pakistan, everyone gossips. Bushra stole an expensive piece of wedding jewelry my deceased Mother gifted me, a family heirloom that was invaluable to me."

"The following week, a relative had a large amount of cash, clothing and jewelry taken." Aaliyaa explained

"We don't say anything when things turn- up missing. In Pakistani culture everyone gossips. The housekeepers make- up stories about how we abuse them or don't pay them fairly. Bushra would run to Aaliyaa claiming she was being mis-treated. In the Pakistani community, speaking out about missing clothing, jewelry, or wedding make up makes you look petty or unkind." Nadia explained.

When I lived in Louisiana with Daniyal, I rarely had extra cash on hand for Sameer and Asad's basic needs. During our worst financial hardships, I returned home to Louisiana with Sameer and Asad with grocery bags of food, I needed for Sameer and Asad taken from my parents' refrigerator. No one knew that I stole medicine or school supplies for Sameer, rarely buying new clothes or nonessential things I wanted for myself. Years ago, I had no knowledge about property disputes between family members of different tribes in Ganish. I didn't understand why I never had money to spend on my children's needs. We seemed to be only getting by- hand to mouth, living paycheck to paycheck in Louisiana. Daniyal was in debt, borrowing money from friends and relatives to fund lawyers over a case involving stolen property.

Sameer's carefree laughter made me temporarily forget the financial setbacks we faced in Louisiana. Sameer's favorite toys were remote cars and small metal cars, he played with on the floor of our living room, imitating sounds of airplanes and trains. A room full of relatives and guests stepped over him. I purchased a stash of metal cars and trucks poor kids sold at local bazaars and sanitized the used merchandise at home. Toy cars, and airplanes were among a pile of stuff I collected at bazaars for a cheap price. Comfortable shalwar kameez I wore at home that fit like pajamas was among the pile of stuff I found bargain priced at bazaars and stored away. Sameer's cousins were around the same age and came over to our house in Faisalabad in the afternoons for play dates. I was comforted knowing I had family support and friends. I would be able to put the financial setbacks I experienced with Daniyal behind me for now.

"This happens with housekeepers a lot in Pakistan with maids from our community who are hired to work in our home, it's very common."

"Housekeepers commonly steal food, cosmetics, and even clothing. Juvenile housekeepers hired to work here take expensive bras and panties. Housekeepers from Ganish struggle for food. We let it go and chose not to say anything or ask for the stolen things to be returned. I still think of asking for my mom's wedding jewelry back. Inaya says I should stay silent on the matter." Nadia explained.

I never saw our new housekeeper, Yasmin or her teenage daughter again after the first day we met. The day before Yasmin left the job employed as a maid in our home, I was sure to thank- Yasmin for giving me a massage and making tea and lunch. I was sure not to mention to the new helper about the stolen foundation and lipstick I brought from America, which happened to be my favorite.

CHAPTER 29

Naima, The Artist

I recognized the exact glittery, large sized, kameez blouse Naima was wearing. Naima must have purchased the same top at a high- end store where Aaliyaa and Farah shopped. Watching black suitcases that all looked like mine rotate in a circle until I was lightheaded, I waited at the baggage terminal for what felt like an eternity. Inside the airport lobby, the air was dry, too humid for me to stay inside. Before Ayaan's college friend, Naima showed up out of nowhere, I was sitting outside on a bench for hours. I must have broken down and started sobbing again from sheer exhaustion and fear of being stranded.

I wandered around the airport in Lahore, seeing Daniyal in every brown skinned foreigner who looked like a cluster of one person, perspiring, searching for luggage and shouting in Urdu. I made my way through a crowd of people. As more time passed, there was still no sign of Ayaan. I became more infuriated for the reasons my brother- in law would come up with to explain why he forgot to pick me up from the airport on time.

"How long have you been sitting alone crying?" The artist asked in a way that meant she was genuinely concerned about me. Naima sat next to me on the bench. "Hardly anyone is here tonight."

"Have you eaten anything?

I recognized, Ayaan's friend, Naima right away. Naima was a familiar face in a crowd of Ayaan's school friends who welcomed me to Pakistan on my first couple of visits to Ganish. Naima showed up with a plate of sweet rice cooked by her mother and a genuine smile. A small statured Punjabi woman who stood a little over five feet tall, introduced herself to me in Urdu. Ayaan's friend was dressed down in a pair of jeans.

I thought back to the same unaffordable shirt Naima wore hanging on a rack, too expensive for me to buy in rupees. Naima must have shopped at name brand department stores where Nadia went to rip-off expensive clothing designs, she sewed by hand for family members. Naima looked like she was in her early twenties. Ayaan's college friend made her way toward me. I noticed a sketch pad she carried at her side. This was Ayaan's way of apologizing.

To a person who must have seen pictures of me fixed up and wearing new shalwar kameez at nice dining establishments and cafes I went to with relatives, I realized how pale and undesirable i looked. Catching a glimpse of myself in the mirror, I stopped strolling around a humid airport in Pakistan to use the restroom, a squat toilet My face was red and puffy from crying, mascara and eyeliner were smeared under my eyes.

"First impressions are the last impression," Nadia used to say. I loathed how Nadia cared about what people who she considered rich or important upper class-families thought of us. I wasn't expecting a stranger to show up. I used concealer in my bag, I bought at the airport to conceal puffy circles before pulling myself together and greeting Naima in Urdu, apologizing for my public display of emotion, hoping Naima wouldn't judge me for my disheveled appearance. Nadia reminded before going to a medical appointment or when eating out somewhere with family, to put on a new pair of shalwar kameez and a natural shade of foundation and lipstick.

Nadia always emphasized how she hated to give off the wrong first impression. The shalwar kameez I borrowed from a neighbor in Louisiana was stained. I didn't bother changing clothes before meeting Ayaan at the airport, who saw me without make up, looking less than pleasing on some mornings.

I was uneasy about speaking to my brother-in-law's friend, Naima or accepting an apology from Ayaan when he was ready. I tried to steady each of my breaths and stop bawling, ashamed to be seen so vulnerable in a public place like the airport lobby. I felt fragile and childlike, plagued with a sense of panic and indirection, a learned sense of helplessness that I used to experience during my marriage to Daniyal.

"How long have you been waiting out here, sitting alone? All other flight departures and arrivals have gone home."

"To tell you the truth Kasra, brother-in-law was afraid to meet you in person. Ayaan was worried you might be upset with him for forgetting your flight arrival time, so he sent me instead. The airport in Lahore is busier than usual during evening flight arrival times, especially at this hour of night. "You need to lie down and shut your eyes for a while."

"Here, let me help you with your luggage," Naima offered, peering around apprehensively, pushing my luggage cart with all the strength she could muster in her frail body. I thought about how amusing a petite woman in glasses looked pushing a luggage cart stacked with heavy suitcases.

Naima told me that after years of living away from her birth country, she spent her first weeks in Pakistan dining out at her favorite restaurants with friends while visiting relatives and shopping malls in Lahore again. Ayaan's university friend shared with me that she was beginning to feel like a tourist in her favorite city of Lahore. Before driving to the airport to pick me up, Naima walked around the city, sight-seeing, wasting away entire afternoons window shopping.

"At least we found you, so we're a little late," Naima said unbothered, reaching over to hug me. There must have been some kind of delay or mix- up with your flight arrival time." I hope you haven't been waiting out here in this dreadful heat for long." The artist explained

"You must have been scared sitting out here late at night by yourself as someone from a foreign country."

"'I hear you write beautiful poetry."

"Ayaan cares about you. I'm sure your in-laws forgot about your arrival and departure times. Cheer up! We are going to have such a good time, I promise. You are considered a part of the family."

For more than three hours, I walked around the airport terminal in Pakistan, thinking about my first time traveling to Faisalabad. My in- laws arrived a couple hours early, searching for me in every person. Sana waited to greet me with a bouquet of flowers.

Lost in a crowd of brown skinned Pakistani's, dressed in colorless salwar kameez. I was virtually invisible, A group of relatives and children waited around the corner for me, eager to fill me in on everything I missed since I traveled back to my home state of Louisiana. After traveling back to the United States, and every trip thereafter, I understood that I became less important. Uneducated Women from Ganish were easily discarded. There was no telling what sin I committed. Farah reminded me of new ways that I insulted Islam. Relatives from Faisalabad gossiped about Daniyal's arranged marriage to a first cousin. Farah spoke in Urdu about her disapproval of love marriages.

"I have been waiting at this airport for a long time, thinking about different areas of Pakistan, regions far from Lahore that tell stories of unrequited love and family betrayal. When you rest up from your journey, I will take you with me to visit each place. I hope you don't mind Kasra, I thought I would observe you for a while so I could eventually make a portrait. It's not every day that an American girl comes to Pakistan in search of something."

"Look around at the littered sidewalks, Is this anything like your America?"

"I want to make a portrait of you, Kasra. I know all the colors I'm going to use, vibrant reds and pale grays to capture tonight's sky and gloomy setting. "My new painting will be called, "traveling to Pakistan, lost at a crowded airport in Lahore. Stop crying so loudly. People are staring at us." Naima smiled through her discomfort, in her best attempt to cheer me up.

I left countless frenzied voice messages with my in-laws from Ganish, calling erratically and leaving indignant voicemails for Daniyal back in Louisiana. I had to borrow a foreigner's phone to call the United States because I had no international plan or phone service that worked when I first arrived in Pakistan. A foreign woman, Sofia approached me when she heard me bawling claiming she worked as an English teacher in Islamabad. The teacher, Sofia, gave me her number and offered me a place to stay in Islamabad if needed. After the third hour, I was fearful that no one would show up.

"Where's brother- in law?" I asked Naima angerily. My fear turned to rage. I finally calmed down. I couldn't prevent the unpleasant emotions from coming to the surface, mixed in with sheer fatigue.

"Do you think we forgot you, Kasra? You must be tired from your flight. You're not thinking clearly. You need rest. Sana spent nearly the entire night decorating your room, buying new shalwar kameez from local bazaars and waiting to celebrate your arrival."

"You look like a little girl when you wear salwar kameez, especially since you lost so much weight. That's what my brother-in-law says about you. He's right."

"One of these days I promise to take you along with me to show you my art gallery. I sell my paintings in major Cities like Karachi, Lahore and Islamabad. Lahore is my favorite city in Pakistan to visit. I make a high- income selling my paintings. I travel around, selling and promoting artwork. You could say I'm like that chai wallah Uncle or vendor you buy your favorite junk food from. I observe compelling people and places around Pakistan asking locals to buy my paintings for a fair price."

"I know what you must be thinking Kasra, I don't have any brothers or a father to look after my safety and well-being. A girl, traveling alone in big Cities, that couldn't mean anything positive for a Punjabi woman from a good caste."

I wanted to tell my brothers friend how fortunate she was to be given freedoms as a woman from Pakistan. I stayed silent, fuming about my in-laws who didn't bother to pick me up from the airport on time. Naima married into an upper-class Pakistani family and lived abroad, visiting Pakistan for a few weeks. My in- laws cautioned me about commuting alone, especially by public transportation to local places around Faisalabad.

Naima was like a few other Pakistani people who wanted to look at a foreigner from Louisiana who didn't blend in with a group of Pakistani's who looked, thought and dressed similarly. The artist, Naima was like the rest of my relatives and friends who drew their own conclusions about why I traveled to their homeland.

For an artist selling paintings, I was someone unique to look at among a crowd of people who talked with the same Punjabi accent. The background noise of the once crowded airport died down. Naima and I were practically the only ones left at baggage claim at an airport in Lahore.

Brother- in laws friend, Naima offered a second time to show me an enjoyable visit in Pakistan by saying things like, "after you rest from your flight, I will invite you to my house and show you all my paintings. I live a couple miles from the airport."

I knew enough about upper middle-class girls in Faisalabad to conclude that wealthy women from modernized cities hired maids, or poor farm workers from rural areas to do almost everything for them. Most hired help who worked for well-off Pakistani women cooked food, drove their employers around, looked after children and purchased groceries. Naima's personal driver was probably waiting to pick me up around the block.

By the time we stacked four heavy suitcases onto a luggage cart and made our way to the parking garage, a long walk from the terminal where my brother's friend picked me up, it was already late. I wanted to sit on a bench outside the airport in Pakistan a little while longer, ruminating over the reasons my relatives would have to explain why no one showed up to the airport. I wanted to return to Louisiana momentarily. Things had gotten bad at home with Daniyal.

Naima was a stranger disguised as a charismatic friend who arrived at an airport in Pakistan. Ayaan' college friend was right, there was probably nothing to worry about. There were most likely decorations, streamers and balloons blown up, taped to walls along with appetizers from a local pastry bakery ready for me when I returned to Faisalabad. Sana must have gone out of her way to throw a surprise welcoming party for me like she did to celebrate Sameer and Asad's birthdays. I laughed to myself when I thought about a kid's party being thrown for me. Aaliyaa was probably cooking food and insisting like each time I traveled back to Ganish, that she didn't need any gifts from America. Aaliyaa only wanted to sit together and talk.

Naima was an independent girl from a city who traveled freely unlike most middle-class girls I met in Pakistan.

I was introduced to a foreign teacher, Sofia, who offered to let me use her cell phone. I needed an international calling card. When Sofia let me borrow her cellphone, I immediately called my brother-in-law, Ayaan, redialing his number a couple more times. When no one answered, l left ranting messages, cursing my brother-in-law through soft whimpers.

How could Ayyan have left me stranded at the airport? Anything could have happened.

My negative emotions seemed justified. Ayaan did this on purpose. I was exhausted and jetlagged from withstanding a sixteen-hour flight. I wasn't thinking clearly. Those were my darkest thoughts, but I don't remember verbatim what I said after to Ayaan that followed a series of unpleasant voicemails, I left on Ayaan's machine bawling and shouting. Expressing any kind of negative emotion or anger was frowned upon for a Muslim woman living in Ganish. Immediately, I felt guilty and remorseful.

When I thought back to all the considerate things Ayaan did for me and my children during my stay in Faisalabad I calmed down momentarily. Calling again and leaving another resentful message didn't make sense. I needed sleep.

Brother-in-law was afraid to face me in person. Ayaan decided to send his artist friend to the airport in Pakistan beforehand, knowing me well enough to realize I would be too upset with bother speaking to him for a long time. I wanted to believe the real reason no one showed up at the airport on time was that there was a mix up with my flight arrival time, a family emergency, or that relatives overslept. The truth I didn't want to say out loud was that I was no longer a valued member of the extended family. I was wrong to jump to conclusions. My brother-in-law likely couldn't stand to see me hurt or disappointed. Ayaan decided to send his artist friend, Naima to meet me first before throwing a welcoming party for me.

Sitting in the backseat of a small car around the corner, I discovered my brother-in law, Ayaan. I hardly recognized him at first. The streetlights near our neighborhood of Faisalabad usually blinked out before I could get a clear picture of our house, around the next block. My feet were grimy from dirt, and debris from polluted roads. Brother-in-law slid down in the back seat of the car. Ayaan was too ashamed to face me. I didn't say anything.

We drove the rest of the way home, about an hour into our home city of Faisalabad in silence. Brother-in-law didn't dare say anything on the entire way to Faisalabad.

"My friend from Pakistan wants to make a painting of you," Ayaan finally said. I spotted our familiar bugaloo style home in the distance. The neighborhood of Faisalabad was peaceful as I remember. A guard ran outside to open the gate. "We should go to an art gallery together, brother-in-law suggested. "My friend Naima from Pakistan invited me too. There's a nice restaurant where they serve the best fried fish in all of Faisalabad. When you rest, we will eat your favorite street food too, I promise," my brother-in-law said grinning.

"What did you think of my friend, Naima?"

I was too hurt to say anything. Being back in our City of Faisalabad was like visiting Pakistan all over again. Ayaan opened the car door, showing me my in laws house while reassuring me that Pakistan was a country that I could always call home. I felt like Pakistan was coming home.

"Be careful when you go inside because it is very late, and everyone is sleeping. We can talk in the morning," Brother-in-Law said.

I wasn't sure if I would be ready tomorrow morning to ask my Brother-in-law about forgetting to pick me up from the airport. Ayaan was smart to send his artist friend to meet me at the airport in Pakistan first. Brother- in law was right, I settled down the next morning, got up early for breakfast and sat out on the terrace. "We're finally here," my brother – in law announced, yawning.

I waited for Ayaan so I could thank him for the invitation but politely turn down his offer to go to the art show and a fancy eating place together. "I would like to go to an art show," I answered instead. I knew the exact dining establishment my brother-in-law was talking about where they made the best fried fish. Along with recognizable outdoor shops and bazaars around, I couldn't wait to visit the seafood restaurants. The following morning, brother-in-law said we would visit every tragic area of Pakistan that told a captivating story about family betrayal and heartbreak. Once my anger directed at him died down, I decided I would join Ayaan. I didn't want to think the worst of my brother or well-intentioned relatives any longer.

"Are you still annoyed that I showed up late to pick you up at the airport?" My brother-in-law asked, bringing me a cup of tea Aaliyaa made.

"I'm not angry anymore," I said sipping from the cup of tea, waiting for his mother to ask me about new shoes I brought from America.

CHAPTER 30

Political Riots: Christianity and Islam

Through the smoke-like fog, I saw an outline of my sister- in law, the image of her was like looking in a dirty window. I understood words she mouthed in her mother tongue of Punjabi. Zarah was motioning for me to leave the diner. I was beginning to enjoy my time living in rural parts of Punjab and could foresee a future for myself, Sameer and Asad. I rarely thought about Daniyal. Before my last trip to Pakistan, I was comfortable and gradually settling into my life in Faisalabad. In mountain regions of Pakistan, smog is visible because it gets trapped in valleys and can't be carried away by wind.

We were in smog season. It was mid-January. A cloud of fog blurred the path in front of me. My future living in Pakistan came to a standstill. Before the day when Zarah showed up at the store in a panic, my future living in Pakistan seemed promising. Rohan, sat beside me on a plastic chair outside his favorite cafe. In the afternoons, we enjoyed walks to the cafe across the freeway. I ordered the same thing every time we dined together, a chocolate shake and fries.

Rohan glanced at the menu before tossing it on the table, looking around un-easy, like he was afraid someone may catch him doing something wrong. Rohan ordered his favorite that afternoon, an ice- cream sundae, fries and a soda. When I ate out with Rohan, I made sure he consumed the entire meal at the eating place before heading home. Housekeepers from Ganish employed by middle class families shared in the habit of hoarding food. Rohan packed away meals in his pockets or bag, until fast food from restaurants got soggy.

For a long time after the deadly protests broke out on the roads of Lahore, I had recurring dreams about losing limbs and other severed body parts. In the middle of the night at random hours, I awoke, taunted by life-like images of myself, bandaged up. My face and arm were wrapped in gauze. In a series of recurring nightmares, I saw myself in a hospital bed, with half a face or arm missing. My children awoke some nights from a series of night terrors. Sleep paralysis was a medical term comparable to wrong English words Sameer used. Inaya had no need for such medical terms. Like the definition of postpartum depression, recurring nightmares and disturbing visions I had during tough times I faced while living in Faisalabad, were defined as Pagal by my mother-in-law. When I was according to Aaliyaa acting strangely, Inaya told other family members I was delirious or simply unwell. I never watched international news channels.

Zarah said the riots were about inequalities experienced by indigenous people from lower castes. Bloodshed spilled over onto the pavement. I saw visions of men carrying weapons of swords and daggers, chopping off arms, and hands of men from different tribes or religious parties. A war that took place over freedom of religious expression was happening miles from where I stayed in Lahore, Pakistan, like a bloody battle from the Victorian Era. I rarely thought about Daniyal anymore as a part of our present or future existence. I chose to live here.

In surreal visions, I stepped over dead bodies, searching for Aaliyaa's brother, Daniyal. I could still hear the screams of men. Sometimes I imagine what took place that day on the roads of Lahore only a few miles from where I sought shelter with Sameer and Asad at a relative's home for five days. No one in the family thought to tell me that a deadly battle on a nearby boulevard of Lahore was happening. Family members never told the truth about a bloody war fought between relatives over property. When things settled down with Abdullah, I assumed an ongoing disagreement over property came down to a family feud. I decided that I never wanted to see Daniyal again. Pakistan was no longer a country I called home.

Once my favorite city in Pakistan, Lahore was no longer considered safe. A country I went to write about unrequited love, didn't exist. No one bothered asking when I would be returning to Ganish this time around. I missed you.

Some poor kids worked odd jobs at a food booth selling produce, employed by upper middle- class families to help with the care of multiple children. Rohan pitched in with household chores. Sometimes I caught Rohan glaring at me, like he was in a trance. Rohan must have never seen a contemporary person who looked nothing like him. On my last day in Pakistan a homeless man, hired to buy weekly produce from bazaars and help Aaliyaa cook large meals for guests, smiled at me. Bilal looked at me as though he was saying goodbye. I finished packing the last of my belongings to catch a flight to Louisiana. On humid afternoons, Rohan traveled by Rickshaw to packed bazaars with a man Malak hired from our village, bargaining with vendors. Rohan's afternoons were spent cleaning up after family members, washing dishes and helping to cook meals for large groups of relatives.

The real reason Zarah asked me to leave Pakistan for good wasn't because of political protests that broke out on the roads of Lahore one random afternoon. It was something else. When I counted down to my flight departure time, my heart sank when I noticed the stark contrast in family members' displays of affection for me. On my last trip to Ganish before heading back to Louisiana, Aaliyaa once offered prayers for a safe journey and heartfelt goodbyes, inquiring about when I would visit Ganish again. On her way to meet me at the airport. Aaliyaa used to make it a point to purchase a garland of flowers for my hair from a food seller before I left for the airport. Aaliyaa didn't offer prayers of protection for me in Urdu this time, waving from the third story terrace, as a final goodbye. I felt like I did something unforgivable.

"You're almost done, hurry up Rohan, Zarah keeps calling."

"No big deal," I thought Zarah was calling and texting all the time because the three of us were caught in the haze of smog that consumed me, making it impossible to see clearly. The surrounding village roads and boulevards were crowded and treacherous. My student showed up unannounced that morning insisting we go to a cafe close to our home, in the city. I remember feeling that I had a clear plan for my life while living in Faisalabad with Sameer and Asad. Before the day at the eating place with Rohan when the fog came upon us, my future while living in Pakistan looked promising.

After resigning from the government school. I wanted to apply to better jobs in Karachi, if I decided to stay in Pakistan. My children were well adjusted and liked going to a private school a few miles from home. Sameer's health was improving. Depending on the change of season, blinding smog came and went. When I walked closer to Zarah, I could sense something was off. Through the thick haze, I waved to my friends from the government school. I didn't realize that on a random Saturday afternoon that would be the last time I would see my friends for a while.

Following an argument with coworkers while harvesting berries, Aasiya Noreen, a Christian woman, was accused of blasphemy or insulting Islam. In November of 2010, a judge sentenced Noreen to death by hanging. The case made it to the high court in Pakistan until various petitions for her release were created. Noreen was eventually acquitted in October of 2018 by the supreme court citing material contradictions and inconsistent statements of the witnesses," which cast a shadow of doubt on the prosecution's version of facts. Christian human rights groups praised the Court's decision. The blasphemy case of Asia Bibi sparked outrage and violence in the Islamic community.

From my time attending catholic church sermons in Ganish with students from a government school, I knew Christians living in Pakistan were the minority. I was surprised to find out practicing Christians made up less than 2% of Pakistan's population. Among the most disadvantaged groups in Pakistan, violent attacks on Christians were not uncommon. Anger of the US led war in Afghanistan is one possible reason for attacks on minority groups like Christians. Anti-blasphemy laws are supposed to protect freedom of religious expression but have been disputed.

In certain social circles, turning away from Islam and its teachings may be compared to using profanity or insulting the holy prophet Muhammad by some Islamic extremists' groups. Violent protesters took to the streets in Lahore one afternoon during my stay, smashing police vehicles and throwing stones at officers who were caught in a rioting mob. I visited Pakistan as a foreigner a handful of times. On a school break, for entertainment, I took Sameer and Asad along with Zarah to Lahore as a reward for Sameer's good grades. I was clueless about problems that existed in tribal communities throughout Pakistan. Zarah was right when she mentioned how little I understood about Pakistani culture, or the problems people living in certain regions face.

I shut my eyes to the now empty highways of Lahore. The freeways of Lahore were less polluted and more regulated than the interstates of Ganish. A familiar block where we stopped for fast food on our drive back to Ganish was now stained with the blood of tribal groups. Feuding tribes killed each other in the name of religion. Everything suddenly changed for the worse.

Zarah yanked me by the arm, guiding me to a rickshaw parked around the corner. We rode the rest of the way home to our city of Faisalabad in silence. I was alarmed by the way Zarah looked at me. When we arrived back at Faisalabad, Zarah sat close beside me on a new furniture set Farah bought for wedding guests. Farah was picky about who she let sit on new furniture meant for important company. Zarah told me I would need to stay in the house for the coming months. "Going outside to places in Pakistan is not safe for you," Aaliyaa alerted me. I reassured my sister- in law of all the ways I was settling into life in Pakistan. I was beginning to adapt to family life, customs and social norms. There was no need for Zarah to worry about my happiness any longer. Eventually, I grew accustomed to the challenges of living in different areas of Punjab as a foreigner.

There was a contagious feeling of discomfort, I could sense from family members. Visits to relatives' homes at Ganish were usually laid back. A roomful of guests sat around lounged out on the living room sofa watching television, relaxed after a meal cooked by female relatives. Male guests seemed preoccupied with meaningless chatter in Urdu. I couldn't pinpoint what was the matter.

"Have you heard about what's been going on in Lahore?" Zarah asked apprehensively.

Without informing me of what was really happening, Zarah excused herself from dinner. Family members that I hadn't yet been introduced to would be ecstatic to meet Daniyal's wife from America. I almost never watched news channels while living in Pakistan. Zarah told me that since we were already in Lahore for shopping, we should drop by a close relative's home for a surprise visit.

On the drive back to Faisalabad, police barricaded off all major highways and roads leading back to our city. For a total of four nights, I stayed with Sameer and Asad at Jamila's house in Lahore. Zarah's big sister, Jamila, went to a Government University on weekdays. Jamila took care of my kids, treating them like special guests in her home, making poori and halwa, setting out a table of traditional cuisines and a pitcher of cold lassi. Sameer and Asad had a hard time sleeping and adjusting to a new environment. Asad woke up again in the middle of the night complaining of another bad dream.

During our last trip to Pakistan, Zarah didn't bother telling me about dangerous riots going on, not far from us where we stayed at Jamila's home in Lahore, "I was afraid that if I told you about protests happening on the roads of Lahore not far from Jamila's house that I would frighten you. I didn't want to influence you enough to make you never want to visit Pakistan again," Zarah explained.

Zarah disappeared to a quiet room, speaking in a low tone of voice over the phone to Daniyal. I didn't know when it would be safe to drive back to Faisalabad. There was no telling how long our family would have to stay at Jamila's house in hiding. I had little understanding of political unrest in Pakistan during overnight visits at a stranger's home. I chose not to get involved in politics and infrequently watched international news channels. Zarah was like Nadia who considered it rude to drop by at the last minute as a guest in someone's home. Nadia preferred to plan-ahead. Little did I know how drastically my plans for living in Pakistan could be altered. Jamila woke my children up early, informing me that they were in a rush to head back to Faisalabad.

"I am sure Daniyal must have told you about deadly riots going on a few miles away in Lahore. You should go back to America, it's not safe to live in Pakistan right now." Zarah explained, trying her best to sound rational, her voice quivering.

In run down territories of Pakistan, known as the ghettos, Christians and other minorities were targeted for publicly rejecting Islam. In Pakistan, there was no such thing as peaceful protests and demonstrations. Islamic extremist took to the streets to violently express outrage toward minority Christian groups. Practicing Christians consisted of poor village women seeking acceptance in a predominately Muslim society. Bickering tribes were being slaughtered openly, not far from Jamilia's home where I lived for five days. The government closed all schools, places of recreation and worship. Most stores and shops closed for weeks. I ruminated for a long time about returning to Louisiana. For a while, there was no place I could travel safely in Pakistan as a person with fair skin and auburn hair. I stood out as a foreigner. I rarely ventured out anyplace far from our city of Faisalabad. A curfew was set by the government until news of a deadly riot in Lahore died down. Government run facilities could reopen safely again in a couple of weeks.

"Lawlessness takes place because of uncivilized people. Small, minded people from backward villages fight over anything, even if it doesn't make sense," Zarah explained during the drive home from Lahore. Chaos in Jamila's neighborhood of Lahore eventually subsided. Police officers reopened major highways leading back to Faisalabad. Our car was stopped at a check point when a security guard handed Ayaan a citation and circled our vehicle, stopping to stand beside me. The police officer tore out a sheet of paper, handing it to Ayaan. Another guard motioned for us to drive forward. We moved into a rural area I recognized. Ayaan drove along unpaved highways loitered with trash. We left behind a fast-paced city for a tranquil life in the country, I missed.

Nothing seems to change for the better. Abas passed away when I was a little girl. I struggled to finish college. Raised by my mother who tutored girls in our home for income to cover living expenses, I lived most of my youth in Ganish. My two small sisters were married off before graduating," Zarah told me. On our drive to Faisalabad, I couldn't think clearly. Road signs back to Faisalabad were covered in blood. Weeks after, I thought back to the day we arrived out of the blue to stay with relatives in Pakistan. My life in Pakistan changed. A few months ago, I was hopeful that I would find a well-paying job teaching English where I would make new friends. I thought of Sofia, the foreigner who taught English in Lahore and offered to let me borrow her phone at the airport. I would have to travel back to Louisiana and face uncertainty.

Zarah was right. I stood out as a foreigner from America. When I tried to blend in with local people; hiding myself in a veil, wearing traditional shalwar kameez, I still wouldn't have passed as a villager or as an Islamic woman from a middle-class family. I was a non-practicing Islamic woman and a target. I spoke in unconventional Urdu and knew little of the native language of Urdu spoken throughout Provinces of Punjab. Sameer and Asad were cultured and spoke and wrote in fluent Urdu, Punjabi and English. Sameer and Asad were well adjusted and attended a local private school in Faisalabad, rarely asking about our life in Louisiana with Daniyal. Sameer looked forward to going to our village home every weekend and visiting Lahore on holidays. My children blended in well with my Muslim family. My two kids prayed namaz, spoke the native language of Urdu fluently and adjusted better than me to life in Pakistan.

"There is no need to worry about your life or Sameer and Asad's future in Pakistan," Ayaan reassured. Brother-in-law recently applied and was accepted into the United Nations. Ayaan traveled to other third world countries as a spokesperson for Pakistani people. During his trip to South Africa, Brother-in-law told Aaliyaa about his new job which involved bringing food, and medical supplies to third world countries in need. During power and water shortages Ayaan's letters home made me hopeful again about a brighter future in Pakistan for my family. When I wanted to give up and return home to the comforts I missed in Louisiana., Ayaans promise of buying a house in Karachi someday made me hopeful again. On visits home to Faisalabad, Ayaan treated the family to fancy dinners at restaurants and places UN members and their families got in free. Brother- in law gave me something to look forward to outside of an abusive marriage to Daniyal in Louisiana. There was a better life that could exist in a place like Pakistan for each of us, one that Daniyal spoke of.

Before political protests broke out in Lahore, Chandra from the Vocational school took me to a Catholic church to listen to sermons. Poor Christian women filled up church pews. Middle- and upper-class families throughout provinces of Punjab saw Christians as poor workers from lower castes who went against Islam and its teaching as the outcasts of society. Practicing Christians in Pakistan were not much different than gays, bisexuals or trans people who came out publicly to Islamic families.

During my time visiting a catholic church in a rural area, I wondered if Christian women who showed up veiled and fully clothed, draped in a black hijab, followed the teachings of Jesus or understood biblical scripture. I had no idea of real threats to Christians or Muslims who defied family and Islamic religion to reject arranged marriages or flee abusive Muslim families. Few defiant middle-class girls dared to marry the person they wanted. Some activists who lived-in forward-thinking areas of Pakistan still fought for justice and equality.

When I stayed at Mahnoor's house with Sameer and Asad during long power outages and water shortages, my friend reminded me that Pakistan was a place I could turn to for support, a country that would always welcome me. There were people who cared about Sameer and Asad, Asma reminded. Through every problem I faced during my stay in Pakistan, like weeklong power losses, property disputes or financial setbacks, I still believed Pakistan would embrace my children with the same acceptance and sense of community that drew me back each time. I was never a good predictor of when the smog in Faisalabad would dissipate.

In moments when I was most hopeful about a future in Pakistan with my children, I was like some disadvantaged village people who had most of their land stolen and could only wait for things to get better. Like the old man selling juice from a pushcart, I passed by a dozen times, I was no one special to tell my students from a government school about a place they could hope to travel someday. I was no different than any middle-class woman from Ganish. Being a foreigner from the United States didn't mean I was privileged. Living in Faisalabad didn't make me immune to problems middle class families faced. I couldn't give poor kids false promises that involved striving for a better way of life.

After life in Faisalabad went back to normal, I sat with Rohan at a local café that same afternoon. My future in Pakistan had reached an impasse. Zarah stood in front of me, with a cell phone pressed to her ear, suggesting we leave my favorite coffee shop. Rohan ordered something different from the menu every time now, burgers, fries and a chocolate milkshake. I waited for the smog to lift.

About the Author

*S*ay You'll Wait For Me is my first book based on a true- to life experience of meeting and marrying an immigrant from Karachi, Pakistan. Say You'll Wait For Me is a cultural journey as I relocate to Faisalabad, Pakistan, a tribal village area of Punjab from my home state of Louisiana with two small children. As I attempt to fit in with a large, boisterous extended family as a foreigner from America who knows next to nothing about Pakistani customs, my haphazard attempts at blending in with my Muslim family turn into a series of comical cultural blunders and missteps. Secretive in-laws appear as well-meaning family members offering Muslim prayers, revealing a series of family betrayals and secrets surrounding an ongoing legal case in Karachi, Pakistan involving the acquisition of ancestral land that spirals out of control in the form of an ongoing family feud.